THE VOCAL ARTS
WORKBOOK

SECOND EDITION

Online resources to accompany this book are available at: https://vimeo.com/channels/vocalarts/videos. Please type the URL into your web browser and follow the instructions to access the videos. If you experience any problems, please contact Bloomsbury at: contact@bloomsbury.com

THE VOCAL ARTS WORKBOOK

A Practical Course for Developing the Expressive Actor's Voice

DAVID CAREY AND REBECCA CLARK CAREY

methuen | drama

LONDON • NEW YORK • OXFORD • NEW DELHI • SYDNEY

METHUEN DRAMA
Bloomsbury Publishing Plc
50 Bedford Square, London, WC1B 3DP, UK
1385 Broadway, New York, NY 10018, USA
29 Earlsfort Terrace, Dublin 2, Ireland

BLOOMSBURY, METHUEN DRAMA and the Methuen Drama logo are trademarks of
Bloomsbury Publishing Plc

First edition published in Great Britain by Methuen Drama 2008
This edition published 2022

Series design by Catherine Wood
Cover image: Wayne T. Carr, *Pericles* (2015), Oregon Shakespeare Festival. Photo by Jenny Graham.

A catalogue record for this book is available from the British Library.

A catalog record for this book is available from the Library of Congress.

ISBN: HB: 978-1-3501-7848-9
PB: 978-1-3501-7849-6
ePDF: 978-1-3501-7850-2
eBook: 978-1-3501-7851-9

Series: RADA Guides

Typeset by Integra Software Services Pvt. Ltd.
Printed and bound in India

To find out more about our authors and books visit www.bloomsbury.com
and sign up for our newsletters.

To our parents, who gave us our voices:

Brian and Elna Carey

and

Owen and Barbara Clark

CONTENTS

PREFACE TO THE SECOND EDITION

We were delighted to be asked by Methuen Drama to produce a second edition of *The Vocal Arts Workbook*. Since its first publication in 2008, the book has found an enduring place in the recommended reading of many actor-training courses in the UK, the United States and across the English-speaking world. In the light of developments in our own teaching and thinking, and in theatre and the performing arts in general, we have taken the opportunity to thoroughly revise and update *The Vocal Arts Workbook* for a new generation of students.

To this end, we have introduced, adapted or replaced a number of exercises, revised many of the *Suggested texts* lists, added to the *Further reading*, adjusted exercises that rely on physical contact between students, and generally made the book more learner-focused. Whether you are in training, starting out as a professional or looking for some fresh inspiration, it is our hope that this new edition will speak to actors at all stages of their career of the importance of vocal artistry in today's world.

FOREWORDS TO THE FIRST EDITION

This book is valuable both for the voice teacher and for the student working on their own voice – for, in a very comprehensive way, it brings together all the factors which are needed to find one's own authentic voice.

I find the book both refreshing and remarkable since it teaches, not by telling you what to do, but rather by first making the reader aware of their own personal bodily responses to breathing, tension, resonance, etc., and to the whole process of making sound in their everyday life. In a most imaginative, and often humorous, way, it arouses our curiosity as to how we each make sound and speech in the variable circumstances of our lives. With this enhanced awareness of our own habits, it then instructs us, through very clear and specific exercises, how to build on this knowledge by managing our tensions and developing our breathing potential; the exercises are always an exploration.

The message that underpins the work is that good breathing not only produces a good voice, but also feeds the actor in their exploration of character and in the truth of that character. In other words, to breathe deeply is to think deeply.

Cicely Berry

Each time we speak, we reveal our nationality, disposition, attitudes, background, idiosyncrasies, familial traits and mannerisms. We carry our lives and childhoods in our voice and this is an important part of the armoury of any artist or any person who wishes to be heard.

Voice is about connecting both our primitive thoughts and our sophisticated ones to a mechanism that can communicate. Having 'a voice in the world', whatever that world is, is the gift we inherit and one we can develop. Voice holds our self-esteem, confidence, comfort and control. It is a physical activity: we 'draw breath' and speak. Without it, as Winnie in Beckett's *Happy Days* says, there is '[n]othing to break the silence of this place'.

Voice is about not having to live in the silence of the lonely imagination, instead sharing our thoughts and sculpting sound so that not only is meaning conveyed, but also the essence of who we are. It is about our possibility. So there is not a person on the planet who will not benefit from making sure that their voice is being true to its master, the inner self.

For actors, of course, vocal skill is crucial – not just for serving personal expression, but also for serving the play we are releasing. It is also crucial to be able to sustain vocal energy over a prolonged time so that neither mood nor fatigue can shake our abilities. It was in this context that I first met David Carey at the Royal Shakespeare Company, when he came quietly into a rehearsal room to observe rehearsals with Cicely Berry, the transformative voice coach of the previous generation. That was about twenty-five years ago, since when he has had many individual sessions with many actors and has always been sympathetic to the myriad problems that strike each performer. In this book he and his fellow writer, Rebecca Carey, draw on their unique experience as voice teachers to give us valuable insight into the process of developing the actor's voice.

The actor's voice is always being tampered with, even as it tries to be the most 'normal'. It is the tool that, along with the spectacular truths held in poetic language, is one of the most distinguishing aspects of our humanity-driven trade. We need voices to be able to perform better than our natures and yet to reveal our natures. We are asked to be the conduits of big thoughts – bigger than normal conversational usage – and so voice work is as much about tuning into our own possibilities as it is about gaining vocal skill. It also has a philosophical dimension and, through it, we open up the possibilities for the listener to be touched more profoundly.

Recently, I performed in Epidaurus, the ancient Greek amphitheatre. A terror of a lifetime to act to 5,000 people, out of doors, and not to have a microphone! I was struck that our colleagues in ancient Greece were undertaking the same activity 2,400 years ago. How did they cope with vocal challenges? I was reminded of the exercises, some of which are presented in this book, the power of breath, the necessary relaxation and heightened awareness of thought and feeling. All this is as true then as now. Technology enhances volume, but only we ourselves can enhance the power of concentrated thought, the distillation of which is carried in the miraculous journey from breath to rhythm. I feel that by reading this book, we start this journey into the air and into ourselves.

Only in testing variation can the actor reach for the heights needed to be a conduit for what is demanded by complicated texts. Acting is the art of transforming both the ordinary and the extraordinary so that it can be heard in a poetic way, and lodges in the listener's mind, haunting them after the event. Actors must develop the voice so that when we have the thought in mind we can communicate it with real 'depth charge'.

For each new generation of theatre practitioners the style of that delivery must change, but not the fact of it. Here we have writers who are offering important insights to us all in a way that our new ears can hear, so that our new voices can speak. Employing contemporary media and tried-and-true training, they present concrete, practical information and in an imaginative way. Using the exercises in this book, one is put in touch with the self-empowering aspect of voice, the chance to extend and expand our range. That is a great gift, to be empowered with old knowledge so one may be more fully in the present. Ultimately this is what *Vocal Arts* offers to actors, students, teachers and any kind of speaker: not just the means to develop technical skill, but also a process to enable fuller expression of the self in the moment of speech.

Fiona Shaw

ACKNOWLEDGEMENTS

We would like to warmly thank the following: Cicely Berry, Jane Boston, Yvonne Burgess and Sarah Lozoff for their insightful comments on our manuscript; Barbara Houseman, Gillyanne Kayes and Miriam Rabkin for their generous advice and support; Steven Ambrose for his diligence and talent in translating our ideas into line drawings; and Matt Bannister and Annie Hemingway for their skilled contributions to the video.

We would like to wholeheartedly acknowledge the contribution that our teachers and our students through the years have made to our understanding of voice. In particular, David would like to thank all his past students of the Voice Studies course at the Central School of Speech and Drama.

Our thanks also go to all at Bloomsbury Methuen Drama – in particular, Jenny Ridout for her initial support and enthusiasm, Anna Brewer and Meredith Benson.

INTRODUCTION

The Vocal Arts Workbook and you

When we think about the arts, most of us think about music, painting, sculpture, literature, dance, drama – all acts of expression which have been given form through the creative application of skill. Speaking can also be considered a form of art – what we call *vocal art*. It too can engage, entertain, challenge, enlighten and inspire. The vocal arts are so commonly practised, though, that sometimes we forget how special they can be. Our voices and the words we speak are fundamentally products of our whole selves – our thoughts, our feelings, our bodies and our souls – this is what gives them their unique potency. To develop our vocal artistry is to develop our creative ability to express and contribute to our common human experience through our voices.

Whether you aspire to use your voice as a professional artist or are just interested in improving how you speak, you can benefit from exploring *The Vocal Arts Workbook*. If you are a student of acting, however, this book is most particularly for you. How you use, train and think about your voice is fundamental to who you will become as an actor. Your voice is where you as a person and the story told by the playwright come together and connect with the audience. At its best, that moment of connection is personal, intentional, generous, disciplined and creative – and voice work needs to be all those things as well. Working with this book will help you to use your voice so that it fully and accurately represents your intentions – just as writers use their words or dancers their bodies. It will give you the skill to express yourself with greater ease and success – to communicate thoughts and feelings with precision and authority.

This book is also intended for use by drama teachers who would like to introduce voice into their curricula or to support the voice teaching they are already doing. We believe that exploring, exercising and playing with the voice can be an exciting component of studying drama at any level. This book can be used as the basis for a designated, year-long voice class at a drama school, or as a starting point to integrate 10–15 minutes of voice work per session into a secondary school acting class, or anything in between. An appendix at the back of the book outlines a couple of suggested curricula that could be used for different periods of instruction (Appendix 2).

Learning and teaching *Vocal Arts*

Work on the voice, in particular, is work on the self, and learners need to feel that they are free to work without fear of judgement. An inquisitive spirit that is open to play and discovery is also vital in voice work. Often, we are our own worst enemies when it comes to vocal expression; we judge, censor and constrict ourselves. As you do the practical work, it's important to give yourself permission to do things and make sounds that are unexpected and unfamiliar. Allow yourself to explore beyond how you usually use your voice and, more significantly, how you feel you 'should' use your voice. Actively seek to discover and *enjoy* possibilities in your voice that you may not have experienced before.

It is important too that you be attentive to the work; it rarely proceeds the same way twice, and you may make different discoveries doing the same exercise from one day to the next if you pay close attention. This work requires both a sense of discipline and a sense of play. It requires the ability to improvise – to run with something that is yielding results or to adjust something that is not. It requires sensitivity to the unfolding of individual growth. None of these are things that we can provide in a book. However, the work also requires structure, which is something we can.

The Vocal Arts Workbook: An overview

This book is divided into five chapters, each of which addresses one of the fundamental principles of vocal expression: **Bodywork** focuses on preparing you physically for work on the voice; **Breath and Voice: Creating Connection** focuses on establishing the essential relationship between your breath and your voice; **Breath and Voice: Developing Supply and Support** looks at developing that relationship so your voice can more easily meet the demands of performance; **Resonance and Range** explores how the pitch and resonance of your voice can respond more expressively to your intentions; and **Articulation and Muscularity** focuses on increasing the effectiveness of your articulation. Each chapter lays a foundation for the work that follows. However, since dividing the voice into categories is inherently artificial, we suggest that you first take a quick read of the whole book in order to get an idea of how the work hangs together and where it is going. Then, usually, it will make sense to go through the book chapter by chapter, although there may be moments when it will be appropriate to return to earlier exercises to reinforce or rediscover basic principles. You may also find that a topic which appears later in the book becomes a pressing issue in the work you are doing; should that happen, turn to whatever section is useful to you and make the most of it. There is a progression that the training usually follows, and some parts of the process will only make sense when others are in place first, but no two learners will develop in exactly the same way, so please use the book to serve your needs.

Each chapter consists of several sections: *Framework*, *Exploration*, *Exercises*, *Follow-up*, *Suggested texts* and *Further reading*. In general, we directly address you, the learner, throughout the book; but we also provide teaching tips which give specific notes for teachers. For example:

Teaching tip
These tips can help you adapt your teaching to suit your students' needs.

Framework

Each chapter begins with a *Framework* section. In it, we offer an introduction to the topic at hand and our approach to it. This includes a description of the relevant anatomy. An understanding of vocal anatomy is not necessarily a prerequisite for good vocal use. In fact, much of our work employs images that have little to do with precise anatomical function. Nevertheless, we have found that having some knowledge of what is actually happening in your body can give you a framework for understanding what you experience in exercises. This is useful because it demystifies the process; you can appreciate that the growth you undergo is not the result of magic but of specific changes in muscle use – and what is specific is repeatable. Ideally, intellectual insight and physical experience can work together to help you translate your discoveries into new habits.

> **Teaching tip**
> You may find it valuable to have students read through the *Framework* section before beginning extensive work on a chapter. Alternatively, you may prefer to have them experience some of the exercises first and then delve into how and why they work.

Exploration

The *Exploration* section of each chapter serves two functions. The first is to give you a sense of where you are starting from in relation to the work of that particular chapter. Understanding how you usually do things will help you begin to explore new patterns of behaviour. It will also help you to recognize when your habits start to change. The second function is to encourage you to think about the issues surrounding your voice in ordinary usage. To fully develop your skill, you need to cultivate awareness of your voice not only as a student in the classroom but also as a human being, if you're an actor, in rehearsal and performance and in daily life. The exercises in this section help you to do this.

> **Teaching tip**
> We suggest that one or more of the explorations be undertaken in the week before work in that chapter is to begin.

Exercises

Vocal art is a practical discipline, so the bulk of this book is devoted to practical exercises. The exercises in each chapter are grouped under headings. Under each heading, there may be several exercises which focus on developing the same skill. This is important because people respond differently to different exercises on different days. Don't panic if you don't 'get it' on the first try of every exercise. By coming at each element of voice production through a couple of exercises, eventually you will find a way to move beyond old habits into a new experience and, with a bit of diligent practice, fresh patterns can become new, unconscious habits.

We often use images in conjunction with exercises because many of the muscles that are associated with the voice are not easy to control directly. Engaging the imagination helps the muscles respond more fully. For example, simply giving yourself the mental command 'Let go' for a tightly clenched jaw will only help it to release so far. Gently massaging the muscles will encourage further release. But visualizing it softening and opening as you massage will help even more. To get the full benefit of all the exercises, therefore, it is important that you engage your imagination as well as your effort.

The exercises are also sometimes very physical and can involve work on the floor, so we would advise you to wear clothing that is casual and easy to move in; track suit bottoms and T-shirts are usually good. If you are working in a class, it will help your teacher observe your breathing and posture if your clothes are not too baggy.

We haven't divided the exercises into categories of 'beginning' or 'advanced'. This is because even the most experienced learner can benefit from a re-exploration of fundamental exercises, and a novice can make discoveries by engaging in more sophisticated work from time to time. Some exercises, however, will be a better fit in a year-long voice class for acting students at a drama school than in a one-term introduction to acting course at a university. Some will be useful for experienced actors wanting to deepen their craft on their own, and others will really only work in a room full of learners. Feel free to focus on those exercises that seem most applicable to your situation and goals.

Teaching tip

If you are teaching from this book, it will help the students immeasurably if you either demonstrate each exercise first or do it along with them. You may choose to have students read the exercises before class so that they have an idea of what steps they will be following. It can also be good for them to read or reread the exercises after class as a way of reinforcing the experience.

For each of the exercises, we give an estimated time. This is an approximation of how long it takes to actually do the exercise. It does not include the time you might take to explain or demonstrate beforehand or discuss afterward – which may be as long as the exercise itself. Some exercises may take less or more time depending on the size of the group.

In the early stages of the work, we suggest that you explore each exercise in a section. As the class progresses through a chapter, we recommend that you devote some time in each session to reviewing at least a few of the earlier exercises in that chapter. As you move on through the book, it is also a good idea to use some exercises from previous chapters as a warm-up for each session.

Follow-up

We recommend that you keep a journal as you work through this book, as it can be a very effective way for you to sharpen your awareness of what you are experiencing in your voice and body. This will help you gain greater insight into which exercises had particular value for you and how you might recreate the positive results. Much of the *Follow-up* section of each chapter is devoted to questions intended to stimulate detailed observation and encourage reflection on the work. More free-form notes on your own impressions and experiences are useful as well.

The *Follow-up* exercises are designed primarily to help you make the connection between vocal use in class and vocal use outside of class. They are usually very simple, but are nonetheless a key component in overall development. To help you maintain your growth after you have completed the course, we've included a vocal workout in Appendix 1.

Teaching tip

In addition to assigning *Follow-up* work, we would encourage you to make time at the end of every class for a brief discussion of discoveries, observations and questions. We have found these conversations to be very effective in helping students become aware of what they have learned in the session.

Suggested texts

The primary task of an actor is to communicate thoughts and feelings through language, and we believe it is important to work with language throughout your training. For that reason, at the end of chapters two through five we have included a section of text-based exercises. Most of these exercises do not focus on any particular passages, but rather on applying the specific skills developed in that chapter to the act of speaking. The material you choose to work with in those exercises is up to you. We do, however, give some suggestions at the end of each chapter of texts that we feel lend themselves well to the exercises described. We have mainly chosen poetic texts because we have found that poetry has a focus, specificity and economy of language that are very useful for facilitating good vocal practice. Furthermore, working with poetry allows you to speak powerful language without having to worry about characterization, given circumstances, objectives or other issues associated with dramatic text. We would encourage you to explore other poems from a variety of historical periods and cultural perspectives; we have found that when you get away from your own rhythms, syntax and vocabulary, you often find it easier to get away from old vocal habits as well. In Appendix 4, we provide a list of recommended anthologies and websites where you should be able to find the texts we suggest and many other excellent poems.

Further reading

We would never try to pretend that this book comprehensively covers every voice issue, so we have included suggestions for further reading on every topic. As mentioned previously, there are many excellent resources available, and we encourage you to use whatever speaks to you in your teaching and learning. Our work is deeply indebted to many outstanding practitioners who have taught and inspired us, and, in Appendix 5, we give a more detailed overview of those experiences and individuals that have shaped our approach to voice work. In particular, we'd like to acknowledge the profound influence that Cicely Berry and Kristin Linklater have had on the teaching of voice in the twentieth and twenty-first centuries.

Video

Many of the exercises we use can be hard to describe, so the video clips that accompany this book give a brief demonstration of those exercises that can be best understood when they are seen and/ or heard. They are designed to supplement the workbook, not provide vocal training independent of it. You can watch them by following the link on p.157. The exercises that appear in the video clips are marked in the book with a 💿. If you are teaching from this book, you may want to watch those exercises before introducing them in class. Your students may also find it beneficial to use the video clips to review after class. If you are working from the book on your own, you should watch each exercise as you come to it in the book, then try it. You can then return to the video to review as needed. What you will see are demonstrations of the essential points. In most instances, when you perform the exercises following the instructions in the workbook, they will take longer. For example, if an exercise involves several repetitions, we have generally shown just the initial cycle of movement or sound. Once you have an image of how the exercise works, you can proceed to explore it more fully yourself.

Working with *The Vocal Arts Workbook*

Physical use

All of us have habitual ways we use our muscles – breathing muscles, postural muscles, muscles of the 'voice box' and speech muscles included. These habits are built up over a long time. They are not necessarily wrong, but sometimes they inhibit the voice's full expressive potential. The exercises in this book are designed to encourage the effective engagement of the appropriate muscles for the production of voice. In order for this to happen, you first need to free yourself of restrictive tensions which keep you locked in old, inefficient patterns. You can then experience a new pattern – one which will allow you to express yourself with greater ease, range and precision.

Changing muscular habits may cause aches and pains to occur or may just feel uncomfortable when a sensation is unfamiliar. It's important to keep an eye on health and safety as you do the work. If you are in a voice class and feel temporarily unwell for any reason, let your teacher know. They may suggest that you sit the work out or ask you to engage with the work to the best of your ability at that time. Do not push yourself to extremes or undertake anything which does not feel safe in your weakened state. Your first responsibility is to preserve your own health – not to please the teacher!

With regard to 'aches and pains', learn to distinguish between the dull ache of muscles that have been exercised and the sharp pain of physical injury. Muscles which are not used to performing a particular function will ache when they are first asked to engage in an appropriate way, or may feel sore the next day – this is a healthy reaction. However, muscles which are made to work beyond their physical capacity or to engage in a way that is dangerous will register a sharp pain – this is a sign of injury. Generally, if in doubt whether something is an ache or a pain, consult your doctor or sit out the exercise.

Breathing exercises can occasionally cause dizziness associated with hyperventilation. If you feel slightly light-headed after an exercise, try holding your hands a few inches in front of your face and looking at your palms for about 30 seconds. If you feel faint, try sitting down with your head between your knees for a minute or two. If you feel very dizzy, try breathing into a paper bag until the sensation diminishes, and then sit down quietly for a few minutes. If the symptoms last for longer than 10 minutes or keep occurring, seek medical advice.

If you suffer from asthma or any other respiratory disorder, consult your doctor before you begin regular exercise. These conditions can often be helped by working on the voice, but occasionally they can be exacerbated. So, be sensible and take responsibility for your health.

If you have a physical disability or an injury, you may need to adapt some of the exercises. For example, if you are a wheelchair user, stretches may need to be adjusted to fit your particular capability;

> **Teaching tip**
> Always check with a new class whether any students have health issues which may affect their ability to perform exercises. Talk with the students and become informed about how specific issues affect them. Don't make assumptions about their abilities – ask them to tell you what they can or can't do.
>
> Undertake a risk assessment of your class, so that you can anticipate measures you might need to take in the unlikely event of an accident.

or, if you have a history of back pain, work on the floor may need to be substituted with work standing or sitting against a wall. We have worked with a number of differently abled students and have usually found that with consultation and ingenuity exercises can be suitably tailored to their needs. If in doubt, however, do not engage in an exercise which might put you at risk of injury.

Voice work and context

In addition to health and safety concerns, there are issues of personal, social and cultural identity and boundaries which we want to address at this point. We wish to explicitly acknowledge that our approach has developed from within the Western tradition of theatre training. Until recently, this training culture assumed that it was acceptable, for example, to require students to wear specific types of clothing, to work in bare feet, to touch each other, to sight read, or to work only with texts from the Western canon. However, many of these practices are rightly being questioned in an effort to make actor training more inclusive, equitable and effective. We sincerely believe in the need for sensitivity towards personal, social and cultural boundaries; in respect for each individual's identity; and in the advantages of encouraging students to bring their own perspectives into the work. Because we cannot anticipate every educational context or individual circumstance in which this book may be used, we would urge you to adapt the work to your own or your students' particular learning culture.

Touch

In recent years, we have had the tremendous good fortune to work alongside intimacy director Sarah Lozoff at the Oregon Shakespeare Festival. She has generously shared with us the principles that underlie her work in choreographing intimate contact between performers on stage and screen, and we have recognized the vital benefits of incorporating them into actor training. Actors' bodies are the vehicles they use to tell stories, and touch is part of that storytelling. Touching has also traditionally been part of actor training, as it is the body that is being trained as well as the mind. Whenever touch happens, however, consent is vital. In a classroom or rehearsal setting, that consent is only meaningful if it is specific, given in the moment, and can be withheld or revoked. So, enrolling in a drama course is not the same thing as consenting to being touched at any time by an instructor or fellow students, and giving someone consent to touch your neck does not mean it's okay for them to touch your leg. Students must ALWAYS have the real option of declining to be touched and instructors must ALWAYS be willing to adapt exercises that involve touch if consent is not given. In our own teaching, we make a practice of telling students what kind of touch we are proposing and asking their consent: e.g. 'Is it okay with you if I lay my hands across your middle back?' In partnered exercises, partners should do the same with each other.

We encourage you to have a discussion in one of your first sessions about what consent is, why it is important, and why it is something that is given specifically not generally. You can also talk about agreeing communally about what rituals and language you want to use as a group to obtain individual consent every time touching is introduced in the work. We have included reminders to obtain consent in every exercise that involves touching.

Teaching tip

It can take a little time to introduce, but we cannot overstate what a positive impact the use of explicit consent has in the classroom. An important factor to consider is the inherent power imbalance between teachers and students and even between advanced or older students and those who are newer that may make students self-conscious about withholding consent even if they really don't want to be touched. It's worth talking about this explicitly. It can also be helpful to actually practise not granting consent and discuss what it feels like to withhold it and be denied it. Talk about what kind of adaptations might be used if a student does not want to be touched, and make it explicit that doing an alternate exercise on one's own is always an acceptable option.

If you sense there are interpersonal factors at play that may make it harder for some students to freely and meaningfully give or withhold consent with some of their peers, do not hesitate to assign partners, pairing them so as to make each student as comfortable as possible. If you are working with a group that is not focused or grounded enough on any given day to do an exercise that involves touching productively, just skip or modify it.

Conclusion

We believe that vocal artistry has universal value. It doesn't have to be the exclusive domain of a select few who practise it only in the confines of the most expensive temples of 'high art'. It is a skill that is needed in any and every community. Person-to-person communication is one of the fundamental joys and responsibilities of being a human being. May you fare well on your journey of discovering your potential as a vocal artist!

1
BODYWORK

Framework

It may seem strange to begin work on your voice with work on your body, but it is your body that produces your voice. In order to tell any kind of meaningful truth with your voice, your whole self needs to be available. Physical tension and unconscious physical habits can shut down that availability. The work of this chapter will help to open it back up again.

In theory, it's not hard to grasp that physical tension is undesirable. We all know how uncomfortable we feel and how disadvantaged we are in situations that make us tense – when the shoulders tighten, the jaw clenches, the breathing becomes shallow and the stomach churns. But even though there are physical tensions that we associate with stress and long to be rid of, there are also physical tensions that we associate with passion, commitment and intensity; and, frankly, on some level we cherish and nurture them. Often, the more physically worked up actors get, the more they may feel they are really acting. The muscles, however, make no distinction: tension is tension, and tension very often gets in the way of effective performance.

Of course, a certain amount of muscular activity is necessary just to sit upright; complete relaxation would be an absurdity. The key question is whether the muscles are engaged in a way that supports your intention or undermines it. Muscles either engage (contract) or disengage (relax). The word tension is used to describe a muscular contraction which is either unrelated to the task (e.g. squinting your eyes to pick up something heavy) or is inappropriately strong. Boxers throwing a punch generate a tremendous amount of energy by strongly engaging certain muscles, but excess contraction in those muscles or surrounding muscles will actually block that energy and could cause a boxer injury. Actors playing a scene of high intensity likewise need to engage strongly, not only physically but also mentally and emotionally, but excess muscular contraction will block their expressive energy by stiffening the body and squeezing the voice. Powerful communication happens when energy flows through a channel (physical, vocal, emotional, mental) that is open, responsive and free.

Of course, just as it is possible to confuse tension with passion and intensity, it is also possible to confuse disengagement with ease and naturalness. In vocal terms, this often means using minimal breath energy and actually increasing tension in the jaw and tongue root, creating a sound that's held back, a little gravelly and flat. Sometimes this is referred to as 'speaking on one's vocal fry'. In and of itself, there's nothing wrong with this kind of casual voice, but if your muscles don't know any other way to function, you're going to be quite limited in your expressive choices as an actor. And it's not the same thing as true relaxation. The relaxation and release that we will work to achieve come not from holding energy back, but from freeing it to come forward; not from tuning out, but from paying attention.

Where do the tensions that get in our way come from? Babies and young children are usually geniuses at employing the exact amount of muscular effort necessary to get the job done. Their bodies tend to be free and beautifully aligned. We use the word 'alignment' to refer to that posture which is most physiologically efficient – that is, the posture which requires the least amount of muscular activity to stay upright. It involves what Alexander Technique teacher Glynn Macdonald calls the 'dynamic relationship between head, neck and torso' (1998: 39).

To see healthy children of two or three walking, crouching, running or simply sitting on a stool is to observe creatures that have an intuitive awareness of good, physiologically efficient posture: they are in balance, their centre of gravity is stable in their pelvis, and their head/neck/torso relationship is in dynamic alignment. But over time – under the influence of various elements of their environment, such as diet, emotional or physical distress, or the myriad unconscious choices about how they want to appear that children and adolescents will make as their bodies and minds grow – the instinctive awareness of the healthy body can become numbed. Stubbed toes teach us not to swing our legs so freely. Teasing or other forms of social pressure can cause us to want to shrink or puff up. Fashion magazines teach us to hold in our stomachs and thrust our hips forward. The body is a sponge; it absorbs all of these influences and holds on to them for a long time. As a result, we can literally become ignorant of the knowledge our bodies were born with: knowledge of how the body feels when it is balanced, knowledge of where our centre of gravity is, and knowledge of how the spine works to support and sustain the dynamic relationship between the head, neck and torso. This kinaesthetic knowledge is vital for the Vocal Arts.

Thankfully, if we listen to our bodies, we can become resensitized to the messages they are giving us, and we can reinforce our instinctive knowledge with more conscious awareness. A number of body practices can achieve this reawakening, but our experience has led us to use a combination of Alexander Technique, Qi Gong (or Chi Kung) and Yoga. Alexander Technique is a programme of physical and mental training created by the Australian actor and voice teacher, F.M. Alexander, and it is founded in the principle that the way we use our body affects the way it functions. By focusing on simple activities like standing, sitting and breathing, Alexander Technique encourages conscious awareness of muscular tensions and behavioural habits in order to develop an improved use of the body. Qi Gong is a Chinese system of exercises designed to unblock energy within our bodies and develop 'internal strength' (Chuen 1991). Again, through simple activities like standing, breathing and stretching, it encourages the release of mental and physical tensions in order to increase the healthy functioning of mind and body. Yoga is an Indian system of exercise and meditation which was originally designed to achieve spiritual union with the Absolute. Today, particularly in the West, its focus on postural stretches and breathing is often used to reduce stress and

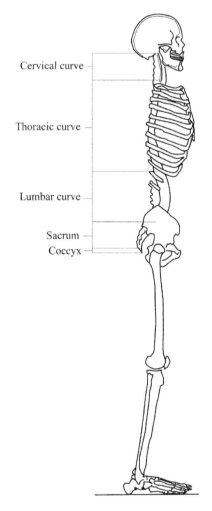

Cervical curve

Thoracic curve

Lumbar curve

Sacrum
Coccyx

Figure 1 The spine and physiologically efficient posture

improve physical and mental fitness. These practices help attune us to what has been called our 'sixth sense' – proprioception, or the kinaesthetic awareness of our body's state of balance, its posture and the muscular activity we use to move through space. As we learn to listen to this kinaesthetic sense, we can become aware of how the head can balance on top of the spine, how the whole body can be aligned to achieve a sense of ease and energy, and how we can use muscles efficiently to enhance our movement potential.

Of particular importance for our vocal practice is the spine. The spine consists of four main sections, all of which are intimately related to areas of the body responsible for producing the voice: there are the seven cervical vertebrae which make up the neck and connect with the voice and speech organs in the head, throat and larynx; there are the twelve thoracic vertebrae to which the ribs attach, and which are thus connected to the lungs and respiratory muscles in the chest; there are the five lumbar vertebrae in the small of the back to which respiratory muscles of the diaphragm and abdomen attach; and there are the five fused vertebrae of the sacrum – the base of the spine – which attaches to the pelvis and so relates to the deep breathing muscles of the abdomen and the pelvic floor. These four sections (plus the coccyx, our vestigial tail bone) create a sequence of gentle curves in the spine that make a dynamic whole (see Figure 1). Distortions of these curves, however, will have an immediate effect on the voice. Too pronounced a curve in the lumbar area, for example, or a collapse in the thoracic vertebrae will affect the management and capacity of breathing. Likewise, if the neck is twisted or shortened, the functioning of the vocal muscles in the larynx will be impaired and the size and shape of the vocal resonators in the throat and head will be diminished.

Efficient alignment of the spine, or good posture, may feel odd to you at first. However, as Kristin Linklater has pointed out in her seminal book *Freeing the Natural Voice* (1976, revised 2006), what feels *familiar* may not actually be what is *natural* – that is, what your body would do if it had not been subjected to stress, strain and habit. Good posture can also make you feel vulnerable. Many postural habits are acquired in response to self-consciousness – about one's height, one's weight, one's body shape, etc. So, raising your head or letting your abdominal muscles relax or bringing your shoulders back may make you feel very exposed. It's okay to feel that way, but it's also important that you have the courage to stick with it. The work of this chapter is not only physical. As you explore what it means to become more released, relaxed and aligned, you will also have the opportunity to discover what it is to be more present in your body and more accepting of your whole self. This will make it possible and safe for you to transform as an actor, thereby becoming a more powerful teller of stories.

Teaching tip

Because the patterns of muscular tension are acquired unconsciously and over time, they can become very deeply ingrained, and the work on releasing them is never really finished. Our approach to this issue is eclectic: progress can be made through actively stretching and manipulating the muscles; through direct, conscious instruction to release; and through focus on images to which the muscles can sometimes respond more profoundly.

On any given day, with any given student, any one of these methods may prove to be more or less effective. It is essential, however, that all of the exercises be entered into with a spirit of active curiosity. Passively going through the motions will bring very limited benefits. Likewise, harsh self-judgement can impede progress. The learning cycle begins when one moves from unconscious incompetence (habitually using muscles in a way that is inefficient without realizing it), to conscious incompetence (gaining an awareness of the inefficient pattern). From there one can work one's way to conscious competence (introducing a new use of the muscles through exercise and focused attention), and finally to unconscious competence (using the muscles in a more efficient way without having to think about it). It is pointless – in fact it may be destructive – for students to berate themselves for not being at a different stage in the cycle; instead, encourage them to develop a calm, detailed awareness of where they are.

Exploration

In the morning, identify three times during the day when you are likely to be under moderate stress; for example, driving to school and looking for parking, presenting a monologue in class, trying to get all your emails answered during your lunch break, etc. Write the following in your journal and plan to have it at hand at each of these times:

Feet	Abdominal muscles
Ankles	Upper back
Knees	Chest
Thighs	Shoulders
Pelvis	Neck
Buttocks	Jaw
Lower back	Eyes and forehead

During the three activities, if possible, or as soon after as you can, take a couple of moments to focus your awareness on each of these areas of your body and make a note of any area in which you feel tight, locked, collapsed, off balance or achy.

At the end of the day, look at your list and see if there is a pattern of tension tending to settle in certain parts of your body. Pick the three areas where you most consistently felt tight or felt the greatest degree of discomfort.

Focus your attention on the first of these three areas. See if you can double the amount of tension in that part of your body. Notice any changes this creates in other parts of your body. Try to take a very deep breath and notice where in your body the breath fills and where it feels blocked. Go back to the original degree of tension and observe the same things. See if you can halve the amount of tension and make the same observations. Repeat the process with the other two areas, making notes throughout. Write your observations in your journal and discuss them in class.

Exercises

Stretching

Stretching is one of the simplest and most effective things you can do to prepare your mind and body to be creative. It feels good, and it's good for you, but you do want to make sure you're doing it safely. If you are working with an instructor, give them, either verbally or in writing, a brief history of any injuries and/or significant illnesses you have. If there are any serious injuries or injuries to the back in particular, the instructor should discuss with you any treatment and instructions you have been given and any adjustments you may need to make. We give some guidelines below, but, if at any point a stretch seems likely to exacerbate an injury, you should simply sit it out.

If you are a wheelchair user or have other physical limitations, work with your instructor (or on your own, if you're working outside of a classroom setting) to find adaptations of specific stretches that will encourage release of muscular tension affecting your breath.

It can also be useful to do a brief check-in at the beginning of each stretching session. Someone who has strained a muscle or sprained a joint may want to sit out certain stretches or exercises; someone who has a bad cold may need to do some of the floor work lying on their side so that they can breathe more easily – all participants should be encouraged to be responsible for looking after themselves. There is no shame in backing away from something that you genuinely feel may be injurious.

A bit of cardiovascular exercise before stretching can effectively warm up the muscles. We find the following swinging exercise particularly useful:

⊙ *Swinging – torso and legs (2 minutes)*

Skip the second part of this exercise if you have problems with your knees.

1. Begin by standing with feet roughly parallel, about hip-width apart, knees soft and arms to the side.
   Start by swinging your arms gently from side to side. Try to keep the rest of your body still without freezing or locking anywhere.
   Let your waist join in the swing, twisting from side to side, but keep your hips still. This is a particularly good point in the exercise to feel a stretch in your ribs and back.
   Let your hips join the swing.
   Widen your stance and let the momentum of the swing pull your heels up off the ground.

2. Widen your stance again and bend your knees in a little lunge as you swing from side to side.

Deepen the lunge until finally you are touching the ground with your hand on either side.

Continue this for at least six lunges.

Continue to lunge, but not all the way to the ground.

Let go of the lunge and simply swing from side to side.

Let your feet be still on the ground as you swing.

Let your hips be still as you swing from your waist.

Let your waist be still as you swing from your shoulders.

Let everything be still except the breath.

In this exercise and all the following stretching exercises, KEEP BREATHING.

Teaching tip

Regarding the opening stance, 'soft knees' may be a concept that is difficult for students to grasp initially. Have them tighten their thighs and reach down to touch their kneecaps to feel what tight knees feel like. Then have them bend their knees and touch their kneecaps so they can feel that bent knees are not the same as soft knees. Then have them stand with just a bit of give in the knees and with relaxed thighs. Ask them if they can then move their kneecaps slightly from side to side with their hands. This is 'soft knees'. You may need to demonstrate and/or help individual students to find this stance.

Granny dance – arms and torso (1 minute)

Begin standing with feet roughly parallel, about hip-width apart, knees soft and arms to the side.

Raise your left arm; at the same time, bend your left knee and raise the foot up onto the toe. Then push your heel down to the floor as you press the palm of your hand up towards the ceiling.

Repeat on the right, and then alternate sides four or five times.

Tilt your torso forward about thirty degrees and continue stretching from side to side four or five times.

Tilt your torso forward another thirty degrees and stretch; then tilt another thirty degrees, so that your chest and arms are parallel to the ground, and continue stretching from side to side four or five times.

Tilt towards the ground another thirty degrees and stretch, and finally come to a roll-down position and reach for the ground as you stretch from side to side.

Partnered stretches – upper back and torso (about 2 minutes each)

I. Find a partner who is somewhere in the neighbourhood of your height. Partners, discuss together if you feel comfortable touching and being touched on the wrists and letting your partner help support your weight. If you are, give consent to your partner. If not, check in with your instructor about modifying the exercise or doing an alternate exercise on your own.

Stand facing your partner with your feet close together; leave about 4–5 inches between your toes and theirs.

Clasp each other's wrists.

Slowly lean away from each other, keeping your bottom in line with your body.

You will be holding up your partner; the stretch is actually easier if you can trust your partner and not try to take their weight without giving yours.

Let your shoulders be pulled forward, and feel the stretch across your upper back.

Hold the stretch for 30 or 40 seconds, and then both bend your knees and lower your bottoms to the floor until you are sitting.

Taking each other's weight again, stand back up together and then gradually come out of the backwards lean and balance on your own two feet.

Repeat a couple of times.

II. Partners, discuss together if you feel comfortable holding hands and letting your partner help support your weight. If you are, give consent to your partner. If not, check in with your instructor about modifying the exercise or doing an alternate exercise on your own.

Stand side by side with your partner, with your feet close to each other and close to your partner's feet.

Hold hands.

Lift your other arm up over your head. Your arm should be next to your ear, not in front of it nor behind it.

Grasp wrists with your partner above your heads.

Lean your hips out away from your partner, taking each other's weight as you do so.

You should feel a nice stretch along your side. Hold it for 30–40 seconds, and then return to standing.

Repeat on the other side.

Teaching tip

These stretches are usually most successful with groups who are working together in a training program rather than in a one-off class.

It can be interesting to have the students do the first stretch once to get the hang of it and then do it again noticing what they are doing with their breathing. Many will find that they are holding their breath. Ask them to do it again while consciously engaging their breathing – keeping it moving all through the exercise. Many will find that this makes the movements of the stretch much easier.

Shoulder stretches (1–2 minutes each)

Begin standing with feet roughly parallel, about hip-width apart, knees soft and arms to the side.

I. Stretch your arms out straight in front of you with the palms facing up, and cross one over the other at the elbow.

Bend both arms. The elbow of the arm on top should be peeking out over the bottom elbow.

Try to touch your palms together – you may only get the fingers of one hand touching the palm of the other, which is fine.

Lift that whole tangle of arms up in front of your face as far as it will go and hold for about a minute (see Figure 2).

Focus on the sensation of releasing and opening in the shoulders and upper back.

This is also a particularly good position for feeling your breath drop all the way to your pelvic bowl.

Repeat with the other arm on top.

II. Stretch the right arm across your chest. Use the left forearm to pull the right upper arm in even closer to the chest.

Hold the position for about a minute.

Remember to keep breathing and focusing on the opening of the right shoulder blade.

Repeat on the other side.

III. Clasp your hands together behind your back, arms straight.

Roll one shoulder back and then the other shoulder back.

Try to lift your hands as far up and away from your back as you can, while keeping your back upright.

Hold the position for about a minute, breathing fully all the while.

Figure 2 Shoulder stretch I

Neck stretch (3–4 minutes)

Begin standing with feet roughly parallel, about hip-width apart, knees soft and arms to the side.

Let your head drop forward. We'll call this position 6:00.

Roll your head around so that the right ear is over the right shoulder and you are facing straight ahead, pointing your face neither to the ceiling nor the floor. We'll call this 3:00.

Roll your head around to the other side so that the left ear is over the left shoulder and you are facing straight ahead, pointing your face neither to the ceiling nor the floor. We'll call this 9:00.

Return your head to 6:00 and then roll it gently between 5:00 and 7:00, feeling the specific stretch of the muscles at the back of the neck and down into the shoulders.

Expand the rolling motion between 4:00 and 8:00 for about 30 seconds, and then expand it again so that you are rolling your head from 3:00 on one side to 9:00 on the other. Continue for about 30 seconds.

Bring your head to a rest at 3:00. Be sure that your ear is over your shoulder and your face is pointing straight ahead, not up or down. Check that your body has not been pulled to the right and you are still standing straight.

Take your right hand – the one that your head is nearest to – and rest it over your head. There's no need to pull on the head, just let the weight of the arm rest there. Imagine that you are carrying a heavy weight in the other hand. This heaviness will increase the stretch along your neck. Keep breathing and hold for 30–40 seconds.

Drop the heavy weight, drop your right hand and let your head roll back around through 6:00 to 9:00. Repeat the stretch on this side.

Let your head roll back around to 6:00. Lace your fingers together and drape your hands over the fat part of the back of your head (known anatomically as your occipital bone). Let your elbows fall down towards the floor rather than holding them out toward the walls. There's no need to pull on the head, just let the weight of the arms rest there.

This is a particularly good position to feel the ribs opening to the breath through your back. Focus on your breathing and hold the stretch for about 30 seconds.

Let your arms drop and allow your head to float up. Register the feeling of release in the neck.

In the 3:00 and 9:00 positions, it can be hard for students to sense if their faces are indeed pointing straight ahead. It is worth taking the time to help them make necessary adjustments. In rolling between 5:00 and 7:00, and 4:00 and 8:00, the motion is not that of shaking the head 'no'; it is that of moving the ear towards the shoulder.

Halloween cat – spine stretch (1–2 minutes)

Get down onto your hands and knees, with your back parallel to the ground and flat like a table.

Curl your tail bone down towards the floor, which will cause your back to arch up towards the ceiling, like a Halloween cat.

Hold the stretch for a moment, but keep the breath moving.

Then, slowly rotate your tail bone so that it points up to the ceiling, which will cause your back to sink down towards the floor, like a broken-down old horse. Your face will naturally lift up, but don't lift it so far that the back of your neck collapses.

Hold the stretch for a moment, but keep the breath moving.

Repeat the movement between the Halloween cat and the broken-down old horse two or three times.

Sun salutation – all over body stretch (5–7 minutes)

If you have problems with your back, you may need to skip step four.

We've encountered several versions of this traditional Yoga exercise and have adapted it specifically for voice work. If you know another version that works for you, use it. Breathing should be strongly engaged, even blown out on the out-breath.

1. Begin standing with feet roughly parallel, about hip-width apart, knees soft and arms to your side.

    On the in-breath, lift your arms out to your side and up until they are over your head, palms facing in. Think of your shoulder blades travelling down your back as your arms go up.

    On the out-breath, reach forward, tilting from your hips until your back and arms are parallel to the floor and flat like a table, and then continue down until your fingers are brushing the floor.

    On the in-breath, hold your calves and pull your chest in to your knees.

2. On the out-breath, step your left leg back and bend your right knee, bringing yourself into a lunge. Keep your chest up and open.

    Hold this position on the in-breath.

3. On the out-breath, place your hands flat on the floor and bring your right foot back to join your left. Your body should be flat like a board, as if you were doing push-ups. Avoid sinking between your shoulders and tilting your chin upwards.

    Hold this position on the in-breath.

4. On the out-breath, bring your knees to the floor and pull your hips back so they are over your ankles. Push your upper body forward, running your nose along the ground, and then push your hands against the floor to lift your upper chest. Keep your shoulders back and down.

    Hold yourself in this position on the in-breath.

5. On the out-breath, curl your toes under and push your bottom up into the air so your body is in the shape of an upside down 'V'.
   Hold this position on the in-breath.
6. On the out-breath bring your left foot forward into a lunge. Keep your chest up and open.
   Hold this position on the in-breath.
7. On the out-breath, bring your right foot forward to join your left so that you are in a roll-down position.
   Hold the position on the in-breath.
8. On the out-breath, keep your knees loose as you roll back up to standing.
9. On the in-breath, lift your arms out to the side and up until they are over your head, palms facing in. Think of your shoulder blades travelling down your back as your arms go up.
   On the out-breath lower your arms.
   Repeat once, and then repeat twice on the other side, moving your right leg into the lunges.

> **Teaching tip**
> **Talk through the actions of the sun salutation while demonstrating once with the students just watching. Also talk them through the actions as you do the four repetitions with them. Model strongly engaged breathing. Many students will raise their bottoms in the air during the pose when their bodies should be flat like a board and will need to be reminded not to do so.**

Floor work

Much of the early work on relaxation, release and alignment is done on the floor, which may seem like a strange way to train as an actor. Being on the floor, however, allows you to observe how your body feels and how your breathing functions when almost all muscular engagement, including that necessary to sit or stand, is stripped away. You can then work on re-introducing only the muscular engagement that you need when you need it.

For most exercises, you can work in supine – on your back with your legs stretched out in front of you and the toes falling away from each other; or in semi-supine – with feet flat on the floor and knees pointing up to the ceiling. In either position, the arms should be to the sides with the shoulders falling towards the floor. This should cause the palms of the hands to open to the ceiling.

Many people will feel most comfortable with a folded scarf or thin book under the head to keep the neck long. The chin should not, however, be forced down towards the chest.

Spending time on the floor can get chilly, so you are advised to put on sweaters and socks before you begin.

If you have back problems or physical limitations that make it difficult or uncomfortable for you to lie on your back, you can do these exercises lying on your side instead. Change the side that you are lying on from time to time. You can also sit, preferably in a chair with good lumbar support.

Floor work is all about calm and focus – mental qualities that are as important in acting as physical relaxation; it's good to take the opportunity to cultivate them. In general, you shouldn't speak during the exercises unless something occurs which demands the instructor's attention.

We start with three visualization exercises which can be used interchangeably:

Visualizations (7–10 minutes each)

I. Start in supine or semi-supine. Imagine lying on the soft, warm sand of a tropical beach. You are under the shade of a palm tree, but as time passes, the shadow will move, and your body will progressively be exposed to the direct sunlight.

First imagine the sun warming your toes. Focus on the image of the toes loosening and softening.

Imagine the sun then shining on your feet and any tension there melting away.

Proceed, step by step, through the following sequence, at each point imagining the warmth of the sun melting any tension:

Ankles	Shoulders
Shins and calves	Upper arms
Knees	Lower arms
Thighs	Hands
Pelvis	Neck
Lower abdomen and back	Face
Ribs	Scalp
Chest and upper back	

When you are finished, stretch and wiggle on the floor, then return to supine and notice your breathing – how often it comes, where it moves in your torso, how much effort goes into it.

II. You've probably come across bean bag chairs or at least bean bags. For this exercise, begin (in supine or semi-supine) by imagining that you are a bean bag person and that you are stuffed to the point of almost bursting with the little Styrofoam balls found in bean bag chairs. You do not need to put any additional tension into your muscles to achieve this state – it describes where you are when you first lie down.

Imagine that there is a seam in your foot and that a small hole opens up in that seam. This will allow a few of those Styrofoam balls to escape. As they fall out of the open seam, the balls that are left in the foot are less tightly packed. They begin to shift as more of them start to pour out of the hole. Gradually, imagine the foot emptying, which allows the balls packed into the ankle to shift and loosen and begin to escape too.

Focus on this image of emptying proceeding up the lower legs, knees, thighs and pelvis.

Imagine a hole opening along a seam in the lower back and the flow of balls proceeding from there to the lower abdomen, ribs, upper back and chest.

Imagine small holes opening up at the tips of the fingers and the balls draining from the hands, the forearms, the upper arms and the shoulders.

Imagine an opening in the back of the neck and picture the neck, jaw and face softening as all the balls from the head roll away.

When you are finished, stretch and wiggle on the floor; then return to supine and notice your breathing – how often it comes, where it moves in your torso, how much effort goes into it.

III. Begin in supine. Imagine your legs are becoming very heavy. Consciously relinquish to the floor all responsibility for 'holding' your heavy legs in any way.

Imagine the arms and shoulders becoming very heavy. Give them also entirely to the floor.

Visualize the face, jaw and entire head becoming very heavy. Imagine that if the floor were made of foam, your head would be sinking into it another half an inch – you don't need to press your head down to do this; just focus on its great weight.

Move slowly into semi-supine.

Now turn your attention to your pelvis. Imagine that, as it is (no need to introduce any additional tension), it is a big slab of butter that has been in the freezer. Because it's frozen, it is hard and brittle. Imagine taking this butter pelvis out of the freezer into a warm room, and visualize it gradually softening, becoming by degrees more yielding and pliable until finally it begins to spread a bit on the floor under its own weight, as a large block of butter will do on a warm surface.

Concentrate for a moment on that picture of the hips softening and widening along the floor.

Next, imagine that your shoulder girdle is also a slab of butter that has been in the freezer. Imagine it too coming into a warm room and progressively softening and then widening.

Turn your attention to your spine.

Feel each distinct bump of your spine along the floor, and imagine the separate vertebrae in the areas that are not against the floor, i.e. the lower back and the neck.

In your mind's eye, picture a small sac between each vertebra (these small sacs do, in fact, exist, but function quite differently from what we will imagine).

Imagine that with every breath you take, a tiny puff of air fills each of these sacs. The filling of the sacs will cause your spine to lengthen, imperceptibly, along the floor. You don't have to pull your spine in any way to make this happen – just work the image.

On the out-breath, imagine the little sacs emptying of air, but the spine staying long against the floor.

Repeat for six or seven breath cycles.

When you are finished, stretch and wiggle on the floor, then return to semi-supine and reconnect to the sense of width across the pelvis and shoulders and length along the floor.

Teaching tip

When leading visualization exercises, it is important to use a tone of voice that is soothing but not narcotic. Walking around the room can help you keep up your own energy and volume. Give each portion of the exercise the time that it needs to develop, but keep the overall pace moving. Avoid long periods of silence. Remind the students that meaningful release requires an active mental engagement with the exercise and that relaxation means freeing the body's potential energy, not falling asleep. It may help some students to work with their eyes open. If possible, dim the lights so that they don't have to squint against the glare.

Even with the best of intentions, however, it is not uncommon for students to fall asleep. If you notice a student has done so, simply standing next to them may prompt them to rouse. Avoid calling attention to sleeping students – the less self-conscious they feel about it, the more quickly they will be able to refocus their attention on the exercise.

Some students may find visualizations disturbing – the images used may seem illogical or may have negative connotations. A simple alternative is the following exercise:

Tension and release (5–7 minutes)

Start in supine or semi-supine.

Put as much tension in the feet as possible – clench them tight, tight, tight for five seconds, then release on an out-breath. You may notice, as you tighten them, that tension creeps into other parts of your body as well, for example, the lower back. Try to keep all other areas as soft and loose as possible and focus on tensing in the feet alone.

Repeat in the following sequence:

Ankles	Shoulders
Shins and calves	Upper arms
Knees	Lower arms
Thighs	Hands
Pelvis	Neck
Buttocks	Jaw
Lower abdomen and back	Face
Ribs	Scalp
Chest and upper back	

When you are finished, stretch and wiggle on the floor, then return to supine and notice your breathing – how often it comes, where it moves in your torso, how much effort goes into it.

The following exercise is very useful after you have begun to experience some release on your own. Working with a partner increases both awareness of one's own tensions and sensitivity to another's process.

✹ *Partnered manipulations (15–20 minutes per partner)*

Each student should get a partner (if there is an odd number, the instructor can pair with a student).

Partners, discuss together if you feel comfortable touching and being touched on the following places: feet, legs below the knee, legs just above the knee, hands, arms and heads. If you are, give consent to your partner. If not, check in with your instructor about modifying the exercise or doing an alternate exercise on your own.

1. Partner A, lie on the floor in supine.

   Partner B, sit next to one of A's legs.

   Partner B, take A's leg at the calf and lift it a few inches off the ground, gently jiggling it, if necessary, until partner A has given you as much of the full weight of the leg as they are able. Partner A, try not to 'help' in holding that leg up!

   Partner B, rest A's leg on your own knee.

   Gently hold A's foot and begin to point and flex it.

   Partner A, send images of softness and looseness to the ankle joint as well as the mental message 'Let go'.

   EVERYBODY KEEP BREATHING

As the joint loosens, partner B can begin making circles or figure 8's with A's foot and wiggling it gently.

Ankles can take a while to warm up, so don't rush it.

B, don't get caught in the same pattern of motion or A may begin to unconsciously help you. Surprise A with unexpected (but not sudden or jarring) movements.

2. Next, partner B kneel next to your partner's knee, facing A's feet.

B, lift and support A's thigh just above the knee with your arm, allowing their knee to bend and lower leg to dangle.

Still holding the thigh upright, move the lower leg through the knee's range of motion. Note that the knee joint moves primarily up and down – do not try to force it to go side to side.

If A tries to help or resists the movement of the lower leg, B can lightly jiggle the leg through the point of resistance or quietly say, 'Let go'.

EVERYBODY KEEP BREATHING

3. After a minute or so, B, still holding onto A's leg with the knee bent, swivel around so that you are facing A's face.

B, you can then hold onto the lower leg and manipulate the hip joint by moving the knee away from the body, across the body, up towards the chest and down towards the ground. You can also rotate the leg within the hip socket.

If there are any areas in the range of motion that feel tight, gently work through them until A is able to let go.

After a minute or so, straighten A's leg, and, still holding on to the lower leg, gently lean back, stretching the leg away from the body in a direction parallel to the floor.

Accepting no help, return the leg to the floor.

4. Repeat with the other leg.

5. Next, sit beside one of A's arms.

Take A's arm at the wrist and lift it a few inches off the ground, gently jiggling it, if necessary, until partner A has given over as much of the full weight of the arm as they are able. Partner A, try not to help in holding that arm!

B, rest A's arm on your own knee.

Gently move A's hand back and forth and, as the wrist joint begins to soften, in small circles.

Don't get caught in the same pattern of motion or A may begin to unconsciously help you. Surprise A with unexpected (but not sudden or jarring) movements.

EVERYBODY KEEP BREATHING

6. Next, work on moving the forearm through the elbow's range of motion.

After a minute or so, hold on to the upper arm and move it through the shoulder's range of motion, which is wide and should be thoroughly explored.

7. After a minute or so, straighten A's arm, and, still holding on to the upper arm, gently lean back, stretching the arm away from the body in a direction parallel to the floor.

Accepting no help, return the arm to the floor.

8. Repeat with the other arm.

9. B, next sit directly above A's head.

Remove any scarves or books and slide your fingers under A's head, cradling it without, initially, lifting it off the floor. A, deepen your breathing while giving the weight of your head to your partner.

B, when you feel A's head start to get heavier, rock it from side to side in a 'no' movement.

When the neck is free, B can then lift the head slightly in a 'yes' nod and move it in circles or figure eights.

A, begin to breathe out on a 'fffff' sound. Then turn it into a 'vvvvv' sound. Finally try humming a bit. Notice if creating sound makes it harder or easier for you to really let go of your neck.

After a couple of minutes, B gently return A's head to the floor.

10. A, now take a moment to scan through your body and notice how it is feeling, particularly in those areas where you had previously identified tension.

A, try to take a very deep breath and notice where in your body the breath fills and where it feels blocked.

Everybody take a stretch and a wiggle as the A partners slowly bring themselves back to sitting up.

Switch over and repeat with A taking B's role.

A, as you now work, see how much you can preserve the physical sensation of release and relaxation you found through having just done the exercise. Remember to keep breathing and use minimal effort to get the job done.

Teaching tip

This exercise is usually most successful with groups who are working together in a training program rather than in a one-off class. It requires a good level of trust between the students, so monitor to make sure that students are all using slow, gentle movements when performing the manipulations. Because there is quite a bit of touching involved, you may want to assign partners who are likely to be comfortable with each other.

Discourage chatting and giggling, although some students may be ticklish and should be supportively coached to try to breathe through the impulse to laugh. Some students cannot resist telling their partners that they are tense in particular areas. Such observations can be counterproductive, however, and may increase tension. Monitor the class dynamic and, if necessary, remind them that this is a non-verbal exercise. All students will need to be reminded to keep breathing throughout the exercise. Note that this is an exercise that can be extended into further breathing or voicing when the students are ready.

Roll-ups

Lovely as work on the floor can be, it's not where you're going to do most of your talking. In order for the release and relaxation work done on the floor to benefit you when upright, attention must be paid to how you get up off the floor and into a standing position. We will look at the whole process in a moment, but a key part of it is the roll-up – that is, moving from standing with your torso and head hanging down to a fully upright position.

If you are in an acting training programme, it may feel like you spend inordinate amounts of time rolling up and down your spine, but this simple activity can be a vital building block for everything you do as a performer. When done with attention and precision, a roll-up can build awareness of and flexibility in the spine, giving you more physical freedom; it can help you find the alignment and balance that allow you to move dynamically; it can bring your breath down into your body and power your voice; and it can focus your attention in the present moment – the cornerstone of great acting.

Whenever you complete a roll-up, take a moment to adjust your alignment:

- Check that you are balanced on your feet. As far as possible, your weight should be neither too far forward nor too far back and should be evenly distributed in both legs. Take a moment just now to stand up and think about your feet. Each foot has three points designed to bear your weight: one at the heel, and two on the ball of your foot just behind your big and little toes. When you are standing upright, imagine your weight being distributed evenly across these three tripod points in each foot.

- Now make sure your ankles, knees and hips are not stiff or braced.

- Pay attention to your pelvis also: imagine the shape that your pelvis makes is like a bowl and see it filled with water. If you shift your weight over to one leg or the other, the water will spill out of the opposite side of the bowl. Similarly, if you tip your pelvis too far forward or back, the water will spill out the other side. Think of keeping the water in your pelvic bowl smooth and even.

- Tell yourself that your back is long and wide; that your shoulders are loose and low; that your neck is long and free; that your head is facing forward and that the crown of your head is going up; and, most importantly, that you are breathing fully.

Well done! You are beginning to experience your aligned posture. From there, a world of expressive choices is open to you.

Getting off the floor and the everyday roll-up (1–2 minutes)

In supine, take a little stretch and wiggle to get some energy moving through your body, and then roll over onto your stomach.

Pull your bottom back over your heels and fold your upper body over your knees. Stretch your arms out in front of you and let your head hang down towards the ground. This yoga position is commonly called extended child pose.

Imagine that your face is heavy and your jaw is hanging down towards the floor.

See if you can walk your fingers out another inch in front of you. Then see if you can leave them there and sink your bottom a bit closer to your heels.

Take a couple of nice, deep breaths, and feel your back opening.

Now, curl your toes under and push yourself back into a squat.

Let your arms rest outside of your knees.

Your head may be pointing down to the floor; if it is, lift and lengthen your neck so that your head is in line with your spine.

In this position, start to bounce on your toes a bit (unless you have trouble with your knees).

With each bounce, imagine your spine, from the base of your skull to the tip of your tail bone, getting a little bit longer. Do this for ten or so bounces.

Then, with each bounce, imagine that your hips are getting a little bit wider. Do this for ten or so bounces.

Finally, with each bounce imagine that your shoulders are getting a little bit wider. Do this for ten or so bounces.

Stop bouncing, and raise your tail bone up into the air – think of it floating its way up. Leave your upper body hanging forward; this is a roll-down position.

Check that your knees are loose.

On the roll-up, imagine that your tail bone is getting heavy and that it is the sinking of the tail bone that causes the rest of the spine to unfurl, like a leaf. Think of the back lengthening and widening as you build each vertebra on top of the other, leaving the head and neck till last.

Finally roll up the neck, thinking of unfurling it too into length. Imagine a surge of energy running between your shoulder blades and up your neck. Feel your weight evenly distributed across your feet.

Take a moment to adjust your alignment.

Whenever you get up off the floor, go through this process of rolling onto your stomach and moving from extended child pose through the squat into a roll-down. Do the bounces too, if they are helpful. Always finish by taking a moment to check and adjust your alignment.

The wall roll-up (about 1 minute)

Position yourself so that you are in the roll-down position with your bottom against the wall.

You're going to take a nice, slow roll-up to standing. As you do so, try to place each vertebra against the wall as it builds on top of the one beneath it. Keep breathing throughout.

To get the lower back vertebrae against the wall, you will probably have to start with your feet fairly far away from the wall and a good bit of bend in your knees. Feel free to shuffle your feet towards or away from the wall as you go and adjust the degree of bend in your knees.

As you move through your mid-back into rolling up your upper back, you will probably find that your lower back, in the lumbar curve, peels away from the wall. This is fine, but do try to keep the sacrum (the bony plate at the base of the spine) flat to the wall.

Don't try to force the vertebrae in the neck against the wall; do find a position for your head against the wall in which the nose is pointing neither up nor down.

When you have completed the roll-up, take a good, deep breath and feel your back spreading softly against the wall.

Roll back down, trying to peel each vertebra away from the wall, one by one.

Repeat a couple of times, being sure to breathe at all times.

Step away from the wall and rock gently back and forth on your feet to find the point where you feel most balanced. Take a moment to check and adjust your alignment.

☉ The zipper (1–2 minutes)

For this exercise you will need a partner who is somewhere in the neighbourhood of your height.

Partners, discuss together if you feel comfortable standing with your backs and bottoms touching each other. If you are, give consent to your partner. If not, check in with your instructor about modifying the exercise or doing an alternate exercise on your own.

Once you are both in a roll-down, position yourself so that your bottom is against your partner's bottom.

Together, you're both going to take a nice, slow roll-up to standing. As you do so, try to bring each vertebra of your spines together one at a time. Imagine that the vertebrae joining are like the teeth of a zipper coming together. Keep breathing throughout.

To get the lowest vertebrae to touch, you will probably have to start with your feet fairly far away from each other and a good bit of bend in your knees. You can shuffle your feet towards or away from each other and adjust the degree of bend in your knees as you proceed.

As you move through your mid-back into rolling up your upper back, you will probably find that your lower backs, in the lumbar curve, peel away from each other. This is fine, but do try to keep your sacrums flat against each other.

When you have completed the roll-up, take a good, deep breath and feel your back spreading softly against your partner's.

Roll back down, trying to peel each vertebra away from your partner's, one by one, like the teeth of a zipper coming away from each other. Again, you may find that you need to shuffle your feet a bit on the way down, which is fine.

Repeat a couple of times, being sure to breathe at all times.

Step away from your partner and rock gently back and forth on your feet to find the point where you feel most balanced. Take a moment to check and adjust your alignment.

Teaching tip

This exercise is usually most successful with groups who are working together in a training program rather than in a one-off class. It allows you to see particularly clearly which students have a tendency to roll up by lifting the back straight up or in two sections rather than moving through all the articulations of the spine. The sacrum is, of course, fused and moves as a plate, and there are several vertebrae in the lumbar curve that also move together, but otherwise, the students' spines should meet point by point. If this is not happening, they may simply be standing too closely together and need to adjust the distance between their feet as they go. They may also need to think of softening their ankles, knees and/or hips. With this and the following partnered exercises you may wish to assign partners if you feel it will make students more comfortable.

Let your fingers do the walking (about 2 minutes per partner)

Find a partner who is somewhere in the neighbourhood of your height.

Partners, discuss together if you feel comfortable touching and being touched on the back. If you are, give consent to your partner. If not, check in with your instructor about modifying the exercise or doing an alternate exercise on your own.

Partner A roll down.

Partner B give partner A's back a little rub down. Check that the head is hanging loosely.

Everybody keep breathing.

Now position yourself behind A and place one index finger on either side of the spine at the base of the sacrum. Slowly walk your fingers up your partner's spine and neck.

A, try to stack each vertebra onto the one beneath as your partner's fingers come to it, neither getting ahead nor falling behind. You will need to have some give in your ankles, knees and hips to do this. Everybody keep breathing!

Repeat with A walking their fingers up B's spine.

☺ Cape shrug (less than 1 minute per partner)

Get a partner. Discuss together if you feel comfortable touching and being touched on the back. If you are, give consent to your partner. If not, check in with your instructor about modifying the exercise or doing an alternate exercise on your own.

Start with partner A in a roll-down.

Partner B walk your fingers up A's spine to a point just between the shoulder blades and stop. A's head and shoulders should still be hanging forward.

Partner A, in this mostly-rolled-up position, imagine that you are wearing a long, heavy, satin cape. Easily shrug the cape off your left shoulder and leave the shoulder back.

Easily shrug the cape off your right shoulder and leave the shoulder back.

Imagine a surge of energy rising up between your shoulder blades and causing your neck to unfurl and roll up until your face is forward.

Repeat with partner B in a roll-down.

Teaching tip

This exercise, which we learned from the movement teacher Debbie Greene, is useful to counteract the tendency to thrust the chest forward in the last part of the roll-up. Many people associate that kind of military posture with 'standing up straight', but it pulls the spine out of alignment, causing an exaggeration in the lumbar and cervical curves. At the end of the roll-up, the chest should be in line with the hips; neither collapsed, nor pulled up and pressed forward.

☺ Sacrum press (about 2 minutes per partner)

Find a partner who is somewhere in the neighbourhood of your height.

Partners, discuss together if you feel comfortable touching and being touched on the following places: the sacrum (the bony plate just above your tail bone), shoulder and forehead. If you are, give consent to your partner. If not, check in with your instructor about modifying the exercise or doing an alternate exercise on your own.

Partner A roll down.

Partner B stand to A's side. Place one hand flat on A's sacrum (the bony plate just above the tail bone). Place the fingertips of the other hand lightly on A's shoulder. You will not be pulling on the shoulder at all; the fingers are there to gently guide and help your partner feel balanced.

Partner A, bounce your knees a couple of times to make sure that they are soft and loose with plenty of 'give' in them; the exercise will not work if they are at all rigid. Think of your whole body as being easy and free like a floppy doll's.

Partner B, on a count of three, apply a good amount of pressure down onto A's sacrum – not enough to make them stumble or feel pushed off balance, but enough to initiate a counter-lever force that will bring them into a roll-up. The fingers of the other hand rest lightly on the shoulder the whole time.

The roll-up will be a bit quicker than many others, but should not be so fast as to feel jarring or violent in any way.

Partner B, leave your one hand on A's sacrum and move the other so that the fingertips rest lightly on their forehead to remind them that the head stays in line with the rest of the body.

Leaving your hands where they are, take A for a walk by applying steady and firm (but not forceful) pressure to the sacrum. You can turn A by applying a bit more pressure with either the heel of the hand or the fingers.

A, imagine that your partner's hand on your sacrum is a little motor that is moving you around the room. Start to hum as you move, imagining that the hum is coming from that motor located low on your back.

After a minute or so, B release A to walk about on their own.

A, imagine that that motor is still propelling you around the room from your sacrum, humming all the while.

After a minute or so of free movement, return to your partner and repeat the exercise for partner B.

As you walk around during the day, thinking of the sacrum as being the motor for your movement and of keeping the neck long can help to align your body and allow it to move more efficiently.

Teaching tip

This exercise is usually most successful with groups who are working together in a training program rather than in a one-off class. It has its origins in one described by Barbara Houseman in *Finding Your Voice* (2002). As the students are being walked around the room, if you see any who are thrusting their chests out, jutting their heads forward, or tilting their chins up and collapsing their necks, individually stop them and help them to adjust their alignment.

Keeping it loose

'Keeping it loose' is a principle that applies at all stages of voice work and to acting in general. When we concentrate, we all have a tendency to get a bit fixed or frozen, sometimes through the torso, sometimes in the joints, sometimes even in the little muscles around the eyes. To break out of this stiffness, it's good to get into the habit of frequently doing a quick scan of your body to notice if there are any pockets of tension that can be released. This is useful not only when doing exercises, but also when sitting at the computer, rehearsing a scene, talking on the phone, or even making dinner.

Massage, physically shaking out, stretching and wiggling can be great ways to break that pattern of getting fixed, and you are encouraged to do them frequently. As with all of the relaxation, release and alignment work, however, it's very possible to go through the motions and achieve very little if you are not also paying close attention to what is happening in your body and consciously engaging with images of softening and loosening.

Partner massage (6–7 minutes per partner)

Teaching tip

Massage is popular and can be very useful. In the hands of students, however, it is usually most effective as a way of helping the body to reconnect to a feeling of looseness and ease that has been deeply explored in floor work exercises rather than as a primary means of achieving release and relaxation. It is usually most successful with groups who are working together in a training program rather than in a one-off class.

Partners who are being massaged should be encouraged to speak out if the pressure being applied is too strong or not strong enough.

Some students may feel uncomfortable receiving massages and can stretch on their own instead. Encourage students to stay focused and avoid being overly intimate when giving massages. Assign partners, if it feels appropriate.

Get a partner who is somewhere in the neighbourhood of your height.

Partners, discuss together if you feel comfortable touching and being touched on the following places: shoulders, back, arms and hands. If you are, give consent to your partner. If not, check in with your instructor about stretching those areas on your own.

Partner A, begin by rubbing down the shoulders and upper back of your partner.

Then, use your whole hand, but particularly the thumb, to massage the area where the neck joins the shoulder.

Work your way along the right shoulder, and then massage down the right arm to the hand. Massage back up the right arm, across the shoulders, and down the left arm to the hand. Massage back up to the area where the neck joins the shoulder.

Partner B, let your head hang forward.

Partner A, gently massage the neck for a minute or so.

Partner B, let the heaviness of your head pull you into a roll-down.

Partner A, massage the mid and lower back.

Finally, do a 'Let Your Fingers Do the Walking' roll-up.

Repeat with partner A receiving the massage.

Joint articulations (2–3 minutes)

We often hold tension in our joints, particularly in the arms and legs. This is a good exercise for beginning a warm-up or for re-energizing the body after floor work. As with many exercises which seem repetitive or become familiar over time, part of the point is engaging the mind and resisting relying on autopilot. Stay in the moment, and keep breathing. It's also okay to have fun and smile.

Begin standing with feet roughly parallel, about hip-width apart, knees soft and arms outstretched to the side.

Loosen your wrists by circling your hands eight times in one direction and then eight times in the other direction.

Now focus on your elbows and circle your forearms eight times in one direction and eight times in the other.

Do the same with your shoulder joints by circling your arms eight times in each direction.

Now stand on the right leg. To keep your balance, it helps to focus on a point in the room about 3 metres in front of you. In this position, begin by circling your left foot eight times in each direction to release your ankle joint.

Now focus on your left knee, circling your lower leg eight times in each direction.

And now your hip joint – circle the whole leg four times in each direction.

Shake out the leg you've been standing on, and repeat these articulations with the right leg. Once you're finished, give yourself a good shake-out all over.

Loose shoulders (about 1 minute)

Begin standing with feet roughly parallel, about hip-width apart, knees soft and arms to the side.

Start swinging your right arm forward in a big circle. Allow your knees to bounce a little with the momentum of the arm movement. Let your breath come into sync with the rhythm of the movement. Send images of looseness and ease to the shoulder.

Repeat on the left side.

Repeat, swinging the right arm backward and then the left arm backward.

See if you can swing one arm backward and the other arm forward at the same time. If you find this difficult, get two partners, one on each arm, to help you.

Loose neck (about 1 minute)

Let your head drop forward, lace your fingers together and drape your hands over the fat part of the back of your head (your occipital bone) with your elbows falling down towards the floor, as in the first neck stretch from earlier in the chapter.

After 30–40 seconds, let your arms drop and allow your head to float up.

Imagine that you are one of those bobble-headed dolls that people sometimes put on the dashboards of their cars: your neck stays long, but your head can make a small, gentle bouncing motion up and down on top of it.

Get a good, gentle, little bounce going, and then rotate your head around to the left, bouncing all the way. Then rotate around to the right and back to centre, maintaining the bobble-headed doll bounce.

Loose hips

I. (about 1 minute)

With the ankles soft and the knees slightly bent, imagine that your pelvic bowl is a cradle. Rock the cradle from front to back ever so slightly – just barely half an inch.

Let the rocking motion gradually grow until your pelvis is moving through an arc of about 7–9 inches. Keep the bottom loose throughout – if you are having to push it forward, make the motion smaller.

II. (about 1 minute)

Imagine you have a very tiny, little hula hoop around your waist. Begin making a tiny hula hoop motion with your hips to get it moving.

Gradually let the imaginary hula hoop and the hula hoop motion grow until they are enormous – as big as they could possibly be.

Move the enormous hula hoop around in the opposite direction. Imagine it gradually shrinking until you are again making a very tiny hula hoop motion.

 III. (5–7 minutes per partner)

Kevin Crawford taught us this excellent exercise.

Get a partner who is somewhere in the neighbourhood of your height.

Partners, discuss together if you feel comfortable touching and being touched on the following places: feet, legs below the knee and legs just above the knee. If you are, give consent to your partner. If not, check in with your instructor about modifying the exercise or doing an alternate exercise on your own.

Partner A, lie on your back, and partner B sit by A's side.

Partner B, do a fairly quick version of the legwork in the 'Partnered Manipulations' exercise on both of A's legs.

Then, crouching in front of A, get a good grip on A's ankles and stand, lifting A's legs perpendicular to the floor.

B, lift A's pelvis slightly off the ground and swing it gently.

Then bounce on your toes, which will cause A's legs to shake slightly.

A, start breathing out on a 'huuuuuuh' sound. Think of the sound as being shaken out of your body from your pelvis.

After about a minute, B lower A's legs to the ground.

B, then get into a crouch and take A's legs by the ankles again. Hold the legs a couple of inches from the floor and swing them gently in an arhythmical and asymmetrical way.

A, start vocalizing, again, still thinking of the sounds as being shaken out of your body.

B, continue for 30–40 seconds and then lower A's legs back to the ground.

Repeat with partner B lying on their back.

Teaching tip
This exercise works best with groups who are working together regularly and have a good degree of trust with each other.

'I'm so excited' (6–8 minutes)

1. Begin with the group in a loose circle, all standing with feet roughly parallel and about hip-width apart, knees soft and arms to the side.

Lean forward slightly from your hips, and begin to shake your bottom. Your thighs and knees will move along with it.

Let the movement grow until your heels are coming off the floor a bit. If you're feeling very energized, you can even turn it into a little jog in place.

Let your upper body hang very loose as you do this – arms and chest bouncing along with the bottom movement.

Keep your neck long. Because you are leaning slightly forward, your head will also be tilted forward a bit; avoid compressing the back of your neck to peer up.

Think of your whole body as a big bowlful of loose, shaking jelly. It will feel a little silly, and that's just fine.

Once the group has established the movement, released into it, and is beginning to really enjoy it, let it start to shake some sound out of your body. Just a 'hah', 'huh', 'hee' or 'ho' to begin.

Feel how the movement of your body encourages a very free and easy release of sound.

Take a little break to catch your breath and stretch.

2. Come back to the bottom wiggling movement and let it get established again.

This time you're going to release not just sound but a voiced thought, and the thought you're going to release is, 'I'm soooooo loose!'

As a group, practise letting that thought bubble up out of your bouncing body a few times, and then go around the circle and do it individually. Again, it will feel a little silly, and that's half the point of the exercise – to get in touch with your inner little kid and enjoy the freedom of silliness.

Take a little break again.

3. Now as a group, shaking your bottoms again, try the thought, 'I'm soooooo excited!' Pretend it's your third birthday – you are THAT excited.

Alternate between, 'I'm soooooo loose!' and 'I'm soooooo excited!' Try to find how to keep the loose energy excited and the excited energy loose.

When an overall energy that is both excited and free is established, go around the circle and take 'I'm soooooo excited!' individually.

Teaching tip

This exercise is usually most successful with groups who are working together in a training program rather than in a one-off class. It is also somewhat advanced in that it brings the students onto voice. Much work on finding open, easy and free phonation will follow, but doing this exercise fairly early can give them a fun sense of how physical and vocal release connect.

Lead the group in coming onto vibration and then onto text. Don't let them get away with breathy, half-hearted sound; model an engaged, fully released sound for them and encourage them to match it. If, however, you can hear that people are starting to push or even scream, take it back down to a light and easy (but not breathy) 'hah'.

This exercise and the one following grew from work done with the Alexander Technique teacher, Glynn MacDonald.

🎧 We will all be stars (5–8 minutes)

Begin with the group in a circle all facing away from one another.

Start with a minute or so of bottom shaking.

While still shaking, release a loose but energized 'Oh!' a few times.

Let the shaking become smaller and release another few 'Oh's' without letting the energy drop.

Let the body become still (but not rigid) and release another few 'Oh's'.

Imagine that all of the energy that went into shaking your bottom is now circling around inside of you just below your solar plexus (above your tummy button).

With an easy, flowing movement raise your right hand up on a diagonal and imagine all that energy inside you pouring out your fingertips in the form of an 'Oh'. (The 'Oh', of course, will in reality come out of your mouth, but play with the image of its energy flowing through your open, loose but energized fingers).

Do the same with your left arm.

Pick up your right foot and picture all the energy in your centre pouring through it on an 'Oh' as you place it back on the ground at a bit of a diagonal from your body.

Do the same with your left foot.

Now, stretch out all four limbs in a star shape and imagine energy pouring from your centre through all of them as you say, 'How do I love thee?'

Turn around so that everyone in the circle is facing in and try it again a couple of times.

If it's going well, try it one at a time around the circle. You may find that, when you are on the spot that way, you tighten up a bit and lose some of the sense of freedom and flowing energy. At this point that's not a big worry. It's good to just notice the difference.

Teaching tip

Again, this exercise is somewhat advanced, but can be very useful for giving students a sense of where they are going with the work. And again, it is important that you model an easy (loose) but full (energized) release of sound. They may need to come back to simply shaking their bottoms and saying 'Oh' a few times between the stages of the exercise to stay in touch with this, which is fine.

Follow-up

Reflective practice questions:

- Is there an area in your body where you have a particularly hard time 'letting go?' Does it respond more readily to stretching, image-based work or direct manipulation?

- What relationship, if any, did you notice between breath and physical release?

- Which exercises left you feeling the most energized? Which left you the most drained?

- What aspects of bodywork do you most enjoy; shrink away from; find challenging?

- Are there correspondences between tension in any areas of your body; for example, does releasing tension in your arms have any effect on your neck? If you didn't notice any correspondences in class, try some out-of-class exploration.

- After doing the roll-up work, did you feel any differences in the way you move? Did any parts of your body feel wider or longer or looser than usual?

- What exercises from this chapter might you use to prepare for a rehearsal or a performance? How might they help you achieve your acting goals?

Exercises:

After a few sessions of bodywork, repeat the *Exploration* exercise. You will probably find that your old tension habits have not disappeared overnight, but you may find that your awareness of them is heightened and that you are able to relinquish them more easily.

As mentioned at the beginning of this section, relaxation, release and alignment work is ongoing. Once the groundwork has been laid through in-depth exploration at the beginning of the course, it's a good idea to revisit at least a few exercises at the beginning of every voice class to prepare the body to work.

Further reading

Houseman, Barbara, *Finding Your Voice*, Nick Hern Books, London, 2002. Chapter 2: 'Body Work', pp. 15–57.

Linklater, Kristin, *Freeing the Natural Voice* (Revised edition), Drama Book Publishers, New York, 2006. Chapter 1: 'Workday One', pp. 31–41.

McCallion, Michael, *The Voice Book* (Revised edition), Faber and Faber Ltd, London, 1998. Part One: 'Body Use', pp. 1–35.

McEvenue, Kelly, *The Alexander Technique for Actors*, Methuen, London, 2001. Part 1: 'The Alexander Technique in the Theatre', pp. 37–53.

Melton, Joan (with Kenneth Tom), *One Voice*, Heinemann, Portsmouth, NH, 2003. Chapter 1: 'The Foundation', pp. 3–19; and Chapter 4: 'The Voice/Movement Relationship,' pp. 77–93.

Nelson, Jeannette, *The Voice Exercise Book*, National Theatre Publishing, London, 2015. Chapter 1: 'Getting to Know Your Voice', pp. 21–3; and Chapter 2: 'Voice Exercises – Stage 1', pp. 34–5.

2
BREATH AND VOICE – CREATING CONNECTION

Framework

Breathing is intimately linked to everything that makes us human. First, we breathe to live, but breath is not only for survival; it is also emotional and expressive. It connects our creative, intellectual, conscious selves with our instinctive, primal, unconscious selves. Furthermore, at its most fundamental, your breath is your voice. Voice is breath transformed into sound waves by your vocal folds, but it is still essentially your breath. And if your breath is not full, free and responsive moment by moment, your voice will not be either.

The work we do in this chapter is designed to make you aware of your habits of breathing, any inhibitions that you experience, and also your potential for responsive inspiration and expressive exhalation. This work will take you beyond the breath of your daily needs and communication to a breath that moves with a character's own impulses and so gives the audience a deeper experience of the character's story.

This requires several stages of training: release work in order to enable a fuller breath and the development of new habits, technical/muscular work to build up the strength and responsiveness of the muscles responsible for respiration, and connecting work to link breath, voice and the thought/feeling impulse.

Vocal anatomy

To understand what is involved in achieving this stronger, more responsive breath, you need to understand a bit about why and how your body breathes. As we began by saying, human beings breathe to live – our bodies constantly need oxygen which they use to create the energy required simply to stay alive. But we also breathe to express ourselves in speech and song – and this requires more oxygen than just sitting still does.

You probably associate the process of breathing with your lungs. Your breath, however, is not actually created by your lungs but by the muscles surrounding them. The lungs themselves have no power to move on their own; they are little more than a collection of tubes and tiny air sacs. When you breathe in, oxygen travels down your windpipe, which divides in two as it enters the two lungs. Those two pipes divide and subdivide over twenty times into smaller and smaller tubes which eventually end in groups of little air sacs called alveoli. Each alveolus (there are approximately 300 million of them in your lungs) is surrounded by tiny blood vessels. The oxygen that has travelled down into these little pouches passes through the walls of the alveoli and the walls of the adjacent blood vessels to enter the bloodstream,

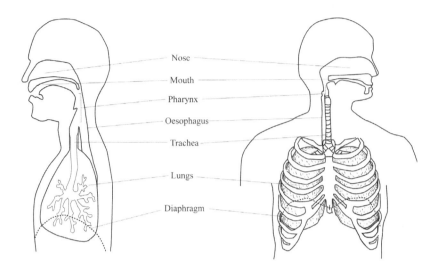

Nose
Mouth
Pharynx
Oesophagus
Trachea
Lungs
Diaphragm

Figure 3 The respiratory system

which will then carry it to individual cells where it will help to create the energy we use to live. At the same time, carbon dioxide (the waste product of this energy consumption), which your blood has been picking up on its travels through your body, passes from the bloodstream into the tiny pouches. From there, when you breathe out, it travels up the tubes, into your windpipe and then is expelled through your nose or mouth (see Figure 3).

So, you might ask, if the lungs don't have any muscle tissue in them and can't move on their own, what is it that causes them to expand, drawing oxygen in, and deflate, pushing carbon dioxide out? The lungs sit on your diaphragm and are attached to the ribcage (or thorax), a structure of muscle and bone which surrounds them in such a way that, when any part of this structure moves, the lungs move along with it. When it moves away from the lungs, the lungs are pulled with it. When it moves towards the lungs, the lungs are pushed inwards. When the lungs are pulled on, they expand; when they are pushed on, they compress. As the lungs expand, the air pressure within them drops and more air rushes in (via your nose and mouth) to bring the pressure back to normal. When the lungs are compressed, the air pressure within them rises and air rushes out (again, via your nose and mouth) to bring the pressure back to normal. Think of an old-fashioned button accordion or 'squeeze box'. When you first squeeze it (like you squeeze your lungs on an out-breath), you decrease the room inside it, increasing the pressure, and so air rushes out, making a musical note. When you expand it again (as your lungs expand on an in-breath), you increase the space inside it, decreasing the pressure, and so air rushes back in, ready to produce the next note. Try *Exploration I* for a human version of this 'squeeze box' image.

As mentioned, the lungs are encased in a surrounding structure of muscle and bone. The most important parts of this structure are the diaphragm and the ribs (see Figure 4). The diaphragm is a large sheet of muscle that lies between the organs in your chest (the lungs and heart) and all the organs in your abdomen (the stomach, liver, intestines, etc.). It consists of two flexible domes connected by a central tendon. The rim of the diaphragm attaches to the bottom of your sternum (breastbone) at the front, all the way around the lower ribs at the sides, and to the lumbar vertebrae of your spine at the back. When you need to inhale, the diaphragm contracts, and the domes are pulled down and partially flattened. This pulls down on your lungs, expanding them vertically. As the diaphragm does this, it pushes down

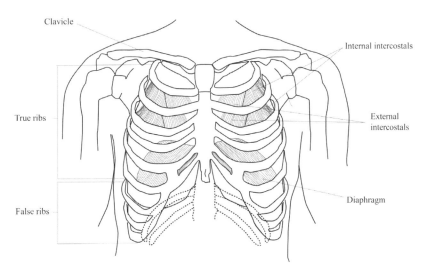

Clavicle

Internal intercostals

True ribs

External intercostals

Diaphragm

False ribs

Figure 4 The thorax

on the contents of the abdomen, causing the slight swelling of the belly we associate with breathing in. In exhalation, the diaphragm relaxes back into its dual-dome shape, passively pushing against the lungs and compressing them as it does so. When you are speaking, the muscles of the abdomen can also engage to push on the organs underneath the diaphragm, thus supporting it and giving extra pressure as it relaxes and pushes against the lungs. The diaphragm itself, however, does no active work at all on the out-breath. Try *Exploration I* again, and notice particularly how your diaphragm and abdominal muscles respond.

When you are simply breathing to stay alive, your diaphragm does most of the work, but in breath for speech your diaphragm does about 75 per cent of the work, and the muscles connected to your ribs do the other 25 per cent. You have twelve pairs of ribs in your chest. The topmost pair lies immediately under your clavicle (collarbone), while the bottom pair can be felt most easily in the small of your back just above your pelvis. To the rear, each rib is attached to one of your thoracic vertebrae via a gliding joint that allows the rib flexible movement. At the front, the top seven ribs attach directly to your sternum; they are known as the 'true' ribs. Ribs eight to ten are indirectly connected to the sternum by means of an attachment to rib seven, and this earns them the name of 'false' ribs; but the eleventh and twelfth ribs don't attach to anything in the front at all, and so are called the 'floating' ribs. For most of its length, each rib is composed of bone, but shortly before the rib attaches to the sternum at the front, the bony portion of the rib ends and a portion made of cartilage begins. (It is this cartilage, then, that attaches to the sternum in ribs 1–7, and that attaches ribs 8–10 to rib 7. The floating ribs are simply bone.)

Cartilage is a softer material than bone and has much more elasticity, so the ribs can move and twist a good deal at the front as well as the back. In the first five ribs, however, the cartilage portion of these ribs is shorter, and the joint with the sternum allows only for a slight rotating movement. This means that these top ribs have a fairly limited range of motion that has been described as being like a pump handle: lifting forwards and up, and lowering back and down (Bunch 1997: 34). Ribs six through ten, on the other hand, have increasingly longer cartilage portions and the ability to rise and fall in a sideways direction, like a bucket handle. This gives them much greater flexibility than the top five pairs of ribs. Since the 'floating' ribs have no forward attachment at all, they have considerable freedom of movement. This is significant because in the areas where there is greater flexibility in the ribcage, there is more room for expansion of the lungs. Equally significant is that this area of greater expansion is in the lower half of the ribcage – precisely the same area to which the diaphragm is attached. The relationship between the movement of the ribs and the movement of the diaphragm is, therefore, an intimate one which can be developed and strengthened with regular exercise. Try *Exploration I* again, and notice this time how your ribcage responds.

The principal muscles that make your ribcage expand outwards are called the external intercostal muscles. They are sheets of muscle that run between the ribs. When these muscles contract during inhalation, they cause the ribcage to swing outwards and upwards, pulling the lungs along with them. The relaxation of the external intercostals, together with the effects of gravity and the elastic recoil of the cartilage in the ribs, returns the ribcage to its rest position, pressing on the lungs and causing us to breathe out. When we are breathing for speech, the external intercostals become active on the in-breath to help us take in the additional air that is needed to speak. On the out-breath, they release in a slow, steady way in order to sustain the voice.

There is another set of intercostals muscles known as the internal intercostals. Like the external intercostals, they are sheets of muscle that run between the ribs, but they lie beneath the externals. These muscles become active during exhalation, particularly to produce the small variations in air pressure that are required for stressing particular words. Contracting them will also press the ribs down further beyond their rest position, thus creating extended pressure on the lungs, and so enabling a continuation of speech where necessary.

As we have said, because the top ribs can't move very much, they can't expand the lungs very much either. Many people, when they think of taking a deep breath, think of lifting up their shoulders (which doesn't help the lungs even a little bit) and thrusting out their chests. This looks impressive, but simply lifting the chest doesn't increase the size of the lungs very much. In fact, when you lift your chest this way, you have to draw your shoulder blades together and probably stick out your bottom a bit. Try it. Both of these things give the lower ribs less room to open up and out, and, as we have seen, it's the lower ribs that are capable of really bringing air into the lungs. The lungs themselves are quite small at the top and much larger at the bottom, and, although they stop at the point of your lowest ribs, opening those lower ribs and allowing the diaphragm to fully descend can cause a sensation of the breath filling much lower in your body. This, not puffing the chest out, is the sign of a full, deep breath.

Much of the bodywork we have already done is important because it allows your ribs and your diaphragm to move more fully and freely. While the lungs themselves fill only the thorax, or upper torso, your whole body is potentially involved in breathing. For example, tension in the hips can lock the abdominal muscles, which then will block the diaphragm from descending fully; misalignment in the back will limit the range of motion in the ribs. The work in this chapter on building a connection to your body's free and full breath and between that breath and your voice will, therefore, include some stretching and visualization exercises to help you grow further in your ability to release even very deeply held tensions throughout your body.

Breath holding

Beyond releasing these habitual tensions, however, we will also ask you to work through a very human tendency to hold your breath. We usually think of holding the breath as something involving a plugged nose and puffed out cheeks that we do underwater, but, in fact, we do it all the time. When we push, pull or lift something heavy, we hold our breath, and with good reason: this breath holding stabilizes the torso, which gives the arm and shoulder muscles a fixed point to work from. When we are afraid, we also hold our breath, which makes sense too. Without the noise of breathing in our ears, we can better hear predators approaching, and with a stable torso we can better throw a punch or sprint away. However, many of the things that frighten us in modern society – e.g. the threat of embarrassment, of failure, of being rejected or misunderstood – are not predators that we're going to have to fight or flee. Nevertheless, we respond to them in the same way that our distant ancestors would have responded to an approaching bear: we freeze our torsos and clamp shut our throats. Furthermore, most of us, whether we are born performers or not, will find at one time or another that standing on a stage in front of other people provokes the same response. It may very well be subtle – just a tiny tightness across the chest or rigidity in the abdominal muscles – but it is a form of holding the breath nonetheless.

In fact, simply standing still and breathing fully may be one of the most challenging things you are called upon to do as an actor. It requires technical skill, courage, patience and faith to release and allow your body to open wholly to the breath. It also may be one of the most important things actors are called upon to do. The breathing impulse is the primary impulse; if you are blocking it, what chance do other impulses have? How can you listen closely, respond subtly, act spontaneously if you're not breathing? How can you connect to an idea or an emotion, much less communicate it powerfully to someone else, if you are disconnected from your own breath? Once the actor has learned to open to their breath, to connect to that primal impulse, the energy of the voice, the text and the performance can then also flow freely.

Breath work

Our work on breath will begin with observation of how that impulse moves the body to breathe when we allow it to. Sometimes, we forget how to work with our own impulses. We stuff our bodies full of air they don't need or we push and squeeze out the last little bit of air, when really it would make sense to just take another breath. So, it's important to learn to listen to your body. To quietly observe how it works when you leave it alone. Once you have done this, you can begin to think about using your breath to support your voice, which is covered in the next chapter.

As you work on opening your body to the breathing impulse through the exercises in this chapter, you will also be working on connecting your voice to your breath. It's entirely possible to make lots of noise on a shallow, tight breath. The voice that results, however, will also be shallow and tight – limited in its range and expressivity. It will often feel trapped in the throat, or squeezed, or simply disconnected from what you are thinking and feeling. The voice that is the product of a full, released breath, on the other hand, will often feel like it is originating deep in the body. It will be easy, flexible and capable of communicating great nuance. This voice is explored simply at first – through small touches of sound connected to the natural rhythm of your breath. It is not, frankly, the most exciting thing you will ever do with your voice. It is, however, the foundation for everything that will follow. Notice what this simple connection feels like; learn to love the feeling, to nurture it and to come back to it again and again to ground your work.

Exploration

I.   **If you have asthma or other respiratory difficulties, skip this one**. Blow out all your breath. Blow and blow and blow until you can't blow anymore; then hold your breath for a second or two until your body insists on breathing in again. As the air rushes in, notice where you feel a strong muscular response. Do it two or three times, focusing your awareness on the abdomen, the ribs to the side, the ribs to the back and the upper chest. Put your hands on those areas to see if you can feel a response from the outside as well as the inside. Note your observations in your journal and discuss them in class.

II.   When you first wake up in the morning, just lie in bed for a few minutes and notice your breathing – how often it comes, how long the little pauses between breaths are, where you feel it filling in your body. Roll over from your front to your back, from side to side; stretch out, curl up and make the same observations in each position. Note your observations in your journal and discuss them in class.

III.   Pick an activity that you do regularly that requires you to concentrate and that is a bit stressful, such as driving, doing homework, checking your bank account. As you engage in that activity during the day, use a little bit of your conscious awareness to notice what your breath is doing. Try to simply observe without interfering, which is not necessarily as easy as it sounds. Do your breaths come more or less frequently than when you were lying in bed? Are they more noticeable higher or lower in your body? Do they ever just stop for a while? Note your observations in your journal and discuss them in class.

Exercises

Teaching tip

The exercises in this chapter are organized under four headings: *Opening the Breath*, *Coming onto Voice*, *Breath and Voice in Action* and *Connecting to Text*. The work on *Opening the Breath* bears very regular repeating through the initial stages of voice training and periodic revisiting thereafter, as do many of the exercises in *Coming onto Voice*. The exercises in *Breath and Voice in Action* and *Connecting to Text* begin to engage the voice's expressivity and are designed to help root it in breathing that is open and easy. The freedom of breath and voice should facilitate freedom of impulse and thought, and vice versa.

Opening the breath

We always come back to the body in voice work, and this section on opening the breath is no exception. We'll be doing more stretching, but it is stretching that targets areas where the muscles that contribute to the breathing process tend to get locked or held. It is, therefore, particularly important not only to keep breathing in these stretches but to focus on allowing the breath to travel deeper and more fully into the body as you hold the stretch.

The work also includes more floor work and visualization. As always, the physical relaxation needs to be coupled with mental focus. Many of the muscles involved in breathing and speaking are not easily released through conscious command. They do, however, respond to images. Exercise your imagination as well as your body to enliven and enrich all your work.

Side stretches (1–2 minutes)

Begin standing with feet roughly parallel, about hip-width apart, knees soft
and arms to the side.

Lift your arms up, and imagine your shoulder blades sliding down your
back.

Imagine that there is a large barrel to your left. Keeping your waist long,
lean over the barrel.

Now bring your left arm down and place your left hand on your right ribs,
which should be getting quite a nice stretch (see Figure 5).

Imagine each in-breath filling your hand.

Continue breathing in this position for 30–40 seconds, and then release
the stretch by relaxing your arms and torso forwards into a roll-down
position. Roll up and repeat the whole sequence to the right.

Bear hug (about 1 minute)

Figure 5 Side stretches

Begin standing with feet roughly parallel, about hip-width apart. Bend your
knees a bit – as if you were about to sit down and were interrupted half way.
Imagine your tail bone curling down underneath your pelvis.

Let your head and shoulders gently drop forward.

Cross your arms in front of you and reach around to your back. Try to hold
the edges of your shoulder blades with your fingertips (see Figure 6).

Your back should be getting a stretch. With each breath, feel the ribs in your
back rise and fall.

Continue breathing in this position for a minute or so.

Rag doll (1–2 minutes)

Begin by standing with feet roughly parallel, about hip-width apart, knees soft
but not bent and arms to the side.

Let your head drop forward, and let the weight of your head pull you into a
roll down, so your legs are straight and your upper body is hanging down, loose
and floppy, like a rag doll.

Figure 6 Bear hug

Bring your arms together in front of your knees, and hold your elbows with
the opposite hands. See if you can let the weight of your arms pull your chest just a little closer to your
knees without forcing the stretch.

Gently rotate your upper body from side to side. As you do, notice if you are holding your breath. If
you are, allow your body to resume breathing.

Return to centre, and notice any sensations of swelling, opening or filling in your lower back as you
breathe in.

Drop your hands, and roll back up.

Open angel I (1–2 minutes per partner)

If you have ever had trouble with dislocating your shoulders, you should skip this exercise.

Find a partner who is somewhere in the neighbourhood of your height.

Partners, discuss together if you feel comfortable touching and being touched on the wrists and letting your partner help support your weight. If you are, give consent to your partner. If not, check in with your instructor about modifying the exercise or doing an alternate exercise on your own.

Partner B stand behind partner A. Partner A should have a fairly narrow stance and B a fairly wide one.

Partner B, take A's wrists in your hands, and gently pull A's hands behind their back.

A, slowly lean forward, giving a third to a half of your weight to B. Let your chest open up, allowing your shoulder blades to be drawn together.

B, you may want to bend your knees or put one foot forward and lean slightly back to help balance A's weight.

A, you should feel a stretch across your upper chest. Notice if you are holding your breath. If you are, allow your body to resume breathing.

Notice any sensations of swelling, opening or filling in your ribs as you breathe in.

After 30–40 seconds, B gently help A come back to standing.

Repeat with partner B in front.

Note: this exercise is demonstrated in the first part of the Open Angel video; see Chapter 4.

Cross arms (1–2 minutes per partner)

If you have ever had trouble with dislocating your shoulders, you should skip this exercise.

Find a partner who is somewhere in the neighbourhood of your height.

Partners, discuss together if you feel comfortable standing very close behind and in front of your partner and holding hands. If you are, give consent to your partner. If not, check in with your instructor about modifying the exercise or doing an alternate exercise on your own.

Partner B stand behind partner A. A, cross your arms across your body, hands reaching to the back.

Partner B, take partner A's hands and very gently pull them towards you.

Partner A, let you head fall forward, and breathe. Notice any sensations of swelling, opening or filling in your upper and middle back as you breathe in.

After 30–40 seconds, B release A's hands.

Repeat with partner B in front.

Note: this exercise and Open Angel I can be done on your own by standing in an open doorway and holding on to the doorframe to each side of you instead of a partner's hands.

☯ Hip sequence (5–7 minutes)

If you have problems with your knees, do this exercise carefully or make adjustments.

1. Place your left foot a good metre in front of the right. The toes of your left foot point forward and those of the right point out at a forty-five-degree angle.

Roll down over your left leg and hold the ankle.

In this position, imagine that you have an inflatable air cushion in each of your hip sockets. Take a good, deep breath, and imagine the breath filling those cushions. Release the breath in a sigh and repeat the breathing cycle two more times.

2. Roll back up, pivot your back foot so the toes are pointing forward, and bend your front knee so that you are in a slight lunge. You will come up onto the toes of your back foot. Don't bend your front knee so far that you can't see your toes.

Bring your arms up over your head with the palms facing each other. Try to lift your fingers another quarter inch and drop your shoulders another half inch.

In this position, imagine that you have inflatable air cushions on either side of your torso, running from your armpit to the bottom of your ribs. Take a good, deep breath, and imagine the breath filling those cushions, expanding your ribcage to the sides. Release the breath in a sigh and repeat twice.

3. Bring your arms down and gently lower yourself down to the floor, folding your left leg in front of you and stretching your right leg straight behind you. You should be sitting up off the floor – a bit like doing the splits, but with your front leg bent under you.

In this position, imagine that you have inflatable air cushions on both sides of your lower back/upper bottom area. Take a good, deep breath, and imagine the breath filling those cushions. Release the breath in a sigh and repeat twice.

4. Bend your right leg behind you as you sit down on the floor, keeping your left leg bent in front of you. You should be sitting up, not resting on your hand.

In this position, imagine that your breath can drop straight down to your pelvic bowl. Breathing in your own time, close your eyes and take a moment to focus on simply being in your body.

5. Swing your right leg out from behind, and place your right foot on the ground above your left knee. Hug your right knee to your chest with your left arm and look over your right shoulder.

In this position, imagine that you have an inflatable air cushion on either side of your upper back. Take a good, deep breath, and imagine the breath filling those cushions. Release the breath in a sigh and repeat twice.

Unfold yourself and repeat the sequence on the other side – starting with your right foot in front.

The empty torso (4–5 minutes)

Start in semi-supine. If you have back trouble that makes this uncomfortable, you can lie on your side instead. If you do so, you should change sides from time to time.

Take a minute or so to release unnecessary tension from your body by imagining your head, your shoulders, your chest, your abdomen and your hips all becoming very heavy on the floor.

Imagine your jaw is becoming heavy and that heaviness causes your mouth to drop open slightly. If you have been breathing through your nose, switch to breathing through your mouth for a while, as this is how we usually breathe when we are speaking.

Focus your attention on your breath and notice it entering and leaving your body at its own tempo.

Imagine that your torso, the area between your shoulders and your pelvis, is a completely empty chamber. No muscles, no bones, no internal organs, no blood vessels or nerves – just a still, dark, quiet, maybe slightly cool space. This is not, of course, true, but the image can help you connect to a sense of openness and freedom in your breath.

Now imagine that coming up out of the top of this empty chamber of a torso is a big empty pipe. This pipe is your neck and throat. Think of it as one hollow round. This pipe comes up out of the empty torso and then turns a corner and opens into the empty chamber of your mouth. While this is also not true, you may notice that the image encourages a slight softening of the jaw, the tongue root and the muscles of the throat.

Turn your attention back to your empty torso. Imagine that at the base, nestled in your pelvic bowl, there is a source of light, heat and energy. We will call it your 'centre'.

Imagine that your centre is constantly gauging how much oxygen you need and is responsible for calling air down to itself and then releasing air back out again. Imagine the air travelling from your lips to your centre and back again through a completely empty channel.

Focus on this image for a few minutes. Notice how your breath and your body respond to it. You, of course, are not *doing* anything; you are simply getting out of the way and letting your body breathe from your centre.

Teaching tip

We learned this exercise from Dudley Knight. It is almost entirely an exercise of the mind, but one that can have wonderful physical benefits. Talking your students through it step by step, constantly bringing them back to the sense of cool space through the torso, throat and mouth, will help them to make a strong connection with the image.

Your students may be working with the term 'centre' in other areas of their training (e.g. movement and acting) and have some confusion about what it is supposed to mean to them. For the purposes of voice work, centre is imagined to be a source of energy and impulse situated at the base of the torso. The idea of giving over to centre, letting it take responsibility for the breath, is useful in establishing a sense of the breath (and later the voice) as originating deep in the body without pushing it down. While it may be a different image and function from the centre that is discussed in other classes, ultimately all the work the students do should be bringing them to a sense of being grounded, free and present.

Once you have introduced the images of the empty torso/pipe and letting centre control the breath, it can be useful to try to implement them while doing various stretching exercises.

The hanging breath I (2–3 minutes)

Start in extended child pose, and take a moment to establish a sense of softness and looseness in your body. Notice your breath.

Come up onto all fours, with your hands directly under your shoulders and your knees directly under your hips. Keep your spine in a stable position, without arching or collapsing as you breathe.

Focus on your abdomen for four or five breath cycles. On the in-breath, imagine that it is completely free to fall towards the floor as it receives the air. You don't need to push it at all – just allow it to open. On the out-breath, notice how gently and easily it floats back towards your spine.

Focus on your lower back for four or five breath cycles. On the in-breath, imagine it swelling slightly, like bread rising in the oven. Again, you don't need to push it at all – just allow it to open. On the out-breath, notice how gravity gently pulls it back down.

Focus on your ribs for four or five breath cycles. On the in-breath, notice where you can feel them swell – probably in the lower ribs to the sides and the back. On the out-breath, feel how naturally they fall back to their original position.

Teaching tip

This exercise also works well with partners, partner A placing their hands on the areas where partner B is focusing on breathing. Be sure to have partners ask each other for consent before touching.

Coming onto voice

The goal in this section is not to make a lot of noise, or even a beautiful noise. It is to get used to engaging your voice while maintaining a full, open breath. As you do so, you may find that your sense of where your voice comes from shifts from your throat and your mouth to your torso. This is a good thing. As we will discuss in more detail in the next chapter, your voice is indeed produced by your larynx, but it is powered by muscles as low in your body as your pelvis. Foster the sense of connection between the energy of your voice and the energy of your breath and body. Foster too an appreciation for how simple and powerful it can be to send your voice into space, carried by your breath energy.

A further goal of this section is not only to connect, but also to coordinate your voice with your breath. There are two kinds of miscoordination that can happen, particularly when we say words that start with vowel sounds. One is to let a little bit of breath escape before closing the vocal folds. This results in a breathy sound and is called 'breathy onset'. An iconic example is Marilyn Monroe singing 'Happy birthday, Mr President'. Try saying, 'I'm excited about airplanes' in your very best Marilyn Monroe voice to get a sense of what this might sound like. The other is to clamp the vocal folds shut tightly before any breath gets to them. When this happens, the air pressure underneath the folds builds up until it finally bursts through with a little popping sound. This is called 'glottal onset' or 'glottal attack'. Try saying 'Uh oh!' as if you were playing with a baby. If you felt a little pop or a bounce at the start of each word, you were using glottal onset. Ideally, the vocal folds should be coming together just as the breath reaches them. This is called 'simultaneous onset'. It's not something you absolutely must use all the time, but practising it will help you develop a coordination between breath, voice and impulse that will be useful to you in many contexts.

In-breath to out-breath (3–5 minutes)

This exercise is the essence of truth and simplicity. We learnt it from Meribeth Bunch Dayme.

Start in semi-supine. Take a minute or so to release unnecessary tension from your body by imagining your head, your shoulders, your chest, your abdomen and your hips all becoming very heavy on the floor.

Focus your attention on your breath and notice it entering and leaving your body at its own tempo. Now begin to notice the point in your breathing cycle where the in-breath changes to the out-breath. Notice also the deepest place in your body where this change starts to take place.

As you become familiar with this point in your breathing cycle, begin to mark the change from in-breath to out-breath with a gentle *huh* sound. Think of touching this sound off from the place in your body where the change starts to take place. Just experience this process for a few breath cycles.

As you become more confident with the sensations of breath and voice, begin to make a more committed and extended sound and let it out on an easy pitch glide so that it sounds like a sigh.

Experience this process for a few breath cycles, and then let the *huh* sound settle on to a sustained pitch – a long *huh* on one note. Remember to stay connected to the idea of the in-breath changing to the out-breath.

With each new breath choose a different sustained pitch to come on to voice.

After several more breathing cycles, return simply to quiet breathing. Notice any changes between how you are now breathing and how you were breathing at the beginning of the exercise.

Teaching tip

This is a useful preparatory exercise for much of the work that is to follow, as it establishes a relaxed connection between breath and voice. For this reason, it is helpful to give it plenty of time for beginners.

Look out for any habits of glottal attack as students begin to make the 'huh' sound. This will be noticeable as a sharp or abrupt onset to the sound, rather like a cough, and is a potentially damaging habit. It means the sound is being initiated in the throat and not at the place in the body where the in-breath changes to the out-breath. To counteract this tendency, just remind students to stay connected to the idea of the in-breath changing seamlessly to the out-breath – there is no stopping of the breath in the throat before making the sound.

☉ Vibrating breath (4–6 minutes)

Start in semi-supine. Take a minute or so to release unnecessary tension from your body by imagining your head, your shoulders, your chest, your abdomen and your hips all becoming very heavy on the floor.

Imagine your jaw is becoming heavy, and that heaviness causes your mouth to drop open slightly. If you have been breathing through your nose, switch to breathing through your mouth for a while.

Establish in your mind's eye the image of the empty torso and the empty pipe. Imagine your centre at the base of the empty torso. Imagine that there is nothing between your lips and your centre as it calls the air down to itself and releases the air back out again.

Now imagine that when that air descends down to your centre, it can pick up some of centre's energy and that that energy will cause it to start to vibrate. That vibrating air will then travel through the empty torso and empty pipe and be released out your lips. It will probably take the form of a small, quiet 'huh'. It's small and quiet because there's not much air coming out of your body at the moment – your centre knows you don't need much oxygen to stay alive when you're lying on the floor. Do make sure, however, that all the air is vibrating, so you get a solid tone, not a breathy, Marilyn Monroe-y 'huh'.

These vibrations travel under their own energy; they don't need any help from you. They are simply catching a ride on the air you would be breathing out anyway, so creating them is no more effortful than breathing.

Try going on to and off vibration a few times to see if you can do so without disrupting the sense of the breath flowing from your centre.

Once you have established a sense of those vibrations easily floating up from centre, you can start to feed centre another stimulus and ask it to give the vibrations different forms – maybe they will come out on a different vowel sound, travel through different pitches or vary in intensity and length. This will cause centre to alter your breathing pattern a bit, which is fine; just stay out of its way and trust it.

Teaching tip

This also comes from work done with Dudley Knight and shares some characteristics with Kristin Linklater's work. When you come to the last step of altering the nature of the vibrations, it can be useful for you to create a sound pattern for the students to follow. Keep it simple, moving, for example, from a 'huh' to a 'huh huh', maybe adding an upward inflection or moving on to a 'huh huh hum' or other vowel sounds, working your way up to easy calls, such as 'hey'.

As you are leading the exercise, listen carefully for any sign that students are 'putting on' a voice or pushing. If it starts to feel at all 'projected' or performed, a simple reminder such as 'It's easier than that' will usually help them find their way to a vocal expression that is simpler and more grounded. Listen too for de-energized, 'throaty' sounds, and encourage students to visualize the vibrations flowing easily up and out the open pipe rather than getting trapped in the bend at the back of the throat.

Once the students have made the connection between breath and voice, it can be very useful to revisit exercises from both this and the preceding chapter and add vibration to them; for example, Swinging, Partner Manipulations, The Hanging Breath, etc. The challenge is to keep the channel open and to continue to imagine the vibrations coming from the same place as the breath: centre.

The open-mouth hum (5–6 minutes)

Start by repeating the first steps of Vibrating Breath, up to releasing a small, quiet 'huh'.

After you have started making some gentle sounds, check to make sure that the passage from your lips through your throat is still open. Practically, this will mean that your jaw is open softly, with about half an inch of space between your back teeth; your tongue is resting in the bottom of your mouth, not touching the roof at any point; and there is the feeling of space at the back of your mouth that is associated with the beginning of a yawn.

Release an energetic 'huh' sound from centre.

On the next breath, extend the 'huh' into a 'huuuuuuuuh'.

On the next breath, release the same sound from centre, and after a second or two, bring just the lips together, leaving space between the back teeth, between the tongue and the roof of the mouth, and at the back of the mouth. This will make a 'hummmmm' sound.

We call this an open-mouth hum.

Teaching tip

The idea of an open-mouth hum is an important one that we will refer to often. To help your students appreciate what distinguishes it from other humming possibilities, it may be useful to try a little negative practice: clamp the jaw shut, push the tongue up against the hard palate, constrict the throat and then hum. Reintroduce space in each of those areas and feel how it changes the feel and quality of the hum.

☻ The lazy day warm-up (10–12 minutes)

If you have any history of back injury, do this exercise with caution or skip it.

1. Lie on the floor on your side. Draw your knees up so that your thighs are at a ninety-degree angle to your torso. Stretch your arms out straight in front of you, one on top of the other.

Slowly raise your top knee into the air. As it rises higher, it will start to pull on your pelvis, which will eventually pull your bottom knee up off the ground as well. Let your pelvis and bottom knee follow the top knee all the way up in the air and over to the other side.

As your pelvis moves, it will also pull on your spine and your shoulder girdle. As it does so, allow your top hand to be pulled across your chest. Keep the fingers of your bottom hand on the floor and draw a large circle over your head with them as you roll from one side to the other. Your head will naturally follow your shoulders and roll over to the other side.

Do this three or four times to get used to the motion.

2. Next, bring the breathing into synchronization with the motion by breathing in as you are lying on your side and then breathing out on a 'ffffff' as you roll from one side to the other.

Think of the motion of the rocking pelvis moving the breath through your body; the motion of the pelvis is the motor for the breath.

If you run out of easy breath before you've finished the motion, don't push or squeeze; just allow the breath to fill again. Over time, your body will learn to sustain the breath over the period of time that it takes to roll from one side to the other. It can't learn to do this naturally, however, if you rush in and force it to squeeze out every last drop of air.

Do four or five movement cycles on the 'ffffff', and then add a touch of vibration, changing it to a 'vvvvv'.

Do four or five movement cycles on the 'vvvvv', and then close your lips around the vibration, changing it to an open-mouth 'mmmm'.

Do four or five movement cycles on the 'mmmm', and then open it into a 'maaaa'.

Do four or five movement cycles on the 'maaaa', and then take a little break to stretch and wiggle.

3. The next step is to imagine releasing a flow of sound from your rocking pelvis, just as you have been doing, but the flow of sound will be taking a particular shape: the shape of chanting the first line of a nursery rhyme.

Do another cycle on the 'maaaa' just to get back into the rhythm, and then allow your breath to fill as you lie on your side, and chant the first line of a nursery rhyme ('Jack and Jill' and 'Humpty Dumpty' are good ones) as you move.

Repeat for at least four lines.

4. Finally, you will speak each line of the nursery rhyme as you roll from side to side, one line per cycle of movement. Do not worry about 'acting' the nursery rhyme or even about making much sense of it at this point. Focus instead on letting your voice move through your body as easily as it did when you were releasing a 'vvvvv'.

Teaching tip

This exercise is a great warm-up on days when no one can face the thought of warming up.

Many students may need a bit of help to grasp the arm motion. Demonstrate it once or twice, and then help students individually. Over the course of the exercise, some students may start to straighten their legs; remind them to keep them bent as if they were sitting in chairs.

⚙ *Vibration pools (6–10 minutes)*

1. Start in extended child pose.

   Take a moment to establish for yourself the sense of the empty torso with centre at the base calling air down to itself and releasing air back out. Your front is fairly closed in this position, and your back is very open; centre, furthermore, is in a different relationship to your mouth, so the process will feel different from how it does when you are lying down.

   Begin releasing a touch of vibration on each out-breath, letting it ride the air that you would be breathing out anyway. Imagine the sound rolling like a marble from centre to fall out your open mouth.

   Extend the vibration to a longer 'huh' for a few breath cycles, and then close just your lips around it so that it pools in your mouth as a 'hummm' for a few breath cycles.

   Alternate between capturing the vibrations with your lips and letting them fall on the floor, in a 'hummuhmuhmaaa'. Imagine that when you open your lips, the vibrations run like water from your centre, form a small pool on the floor in front of you and then gradually roll away.

   Try some 'bubububububah's', keeping the lips very loose and floppy as you do. Play around with lengthening and shortening the sound and moving it through your pitch range as well. Imagine it flowing from centre at all times.

2. Roll your toes under and push yourself into a squat, letting your head continue to hang forward. Go through the process of finding just a touch of vibration at centre, then extending it, trapping it on your lips, and releasing it in a pool on the floor.

3. Float your bottom up into a roll down and repeat the same process. This is a particularly good position for getting a sense that the sound is just falling out of your body.

4. Roll up your spine, wiggle and shake. Take a moment with your eyes closed to re-establish the image of the empty torso, of the empty stove pipe of a throat turning a corner into the empty cavern of the mouth, and of centre. Begin releasing a touch of vibration from centre, and give yourself a few breath cycles to establish it. Then you can start to play with giving the vibrations different forms – extending them, changing the vowel and pitch, etc.

Teaching tip

As in the floor work, it is of great help to the students for you to model the sounds in the last step and have them echo you.

⚙ *Three suns (6–8 minutes)*

This is an adaptation of a Qi Gong exercise. Qi Gong exercises take many forms but all are useful for synchronizing breathing and movement in ways which increase internal energy. We have added the element of voicing to this exercise.

Begin by standing with feet roughly parallel, about hip-width apart, knees soft and arms to the side. Cup your hands together in front of you, palms upward and hold them just below your navel.

As you begin to breathe in, raise your hands vertically to chest height in time with your breathing. Keep your shoulders and chest relaxed and let your breath fill down to centre. Remember, your chest should not rise with your hands. When you feel the in-breath change to the out-breath, turn your hands over and, as you breathe out, lower your hands again to just below your navel.

On the next breath, repeat the same motion on the in-breath; when you feel it change to the out-breath, turn your hands outwards and, as you breathe out, send your hands forward and out to the side in a breast-stroke movement before lowering your arms to your side.

As you begin to breathe in for a third time, raise your hands vertically to chest height again. But this time keep breathing in and, as you do so, turn your hands over so that you can raise them vertically above your head. Then, when you feel the in-breath change to the out-breath, turn your hands outwards and, as you breathe out, lower your arms to your side.

Repeat the exercise until you feel that the breathing and the movements are synchronizing naturally. All movements should be performed continuously so that there is nothing abrupt or staccato about the process.

Once you have established the cycle of synchronized breath and movement, you can begin to add sound to the out-breath. Start by simply breathing out on a 'ffffff' sound for one complete cycle, and then add a touch of vibration, changing it to a 'vvvvv' for the next cycle. Use an open-mouth 'mmmmm' for the next cycle, and then change to vowel sounds – students can choose their own or the instructor can use the following vowel sequence: OO, OH, AH, AY, EE.

Teaching tip

It will help the students if you model the whole process for them before they begin the exercise.

As students get more experienced in this exercise and develop greater physical awareness, you can have them rise up on tiptoes as they breathe in and lower their soles to the floor again as they breathe out. This has the added benefit of increasing the engagement of the breathing muscles.

The archer (6–8 minutes)

This is another adaptation of a Qi Gong exercise to which we have added the element of voicing.

Begin by standing with feet roughly parallel, slightly wider than hip-width apart, knees slightly bent and arms to the side.

Now raise your left arm out to the side, with your palm facing outwards and fingers raised to the ceiling, as if signalling 'Stop'.

At the same time, cup your right hand at your waist just above your right hip. The stance will look rather like an archer holding a bow.

Breathe in and turn your head to look at the fingers of your left hand as you do so.

As you breathe out, let your outstretched arm travel round in front of you until it is parallel with your right shoulder. Keep watching the fingers of your hand as it moves, and send the breath to your fingertips.

As you breathe in again, change the position of the arms, drawing your cupped left hand down to your waist just above your left hip, and raising your right arm to the right, with your palm facing outwards and fingers raised to the ceiling.

Now, as you breathe out, let your outstretched arm travel round in front of you until it is parallel with your left shoulder. Keep watching the fingers of your hand as it moves, and send the breath to your fingertips.

Change the position of the arms again on the in-breath.

Remember that part of the exercise is to synchronize your breathing with the movements, so repeat the exercise until you feel that the breathing and the movements are coordinating naturally. As in Three Suns, all movements should be performed continuously so that there is nothing abrupt or staccato about the process.

Once you have established the cycle of synchronized breath and movement, you can begin to add sound to the out-breath. Start by simply breathing out on a 'ffffff' sound for one complete cycle, and then add a touch of vibration by changing it to a 'vvvvv' for the next cycle. Use an open-mouth 'mmmmm' for the next cycle, and then change to vowel sounds – students can choose their own or the instructor can lead using the following vowel sequence: OO, OH, AH, AY, EE.

Think of your vocal energy flowing from your centre to your fingertips in an easy, unbroken flow.

> **Teaching tip**
>
> As in Three Suns, it is of great help to the students for you to model the whole process for them. You should monitor the students to ensure that they stay aligned and maintain their balance. Students often want to lean towards or away from the direction of their arm, or they will poke their heads forward, raise their shoulders or collapse their chests. Some verbal reminders to stay long, relax their shoulders and keep their weight balanced on both feet should address these issues.

Breathing the space (5–7 minutes)

Begin by standing in an aligned position with feet roughly parallel, about hip-width apart, knees soft and arms to the side.

Connect your visual awareness to your breathing in the following way: let your eyes focus on seeing the detail of each part of the room you are working in and let the in-breath be a response to that room as you 'breathe in' the space.

Now let the out-breath out on a 'fffff' sound and send the sound out into the room.

Think of having an effect on everything you can see in the space. Look at the specific details of objects, people, surfaces, colours. Receive these on the in-breath and communicate with them on the out-breath. Don't lose focus and generalize – stay aware and be specific.

Add vibration to the breath by changing to a 'vvvvv' sound and then an open-mouth 'mmmmm'. Vowel sounds can then be explored – students can choose their own or the instructor can lead using the following vowel sequence: OO, OH, AH, AY, EE.

Once you have added vibrations, start to move through the space – let the sound take you to a specific part of the room on the out-breath. Let the in-breath help you find another part of the space to move towards.

Explore different levels in the room and in your voice – allow the pitch of the sound to move.

Explore different rhythms and dynamics of movement and let the voice respond to these.

Teaching tip

This is a useful exercise for connecting students to the need for a bigger and more sustained breath in relation to the physical space. It can be applied at a later stage to theatre spaces as part of a warm-up before a performance.

I am here (4–6 minutes)

This exercise is designed to apply your developing awareness of release, alignment and breathing to a simple act of communication with intention.

1. Begin by standing in an aligned position with feet roughly parallel, about hip-width apart, knees soft and arms to the side. Be aware of your presence in the room while you focus on your breathing.

   Imagine your weight being distributed evenly across the three tripod points in each foot. Now make sure your ankles, knees and hips are not stiff or braced. Pay attention to your pelvis also. Tell yourself that your back is long and wide; that your shoulders are loose and low; that your neck is long and free; that your head is facing forward and that the crown of your head is going up; and that you are breathing fully.

   You are now going to focus on a specific thought: *I am (whatever your first name is), and I am here.* Connect this thought to your breathing cycle by allowing the thought to form as you breathe in and imagining yourself communicating the thought as you breathe out.

   Once you have established this connection, allow your jaw to open on the out-breath and let the breath flow out freely through an open channel. Close your jaw to breathe in again and repeat the process, paying particular attention to keeping the connection between the thought and the breathing cycle.

2. Now, as you feel more confident with this, begin to add the articulatory movements of your statement to the out-breath. The aim is not to make any audible sound at this point, but simply to mouth the words with your tongue and lips as you breathe out.

3. Once you have established the connection between thought, breath and articulation in this way, you can start to introduce voice to the process. Begin quietly, so that you are only speaking to yourself. Make sure that you stay aligned, released and connected to your breath. Notice any habitual tensions that may creep in as you start to speak, and work to release these.

   Gradually increase your commitment to your statement so that your voice becomes more and more present in the space. There is no need to compete with other students in the room – this would increase vocal tension. Instead, increase your intention to state who you are and where you are, and the vocal commitment will follow.

   Explore how fully you can commit to your statement while staying aligned, released and connected to your breath.

Teaching tip

This exercise is best used once students have gained some facility with alignment and breath work and after they have already warmed up the body and breath. It can then be used at any point in their training as a means of connecting them to a sense of their presence. It can also be adapted to character and text work; for example, instead of using their own names, students can speak in character and/or use a short piece of text in addition to their statement.

While this is a simple exercise on the surface, it can be quite profound for students who find it difficult to assert themselves. It is therefore important for everyone to be respectful of the process and avoid competitive or negative judgements of others' abilities.

Onset exercises (10–15 minutes)

1. Make the sound 'huhhh' just on breath – don't actually engage your voice. This is the feeling that comes with breathy onset. Make a very aggressive 'uh oh' sound just on breath – don't actually engage your voice. It should take quite a bit of bouncy breath, and you should feel a little pop in your throat. This is the feeling that comes with glottal onset. Be attentive to either of these feelings creeping in as you do the following exercises. If they do, back up and try the exercise again.

   Release an extra breathy, voiced 'heee'. Then release a strongly popped, voiced glottal 'ee'. Now think 'heee', letting your mouth and larynx get ready to make the 'h' sound, but then simply say 'eeee' without the 'h'. This is the feeling that comes with our target: simultaneous onset.

2. Stand in front of a wall and imagine that there is a reserve of vibrations down at your centre and that your torso, throat and mouth are completely empty.

   Chant the following, imagining that as you do so, the vibrations are flowing from your centre and carrying on to touch the wall in front of you. As you chant, be sure that the sound is continuous, that there are no breaks between words:

   Each eagle eats evil eels.

3. Now speak the sentence, still imagining the vibrations flowing out of you and touching the wall and still connecting the words to each other in a continuous stream of sound.

4. Finally, speak each word of the sentence one at a time, still sending the vibrations to the wall, leaving a slight break between words. Ideally, there will be neither a little release of breath before each word, nor a little pop. If you're having trouble getting past the aggressive, glottal attack, try thinking of a soft smile at the very back of your mouth as you start each word. Or try thinking of an H sound before each word but not actually making it. If you're having trouble getting past the breathy onset, think of the vibrations being released from the middle of your nose rather than your mouth (a silly image, but a useful one).

   Repeat the process with the sound 'i' as in 'him', using the sentence:

   In Indiana insects itch incessantly.

   Repeat the process with the sound 'e' as in 'hem', using the sentence:

   Emily ended excellent enterprises.

   Repeat the process with the sound 'a' as in 'hat', using the sentence:

   At Alice's attic ants atrophy.

Repeat the process with the sound 'uh' as in 'hut', using the sentence:

'Aggressively upwards', announced another understudy.

Repeat the process with the sound 'ah' as in 'harmony', using the sentence:

'Are aardvarks arms armoured?' Arthur articulated.

Repeat the process with the sound 'awe' as in 'hawk', using the sentence:

It's all awfully awkward.

Repeat the process with the sound 'ay' as in 'hay', using the sentence:

Abel ate eighty-eight acorns.

Repeat the process with the sound 'I' as in 'high', using the sentence:

I identified idealistic ideas.

Teaching tip

Onset exercises are usually most successful in the context of vocal training that extends over a year or two rather than just one term.

It's worth taking the time to listen to each student do at least one of these sentences to identify who might be having trouble with onset. The students themselves may not be able to hear or feel the difference until you coach them through it individually. You may choose to work with three or four of the above sentences and then have students make up some of their own.

Breath and voice in action

The preceding exercises will have provided you with a strong technical foundation for connecting the voice and the breath. The exercises in this section allow you to start to play with that connection and explore its expressive potential. Don't feel, however, that you need to have mastered open breath and grounded voicing before working in this section. It may very well be that you first experience a really powerful sense of the connection between your body, your breath and your voice through these more playful exercises. Returning to the more technical exercises will then help you to achieve that sense of connection more consistently.

Breath play (2–3 minutes each)

I.

1. Get a partner and stand about five feet away from each other.

    Partner A wave to partner B while exhaling. You can make the exhalation a bit bigger than usual just to make sure that you're connecting to it.

    A, now wave to B while inhaling – again, perhaps a slightly bigger inhalation than usual.

    A, now wave to B while holding your breath.

    Discuss the different feeling of the three waves.

2. Now move in so you are just a couple of feet away from your partner.

    B, put your hand behind your back. Pretending you have something in it, take your hand out from behind your back and offer it to your partner on a nice, full out-breath.

Repeat on a nice, full in-breath.

Repeat holding your breath.

Discuss the difference in the three.

II.

If you have asthma or other respiratory difficulties, you may want to sit this one out.

Stand comfortably and take a moment to become aware of your breathing; make sure that you are allowing the belly, back and ribs to open to the in-breath but are not pumping up your shoulders and chest. Likewise, there should be no caving in of the chest and shoulders on the out-breath.

Observe your body's natural breathing pattern for four or five cycles.

Start to shorten your out-breath and extend your in-breath until they are as short and as long, respectively, as they can be.

Reverse that pattern, shortening your in-breath and extending your out-breath.

Try three short, sharp in-breaths in a row followed by one long out-breath. Extend it to six or seven staccato in-breaths for each long out-breath.

Reverse that pattern, using staccato out-breaths and long in-breaths.

Try three or four short in and out-breaths followed by one long in and one long out.

Do one full minute of playing with different breathing rhythms, trying anything that comes to mind and investigating it until you are inspired (pun intended) to move on to something else.

Discuss what kinds of feeling, thoughts, images were evoked by the different rhythms.

Teaching tip

Students may have very different responses to the various breaths – some may find action on the in-breath to be warm and inviting, while others may find it off-putting. Some may find that breathing in rapidly makes them feel panicked, while others may find it relaxes them. There's no one correct interpretation. The point to be made is that breath is connected to our thoughts, our feelings and our interactions with other people. It influences and is influenced by everything we do.

Group sound

All the exercises under this heading are useful for warming up a group at the beginning of a session. Through engagement in cooperative vocal and physical activities, they can help to foster group connection, focus and energy.

I. (4–7 minutes)

Start standing, the group in a circle. Take a moment to check your posture, and get in touch with your breath and how you are feeling at this moment.

Now, one at a time, take it in turns to go into the middle of the circle and perform a combined voice and movement expression of how you are feeling. For example, if you are feeling sleepy, you might flop on to the floor making a yawning sound; or if you are feeling happy, you might jump in the air laughing.

After each person has performed their action, everybody else has to repeat it as precisely as possible.

Teaching tip

In introducing this exercise, it will be helpful if you can start the whole sequence off with a demonstration. Some students may start by expressing tired, half-hearted, shy or negative feelings. If this is the case, it may be helpful to require a second (and even a third) round of the exercise in which everybody has to do the opposite of what they did in the first round. With more boisterous groups it may be necessary to point out that this isn't an opportunity for a competition!

This exercise can also be used as an icebreaker for groups who don't know each other, with students saying their names in combination with the movement.

II. (4–7 minutes)

Start standing in a circle. One person, begin a repetitive movement with your hands. Add a sound inspired by the movement – for example, something like trilling your tongue while circling your hands in front of you. Take 10–15 seconds to play with the sound/movement combination and let it establish. Then, turn to the person on your right, who will start to copy your sound/movement.

Once that second person has established the sound/movement, the first person can stop, and the second person can start to transform the repetitive hand movement and accompanying sound into something new.

Continue passing the sound and movement around the circle, with each person transforming them into something new.

III. (5–15 minutes)

Thanks to Frankie Armstrong for the general structure of this one.

Start standing in a circle. Everyone turn so that your left shoulder is in the circle and you are facing the back of the person who was to your right.

Take an imaginary shovel in your hands. Mime shovelling a pile of dirt from the centre of the circle to the outside. Find a rhythm for the movement so that you are rocking on to the front foot and then on to the back foot as you make easy, stylized shovelling motions – it should not be too strenuous. **If you experience any pain in your knees or hips, step out.**

When the beat is established, the instructor releases a call that fits in the rhythm of the movement: 'Hey-yo', which everyone echoes on the next movement.

The instructor then releases a different call in rhythm with the motion, which everyone echoes – something like 'Hee hee ho' or 'Mamamamamameeee' – any combination of sounds that fits in the space of a cycle of movement.

After the instructor has set the pattern, go around the circle, with each person leading a call and the group echoing.

Don't try to decide in advance what your call will sound like – just follow the rhythm and trust that the sound will be there. Some calls may be very scat-like, others may be the release of a single vowel on a single note. The important thing is that you are staying open to the sound.

Do a couple of rounds, switching sides when your hips get tired.

Try each person giving three calls and responses in a row before moving on.

Try repeating each call three times, adding harmonies or embellishments.

Try having every other person in the circle sticking with a drone (something like 'EEEE' on one medium low note) and the others playing with calls and responses on top of it.

Try not going around the circle but letting anyone who has an impulse offer a call at any time while some of the others drone and some respond.

Teaching tip

This exercise can be anything from a 5-minute part of your warm-up – used to get the body, breath and voice working together in an easy released way – to a much longer, deep exploration of sound, rhythm and impulse, depending on where your students are and what your goals are in any given session.

Connecting to text

The distance between lying on the floor saying 'Huh' and performing a complex text on a stage can seem vast. However, the relationship between releasing a sound that is free and grounded in the breath and speaking a word in a way that is truthful and engaging is very intimate. The exercises that follow will help you make that connection. In them, your job is to maintain the link that you've been developing between your voice and an easy, full breath as you speak a simple text – no more, no less.

These are exercises that will prepare you to perform, not performances themselves – remember that as you work. Focus on keeping your body open to the breath and the channel for your voice free from constriction. As you strengthen your ability to stay physically open and centred from moment to moment, you will also strengthen your ability to be responsive to the text – to be mentally and emotionally 'present'. This will ultimately be invaluable to your acting, but don't think too much about that product; enjoy the process.

Teaching tip

Assign a piece of text to each of the students. You may have them all work with the same one or two pieces, or assign different texts to different students. The advantages of the first are that it can be easier to work as a group if everyone is on the same text, and students can learn from each other's discoveries about the language. The advantages of the second are that it can weaken the tendency students have to compare their work with others, and you can assign texts in response to students' specific needs and interests. If you wish to look beyond the suggestions we make at the end of the chapter, try to find poems and/or prose passages that are relatively short and clear. They should be lively and vivid, but not intensely emotional.

The texts should be memorized – the time spent working on the language in the process is invaluable. At this point, however, the ability to rattle them off perfectly is not the point. We would advise allowing students to hold their texts in case they need to glance at them as it helps to alleviate the anxiety that can come when one is asked to recite. If you have any dyslexic students, they may find it helpful to receive the text well in advance of the day when they will need to use it in class.

Ideally, sessions on connecting to text would start with a thorough warm-up using exercises from earlier in the chapter and then move on to individual work. Students can benefit greatly from watching each other and hearing how effective connected breathing and voicing are. Have each student simply speak the text once, and then choose from the following exercises according to what they seem to need. The general goal is to help students keep the breathing free through the ribs and abdomen and away from the shoulders and upper chest. The voice should also be easy and open. You may feel inspired to introduce a new image or an element of another releasing, aligning, opening or connecting exercise. Your own thoughtful, creative responsiveness will only encourage the students'.

Each of these exercises will take 2–5 minutes depending on the length of the text. As you perform the exercise, notice the effect it has on your experience of speaking the text: it may be easier to speak; it may feel fuller of sound; it may feel truer to your intent in speaking; it may feel more *connected*. If you don't feel any change, ask your teacher or fellow students if they perceived any difference – it is likely that they did. **Take the time to establish consent before any of the following exercises that involve touching.**

I. Speak the text with a partner resting their hands on your shoulders to remind you that they are not part of the channel that breath, voice and thought flow through most effectively.

II. Roll down and begin speaking the text while a partner gives your lower back a massage. Continue speaking as your partner walks their fingers up your spine, bringing you to standing.

III. Get a chair and two partners (three if you want someone to hold your text for you). Sit in the chair with your partners standing either side of you. Each partner should take an arm and gently move it as in the Partnered Manipulations exercise from the first chapter. Now, speak the text, thinking of relinquishing control of your arms while doing so.

IV. Stand in a comfortable, aligned position. Hold the text in your hand. Breathe in as you silently read the first line. Breathe out imagining yourself speaking it. Breathe in again, and then speak the line as you breathe out. Repeat all the way through the text.

V. Stand in a comfortable, aligned position. Chant a line of text, imagining it flowing in an unbroken column from centre; then speak it. Continue alternating chanting and speaking all the way through the text.

VI. Sit facing a partner. That partner should look you in the eye as you speak the text and focus simply on tuning into the rhythm of their own breath while sending the thought, 'Breathe, connect, breath, connect' to you.

Follow-up

Reflective practice questions:

- Can you identify exercises or situations in which you tend to fight your breath – to trap it high in your body or hold it altogether?

- Can you identify exercises or situations in which are you able to let your breath flow freely and easily?

- How do those two kinds of breathing feel different physically?

- Did you feel any anxiety in the stretches that constricted one area of your body? How did you get past that anxiety? Did the breath move to another area of your body? Where?

- Have you made any discoveries about your breathing that might relate to other aspects of acting? If so, what are some ways you might implement those discoveries?

- How does thinking of your voice as originating with your breath, at the base of your torso, change how your voice feels to you? Or how you feel about your voice?

- What does 'get out of the way of your voice' mean to you?

- In which exercises did you feel that you were producing your voice with the least amount of resistance, strain and effort? Is it easier to do lying down or standing up?

- When playing vocally, what kinds of sounds do you gravitate to – low, high, loud, soft, creaky, staccato, smooth? Why do you think you favour them?

- Does introducing language make it harder or easier for you to feel that your body is open to the breath and the breath and voice are connected? Why do you think that is? How do you think you can bring the connection you feel in one kind of exercise to the other kind of exercise?

Once you have begun to experience what it feels like to open fully to the breathing impulse, you can practise it any time, anywhere without anyone noticing. In your acting classes in particular, try taking just a moment before you begin a scene or an exercise to send your awareness to your breath.

Try to make bringing yourself gently and easily onto voice part of your everyday routine. Release a few 'huh's from centre in the shower in the morning, or send some nice, open 'hi's to yourself in the bathroom mirror. The muscles that produce your voice are like any others, and they need to be warmed up gently. You would never jump out of bed and run a marathon, so don't jump out of bed and start rehearsing Jacobean revenge tragedies without warming up a bit. Take the time to connect.

Suggested texts

Elizabeth Bishop	'Close, Close All Night'
Robert Burns	'A Red, Red Rose'
Lucille Clifton	'Good Times'
Wendy Cope	'The Orange'
Elizabeth Daryush	'Still Life'
Emily Dickinson	'The Soul selects her own Society'
Rita Dove	'Exit'
Robert Frost	'The Road Not Taken'
Langston Hughes	'Dream Deferred'
Denise Levertov	'Living'
Vikram Seth	'All You Who Sleep Tonight'
Derek Walcott	'Love After Love'
William Carlos Williams	'This Is Just to Say'
W. B. Yeats	'The Lake Isle of Inisfree'

Further reading

Armstrong, Frankie, 'Gossip Hoeing', in *The Complete Voice & Speech Workout Book & CD*, Janet Rogers, ed., Applause Theatre and Cinema Books, New York, 2002, pp. 140–1.

Houseman, Barbara, *Finding Your Voice*, Nick Hern Books, London, 2002. Chapter 3: 'Breath and Support', pp. 59–73.

Linklater, Kristin, *Freeing the Natural Voice* (Revised edition), Drama Book Publishers, New York, 2006. Chapter 2: 'Workday Two' and Chapter 3: 'Workday Three', pp. 43–86.

Nelson, Jeannette, *The Voice Exercise Book*, National Theatre Publishing, London, 2015. Chapter 1: 'Getting to Know Your Voice', pp. 16–20; and Chapter 2: 'Voice Exercises – Stage 1', pp. 36–7.

3
BREATH AND VOICE – DEVELOPING SUPPLY AND SUPPORT

Framework

In the previous chapter, we worked on letting the breathing impulse be full and free, and on developing a connection between an easy, open flow of breath and an easy, open flow of voice. This connection is the foundation for all manner of vocal artistry. To build on it and unlock a greater range of expressive potential in your voice, we next will focus on developing breath supply and support. This work will help you use your breath and voice intentionally to perform with power and sensitivity in many kinds of arenas.

What, exactly, do we mean by supply and support? Breath *supply* is concerned with how, once we have sufficient air in our lungs, we maintain the flow of air from the lungs to the vocal folds. This will largely determine how long we can sustain our vocal vibrations. Breath *support* is concerned with how we adjust the intensity of that air flow to increase (or decrease) vocal power. This will largely determine the strength of those vibrations. To explore why this is important to someone who wants to use their voice expressively, we need to take another look at some vocal anatomy.

Vocal anatomy

As we discussed in the last chapter, your voice is the result of your vocal folds moulding your breath into sound waves. Your vocal folds are two folds of fibrous tissue and muscle situated inside your larynx, just behind your Adam's apple – which, despite its name, both men and women possess: it's just often less prominent in cisgender women (see Figure 7). The folds are between 17 and 23 millimetres long and are attached to several of the cartilages which make up the larynx. If you lightly place your fingers in the middle of your throat, you can feel the larynx move up and down when you swallow.

The primary function of the vocal folds is not to create our voices: it's to protect our lungs. The vocal folds act like a valve which opens and closes the space between them (the glottis), controlling what enters or leaves the lungs. Both air and food enter our bodies through our mouths (of course, air can also come in through the nose, but then it just drops from there to the back of the mouth). Usually, our tongues push the food over the epiglottis – a cartilage which folds down over the larynx when we swallow – and it slides down the oesophagus into the stomach. Sometimes, however, this doesn't happen as smoothly as it should, and little bits of food drop down the windpipe instead. If this happens, the vocal folds are designed to snap shut, closing the glottis and forming a block in the middle of the windpipe, ready to catch anything that might have gone down the wrong way. If we then sharply expel some breath (by coughing), those bits of foreign matter will get blown up off the vocal folds and then

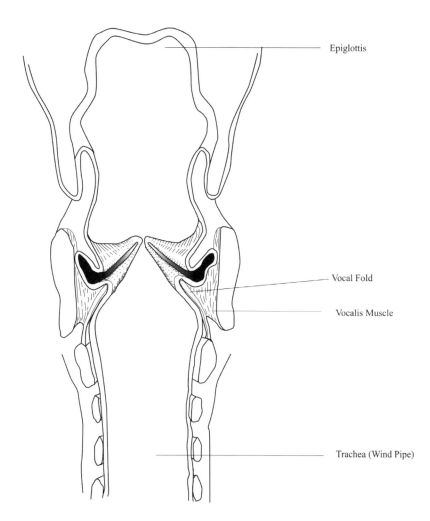

Figure 7 The vocal folds

pushed by the tongue back down the oesophagus where they belong. That's what happens when you 'swallow the wrong way' and have a coughing fit. When you breathe, on the other hand, the muscles of the larynx draw the vocal folds away from each other, opening the glottis so that the air can get through.

As a kind of bonus feature, however, when the vocal folds are brought together with just the right amount of pressure and air passes through them, they can create sound. Try bringing your lips together loosely and then blowing through them. Because of the elasticity of your lips, if enough air pressure builds up behind them when they are shut, they will eventually blow apart. Also because of their elasticity and the laws of physics, once they've been blown apart and the air pressure is released, they will then fall back together until the air pressure builds up behind them again. This blowing-apart and falling-back-together cycle breaks the air flow up into little puffs, which creates a trilling noise. The same principle applies to the vocal folds. When they are brought together lightly as we breathe out, the air pressure builds up underneath them until they are blown away from each other. They then fall back towards each other until the air pressure builds up and forces them apart again. On a pitch of middle C, this cycle happens 261 times a second!

You need a certain amount of air pressure to make this whole system work, and this is where supply and support become important. The longer the sound you want to make, the longer you need to maintain the air pressure (supply); and the stronger the sound you want to make, the greater the air pressure you need to create it (support). There are two ways to create that pressure. One is to use your muscles of respiration to create a longer and stronger flow of air. The other is to constrict your larynx, clamping the vocal folds together tightly so that more air pressure has to build up underneath them before they're blown apart. When using your voice, increasing the flow of air at the source is an infinitely healthier and more efficient way to create greater air pressure than resisting it with the folds. If the folds are clamped shut tightly, they will blow apart from each other and fall back together violently. Your vocal folds are like any other tissue in your body and will eventually become irritated if they're banged and slammed around too much. This can lead to some permanent vocal damage if left untreated (see Appendix 3: Vocal Health).

In order to get an effective supply to power your voice from your core, the muscles of inhalation need to move not only freely, as we worked on in Chapter 2, but also quickly and vigorously. In particular, actively engaging the intercostal muscles that run between and move the ribs is valuable in order to develop the supply of air.

The most important muscles for turning that supply of air into support are the abdominals. The phrase 'abdominal muscles' is a bit misleading. The 'abs' that we work on when we go to the gym to get a 'six pack' are just one of four layers of abdominal muscles and are not the ones that help the most in breathing. The other three layers are beneath the six-pack abs. They run from your lower ribs all the way down to your pelvis, and two of them also wrap around your sides and continue across your back to your spine (see Figure 8). So, support from the abdominal muscles isn't just something that happens in your belly; your sides, your back, even the muscles of your pelvic floor can get involved. In some contexts, these muscles are referred to as your 'core'. Certain fitness regimes call for keeping the core 'tight'; when working on the voice, however, you want to be able to release these muscles on the in-breath and engage them gently on the out-breath.

The contraction of the abdominal muscles as you breathe out pushes the stomach organs beneath them in and up against the diaphragm as it relaxes back into its dome shape. This provides a firm, constant pressure against the lungs, which creates strong, steady air pressure against the vocal folds (what's known as sub-glottic pressure).

Building coordination

Taken together, the work in this chapter will help you coordinate responsiveness in the ribs and engagement of the abdominal muscles to create the kind of airflow that powers and sustains a dynamic and flexible voice. While this is something that needs to be practised methodically, it is not a question of teaching your body to do something that it is not intrinsically designed to do, like learning to ride a bicycle; it's a matter of building on something the body already knows how to do and practising to do it better, like training to run a marathon.

So, technically, what happens when both supply and support are engaged and in balance? As we have seen, the diaphragm and intercostal muscles are the active instigators of the in-breath: their activity expands the capacity of the lungs, creating the potential supply of air for phonation. It is the relaxation

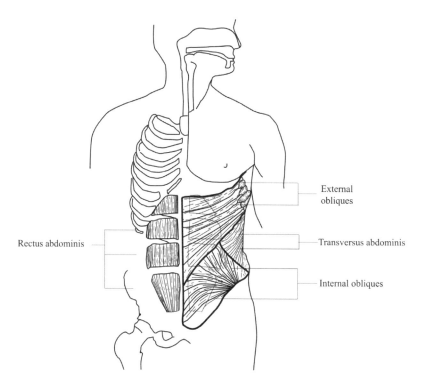

Figure 8 Abdominal muscles

of these muscles which instigates the out-breath, and so how these muscles relax will determine how efficiently that supply of air is used. For example: if, once we have breathed in, we simply stopped engaging the diaphragm and intercostal muscles, the pressure exerted on the lungs as a result of their sudden relaxation (and other physical forces such as gravity) would cause the air to rush out quickly, as in a sigh. Try it now: sigh out on a deep breath without voice. Notice how you took a deep breath in, and then just let it all go again as your breathing system collapsed. We can certainly produce vocal vibration with this air. Try it for yourself now: sigh out in the same way, but add some voice. You probably noticed several things about this sound: it didn't last very long, it lost power/intensity and it dropped in pitch. Try it again and listen. If we change our intention from sighing to sustaining an AH sound – try it now – we can produce a much longer sound with relatively little change in intensity or pitch. Did you notice how your muscles of respiration behaved differently? Try it again. Our change in intention causes us to change the physical usage of the respiratory muscles. When the system is working efficiently, this change involves a controlled relaxation of the intercostal muscles and an active engagement of the abdominal (and perhaps pelvic floor) muscles. The controlled relaxation of the intercostals (as opposed to their collapse) enables us to maintain an even flow of air over time. The engagement of the abdominals provides the muscular support underneath the relaxing diaphragm to create sufficient air pressure for a sustained intensity of vocal vibration. The goal is for this engaged and coordinated breath to become second nature – not just a physical habit, but a way of connecting deeply with thoughts, intentions and emotions as you prepare to communicate them.

Note that as we start to increase the power of the airflow, the work that we've done on staying relaxed and connecting the voice to the breath will become particularly important. It's no good generating lots of energy with the respiratory muscles only to block or strangle that energy with tension in the upper back, upper chest, shoulders, throat, neck or jaw. Continue to work with release exercises and images, cultivating a sense of ease and freedom in your work. Continue too to think of your body opening to the breath and your voice coming from your body. And, above all, continue to trust that you don't have to feel energy in your throat to have an expressive or powerful voice.

Supply, support and acting

For actors, the creation of a good, strong, steady flow of air together with easy, appropriate engagement of the muscles in and around the larynx is not only desirable for creating strong, steady sound; it's also good for your acting. A solid muscular support for your voice also creates a solid muscular support for the ideas and emotions your voice is communicating to the listener. When the big muscles of your respiratory system don't engage, your larynx and also all manner of other smaller muscles in your neck, jaw, even forehead try to pick up the slack. Trying to channel all the energy of your intentions through those smaller muscles, however, will lead to a forced, pushed quality in both your voice and your acting. Grounding the energy of the breath deeper in your body will help you to ground your actions, giving them a sense of purpose and truth. It's no coincidence that 'inspiration' is another word for breathing in. And if inhalation – supply – is the moment of inspiration, then exhalation – support – is the moment of expression. Ultimately, these two principles of breath take us to the most fundamental principles of the acting process itself.

Exploration

I. Find something that makes you laugh – maybe watch a favourite sitcom, stream a funny movie, or call a friend with a great sense of humour. When the giggles have started, notice what's happening in your torso. Where is the centre of the action? Where else do you feel movement? If you're lucky enough to be reduced to gasping for breath, where does that gasp originate? Where does the air go?

II. **If you have back problems, you may want to skip this one.** Find something heavy you can push around your living room or a studio – a large armchair, a heavy table, a chair with a stack of books on it, etc. Think of putting all your power in your arms and push it around a bit. Think of putting all your power in your chest and push it around a bit. Think of putting all your power in your lower abdomen and hips and push it around a bit. Which focus gave you the most power? Note your observations in your journal. We'll be looking at how finding power in the lower torso relates to voice work in the exercises below.

Exercises

Teaching tip

The exercises in this chapter are organized under four headings: *Engaging the In-breath, Engaging the Out-breath, Supporting the Voice* and *Supporting Text*. Of course, work on the in-breath enhances the out-breath, and vice versa, so it's beneficial to move between these two sections quite freely. The work on supporting the voice and the text is best broached once the students have a good working sense of how to engage the muscles of respiration. It will help them connect that engagement with the act of expression and explore the possibilities of a strongly supported voice.

Engaging the in-breath

When we are breathing just to stay alive, the inhalation lasts about 40 per cent of the breathing cycle. When we start talking, the inhalation happens more quickly, taking up only 10 per cent of the cycle (Borden and Harris 1980: 66). We also use a greater volume of air when speaking, both taking in and expelling up to 125 per cent more (Mathieson 2001: 58). This means that the muscles we use to breathe in have to do more work more quickly when we're talking. As we discussed in the last chapter, the primary muscle of inhalation is the diaphragm. We'll do some work on identifying and engaging the diaphragm here, but it is, fortunately, a muscle that engages very well on its own; in fact, you couldn't stop it from contracting for long if you tried. The main thing that gets in the way of the diaphragm is tension in the muscles of the abdomen, lower back and pelvis. If these muscles are rigid, they will hold the internal organs up against the diaphragm and it won't be able to descend very far. Try pulling in your stomach and clenching your bottom as tightly as you can and then inhaling. You can feel the diaphragm fighting to descend and not getting very far. We've done a good amount of work on stretching, softening and releasing those muscles, and it will be important that you continue to foster a sense of openness and freedom in your pelvis, stomach and lower back.

The other muscles that can help your body get more air more quickly are the intercostal muscles that move the ribs. As with any other muscles, these can be strengthened and trained to work more efficiently with practice. And, as with any muscles, working *efficiently* is not the same thing as working *effortfully*: pushing, straining or locking. On the contrary, the goal is to find ease and freedom of movement. While we will be isolating the ribs initially in order to explore their range of motion and contribution to breath, ultimately the ribs and diaphragm coordinate not only with each other, but also with the impulse to communicate to create a full, effective in-breath.

Teaching tip
The Side Stretches, Bear Hug and Hip Sequence from the *Opening the Breath* section of the previous chapter are particularly good warm-ups for rib work. Sun Salutation and Granny Dance from the *Stretching* section of the first chapter are also good preparation for work on the in-breath.

☺ *Find your ribs (3–4 minutes per partner)*

1. Find a partner who's somewhere in the neighbourhood of your height.

   Partners, discuss together if you feel comfortable touching and being touched on the following places: the lower ribs to the side, back and front. If you are, give consent to your partner. If not, check in with your instructor about modifying the exercise or doing an alternate exercise on your own.

Partner B, position yourself behind partner A.

B, place your hands on A's sides with your thumbs pointing back towards you. The bottom edge of your pinkie should line up with the bottom edge of A's ribs on either side.

A, blow out all the air you can while B presses gently on your ribs. When you've come to the end of your breath, pause for a moment, and then think of your ribs widening into your partner's hands as you breathe in. You might imagine that they are expanding like balloons.

Focus too on keeping the shoulders and upper chest soft and quiet.

B, maintain steady pressure, but don't try to push against A's rib expansion. If you notice the shoulders rising, you may place one hand gently on a shoulder as a reminder that they can be still while the ribs move.

Repeat twice, A trying to engage the ribs even more strongly in widening each time.

2. Now B, move your hands forward, so that just your thumbs are hooked around A's sides and most of your hands are stretched across the front of A's lower ribcage, your pinkies lining up with the bottom edge again.

A, again blow out all your breath and then think of your ribs expanding into B's hands as you breathe in. You might imagine them as being like flowers that are opening in fast motion.

Repeat twice, remembering to keep the shoulders and upper chest disengaged.

3. Finally, B move your hands around to A's back, so that just your fingertips are wrapped around their sides and most of your hand is cupping their ribs to the back, the bottom edge of your hand lining up with the lower border of the ribcage.

A, again blow out all your breath and think of your ribs expanding into B's hands as you breathe in. You might imagine that they are like bread dough rising in fast motion.

Repeat twice, keeping the shoulders and upper chest mostly still.

Discuss what, A, you felt happening from the inside and, B, you felt happening from the outside.

Trade places and repeat the entire exercise.

Teaching tip

This exercise raises students' awareness of the activity of the ribcage. It can be done in a number of positions: sitting on a chair, kneeling on all fours, folded over in extended child pose and standing. It is worth exploring each of these positions in sequence, as students will often find that they are more aware of some rib activity in one position than in another. You may wish to assign partners.

◉ Cow belly (2–3 minutes per partner)

1. Find a partner.

Partners, discuss together if you feel comfortable touching and being touched on the following places: the stomach just below the tummy button and the back. If you are, give consent to your partner. If not, check in with your instructor about modifying the exercise or doing an alternate exercise on your own.

Partner A, take up a position on your hands and knees so that your spine is straight and long – neither arched nor collapsed.

Partner B, place your hands on A's back, so that your finger tips are wrapped around A's sides and most of your hand is cupped around A's ribs to the back, the bottom edge of your hand lining up with the lower border of the ribcage.

A, blow out all your breath and then think of expanding your ribs into B's hands as you breathe in.

Repeat two or three times until you can feel that the ribs are strongly engaged.

2. A, now bring your focus into your belly. While keeping your spine straight and long, relax your abdominal muscles so that your belly just hangs from your spine, like a cow. Don't be vain – let it all hang out!

B, kneel beside A, so that you can place one hand on their spine to remind them to keep it stable. Place your other hand immediately under A's relaxed belly.

A, while using your abdominal muscles to lift your belly up towards your spine, blow out all the air you can on a long SH sound. B, keep your hand in the same position relative to the floor – that is, don't move it with A's belly.

Now, A, relax your stomach muscles and let your belly drop back down into B's hand as quickly as possible. As you do so, you should be able to feel your lungs fill with air again.

Repeat this exercise several times until you feel confident in the connection you are building between your breath and the activity of the abdominal muscles. Remember, your abdominal muscles are active as you breathe out, and they relax as you breathe in.

A, discuss what you felt happening from the inside and, B, what you felt happening from the outside.

Trade places and repeat the entire exercise.

Teaching tip

Some students find this exercise counter-intuitive, and so may push the abdominal muscles out as they breathe out and pull them in again as they breathe in. It will be helpful for you to go round and check individually so that you can correct any mistaken perceptions. The touching involved in the exercise is fairly intimate, so you may wish to assign partners who will be likely to be comfortable with each other.

⊛ Find your diaphragm (4–5 minutes)

This exercise was inspired by Barbara Houseman's work.

Begin standing with your feet roughly parallel, about hip-width apart; knees soft; back and neck long.

Place your hands flat on the front of your pelvis, your thumbs should be at the base of your stomach and your pinkies at the very top of your thighs.

Take three or four breaths, and imagine that with each inhalation the area under your hands is softening, like ice cream slowly melting.

Move your hands around to where your back starts to become your bottom on either side (don't hunch your shoulders in the process), and take another three or four breaths imaging a softening under your hands with each in-breath.

Place the backs of your hands against your waist on either side, below the ribs, and repeat the pattern of breathing and softening.

Move your hands so that they are flat against your lower belly and repeat.

Lightly place the fingers of one hand about half way between the end of your breastbone (you may need to feel around for it a bit) and your navel.

Keeping your pelvis, back and lower belly as soft as possible, let out a few panting breaths. The movement that you feel under your fingers is the result of your diaphragm engaging and releasing as you pant.

Speed up the panting a bit, monitoring to make sure that your shoulders and upper chest don't start bouncing along with the breath. It can help to use Kristin Linklater's image that your diaphragm is a trampoline and a tiny person is jumping on it with each breath.

Play with increasing the tempo of the panting and then slowing it back down.

Be sure to take a break every 20–30 seconds and return to your regular breathing pattern.

Try a few sighs, imagining that your diaphragm is like a wave swelling up in you with each in-breath and running out again with each out-breath.

Finally, return again to your regular breathing and just register the sensation of your breath moving through your body.

☙ Breath and thought (6–8 minutes)

Form a circle with the group.

Begin standing with your feet roughly parallel, about hip-width apart, knees soft, back and neck long.

Think of something nice to say to the person to your right.

When the instructor counts to three, turn your head and say your nice thing.

Did you breathe in as you turned to speak? Where did your body open to receive the breath? How much air did you actually get in? How deep in your body did you feel the impulse go?

Return to neutral and to the thought of the nice thing you want to say to the person on your right. Check in to make sure that your hips, bottom, lower back and lower abdomen are soft and ready to open to the breath.

Place the backs of your hands against the sides of your ribs.

Breathe in, and feel your ribs pulsing open under your hands.

On a count of three again, breath in, opening your ribs, and turn your head to the person on your right, as if you were going to say your nice thing, but don't actually speak.

Practise joining the *intent* to speak to the movement of the head and the pulsing open of the ribs without actually speaking once more.

Finally, on three, breathe in, opening your ribs as you turn your head, and then say your nice thing. Discuss the difference.

Walk around the room. When the instructor says, 'Now', stop walking, look at someone across the room, consciously engage your in-breath through the ribs as you think of something nice to say to that person, and then say that nice thing.

Repeat three or four times.

Next, as you walk, think of a line from a scene or speech that you are working or have worked on.

When the instructor says, 'Now', stop walking, engage your in-breath as you connect to the impulse behind the line, and then speak it.

Repeat three or four times.

Discuss any discoveries, particularly about the relationships between breath, voice and thought.

Engaging the out-breath

The engagement of the muscles of respiration on the out-breath is the basic mechanism of 'support'. The word 'support', however, can unfortunately conjure images of rigidity and force – great iron girders, or weightlifters straining under barbells – which are not helpful ways of thinking about breath. Respiratory support needs to be dynamic, responsive and in harmony with how the body breathes naturally.

In this section there are some exercises on extending the out-breath. The goal of these exercises is not to count to a certain number or be able to speak a certain amount of text on one breath **at any cost**. In the first instance, being able to speak for a long time on one breath is not in itself a particularly interesting skill. It's good to be able to keep your air flow and vocal energy up through a long thought, but sustaining sound is not the same thing as communicating effectively; it's only a tool. Furthermore, if you are straining and squeezing to get that last little bit of text out without taking another breath, you are probably diminishing rather than enhancing your ability to communicate – your voice will have less flexibility and your thought will lose its grounding. So, as you work on extending your breath, have patience with yourself and work with your body's impulses. If you are only able to count to six before you feel the need to squeeze your chest and push the sound out with the back of your neck, then stop at six. Work your way up to seven and beyond by learning to work with the impulse to engage your abdominal muscles rather than by forcing the last drop of air out of your body using any means necessary.

> **Teaching tip**
> Because breath support is most efficient when it works with the body's natural breathing impulses rather than against them, it can be useful to preface work on engaging the out-breath with some exercises from the previous chapter on opening the body to the breath.

Straw phonation I (5–6 minutes)

Take a normal drinking straw (eco-friendly, where possible), and place it about an inch into a glass of water. Now, with plenty of abdominal support, start blowing bubbles in the water through the straw while humming on one pitch. Keep your lips firmly closed around the straw so that no air escapes around it, and don't let any air escape through your nose either. Think of sending all your sound down the straw and into the water. Work at this until you can make the bubbles come in a steady stream.

When you feel confident making sound in this way, try changing the pitch by gliding gradually up and down your range, while continuing to make a steady stream of bubbles.

When you've got the hang of this, remove the straw from the water and continue playing with humming through the straw. Add in some 'car-revving' changes in pitch and loudness, making sure that the abdominal muscles are responsible for the changes and not your throat muscles.

> **Teaching tip**
> Straw phonation exercises are good for achieving a fully supported sound with forward placement, and so are very useful for a quick 10-minute warm-up once students have mastered the technique. They help to alleviate vocal fatigue by encouraging the vocal folds to vibrate with less effort, and this, in turn, helps bring out the

natural resonance of the voice. You can find plenty of video demonstrations on the internet. As of the time of writing, www.voicescienceworks.org is a good place to start.

Birthday candles (3–4 minutes)

This exercise was inspired by Michael McCallion's 'Blowing out Candles' exercise.

Begin standing with your feet roughly parallel, about hip-width apart, knees soft, back and neck long.

Hold up your left index finger about six inches in front of your mouth and place your right hand flat against your lower belly.

Pretend that your finger is a birthday candle and blow it out. Notice where and how your muscles engage under your right hand to support this short, forceful explosion of air.

Hold up two fingers and blow them out one after the other.

Repeat with three, four and five fingers.

Put both hands around the sides of your lower waist and repeat (imagining the birthday candle since there's no finger for you to focus on). Notice how the muscles engage in this area.

Move your hands around to your back, still at the level of your lower waist, and repeat.

Go back to holding up one finger, and this time blow it out with a 'fff' sound, engaging your abdominal muscles in the same way that you did when you were blowing it out with breath.

Focus on the stomach (all the way down to the pubic bone), the lower waist and the back in turn.

If you feel any tightness or sense of effort creeping into your throat, stop, yawn and imagine that it is an empty passage.

You may feel a burst of energy coming up from your pelvis – this can be very useful.

Blow out two then three then four then five 'candles' on a 'fff'.

Blow out a couple of candles on a 'vvv'. Now try a 'hey.' Go back and forth between 'hey' and 'hah'. Throw in a 'hee' or a 'hoo'; play around a bit, maintaining the strong connection between the energy of these muscles of support and the energy of the sound.

The column of air (7–10 minutes)

Start in supine or semi-supine.

Take a minute or so to release unnecessary tension from your body by imagining your head, your shoulders, your chest, your abdomen and your hips all becoming very heavy on the floor.

Imagine your jaw is becoming heavy and that heaviness causes your mouth to drop open slightly. If you have been breathing through your nose, switch to breathing through your mouth for a while, as this is often how we breathe when we are speaking.

Visualize your throat as an empty pipe and your torso as an empty chamber with a source of energy at the base: that is, centre.

For a minute or so, just observe how centre moves your empty torso as it calls air down to itself and releases air back up: the gentle rise and fall of the stomach; the slight feeling of expansion and release in the hips, around the back and in the ribs.

Slip your lower lip under your top teeth as if you were going to make the sound 'fff'. Simply continue to breathe, and focus on the feeling of the air sliding between your teeth and your lip.

Start to extend your out-breath so that it becomes a little bit stronger and a little bit longer. As you do, picture the air running between your centre and your lips. Think of it as being like a column of water springing up from a drinking fountain. When you feel the impulse to breathe in, breathe in – air is free, and there's little to be gained from fighting your impulses.

Notice how your body supports the flow of this fluid column of air up from centre to your lips on the exhalation and then responds to the impulse to let more air in on the inhalation. Now, imagine that this column of air continues beyond your lips, running from centre up to the ceiling. Avoid lifting your chin as you do this.

You will probably notice that your body is doing what it does when you just lie there and breathe but is doing it more energetically – your abdominal muscles are drawing the belly in on the out-breath and then are quickly releasing it on the in-breath. You may also feel your ribs springing open on the in-breath and gently pulling in on the out-breath.

After a couple of minutes of observing your body support the column of air on a 'ffff', imagine the air starting to vibrate, which will change it to a 'vvvv'.

It may help you connect to the image of an unbroken column of vibration if you lightly place your fingers low on your breastbone, then higher on your breastbone, then on your throat and finally under your chin to feel the slight 'buzz' moving under your fingers. Remember that the origin of this vibration is at centre.

After a couple of minutes of working with the 'vvvv', take a stretch and a wriggle.

Return to the 'vvvv' for two or three breath cycles, then close your lips around the vibrations, creating an open-mouth 'mmmm'. Continue to work with the image of the sound flowing from centre and the sense of your breathing muscles easily engaging to support it.

After a minute or so of working with the 'mmmm', open your lips and allow the vibrations to flow out of your mouth as a 'maaah'. Work with the 'maaah' for a minute or two. If at any point you find yourself disconnecting from the sense that there is a steady column of vibration flowing up from centre, go back to the 'vvvv' or the 'mmmm' to re-establish it.

Stretch and wriggle as you finish the exercise.

Counting

If you have asthma or any other respiratory difficulty and feel a tightness in your chest or other discomfort at any point, stop the exercise and return to your normal breathing pattern.

I.   (5–6 minutes)

Start in supine or semi-supine.

Take a minute or so to release unnecessary tension from your body by imagining your head, your shoulders, your chest, your abdomen and your hips all becoming very heavy on the floor.

In this and the following exercises, you will be working with your body's natural breathing pattern but shaping it in a specific way, so take a minute or two to simply observe how your body breathes when it is left entirely to its own devices before you start introducing intentions. You want to work with your body's impulses, not against them.

When you feel comfortable and connected to your breath, begin to engage your breathing system more actively by focusing on your ribcage. Place the backs of your hands firmly against your lower ribs to either side. Breathe out fully, and then actively engage your intercostal muscles to widen your ribcage as you breathe in – remember that the focus of activity is in the lower ribs, and not the upper chest or shoulders.

As you develop this connection with the ribcage, begin to extend your in-breath over a two count and breathe out on 'ffff' over a four count. Your ribs, sides and back, will be gently opening and releasing as always; they will simply be doing so over a designated period of time.

When you feel comfortable with the two/four count, extend the in-breath to a three count and the out-breath to a six count. If you feel that you are stuffing your ribcage with air on the in-breath or having to squeeze the air on the out-breath, send your body images of softness, lightness and ease. If you still feel uncomfortable, switch back to two and four and simply pause while your instructor counts three and six.

When you feel comfortable with the three/six count, extend the in-breath to a four count and the out-breath to an eight count. As always, if this is uncomfortable, drop back to the lower count and then gradually try to work your way back up.

After a couple of minutes of working with the four/eight count, take a stretch and a wriggle.

Return to the four/eight count for a few breath cycles, and then leave the in-breath at four, but extend the out-breath to ten. Work with this for a couple of minutes until it feels comfortable.

Next, cut the in-breath to a three count. Your body will have to bring the air in more quickly, so you will have to engage the ribs just as the impulse to inhale kicks in. Work with this for a minute or so.

Take a stretch and a wriggle as you finish.

II. (8–9 minutes)

Start in supine or semi-supine.

Begin as before by taking a minute or so to release unnecessary tension from your body and simply observe how your body breathes in this relaxed position.

When you feel comfortable and connected to your breath, begin to engage your breathing system more actively, this time by focusing on your abdominal muscles. Place your hands on your stomach, and notice how it rises and falls with your breath. Now, as you breathe in, think of filling down to centre over a two count and breathe out on 'ffff' over a four count – imagine the breath as a column of air running from centre, between your teeth and lip, and on up to the ceiling.

When you feel comfortable with the two/four count, extend the in-breath to a three count and the out-breath to a six count. If you feel that you are stuffing your belly with air on the in-breath or having to squeeze the air on the out-breath, send your body images of softness, lightness and ease. If you still feel uncomfortable, switch back to two and four and simply pause while your instructor counts three and six.

After a couple of minutes working with the three/six count on 'ffff', switch to working with 'vvvv' for a few breath cycles. Then close your lips over the vibration and create an open-mouth 'mmmm' for several breath cycles.

Now fill down on a three count and speak the word 'one' on the out-breath, feeling the abdominal muscles engage in a little pulse of support at the same time. Repeat until this feels comfortable and easy.

Now fill down on a three count and say 'one, two', feeling a separate abdominal pulse on each word. Repeat until this feels comfortable and easy.

Gradually build up to a sequence of counting from 1 to 10, making sure that you take time to fill down on a three count and that you feel a separate abdominal pulse on each word.

Take a stretch and a wriggle as you finish.

III. (9–10 minutes)

Start in supine or semi-supine and release into the floor.

When you feel comfortable and connected to your breath, begin to engage your breathing system more actively, but this time focus on both your ribcage and your abdominal muscles. Place one hand on your lower ribs at the side and place the other on your stomach.

Now, stretch your in-breath over a two count and your out-breath over a four count. Your abdomen will be rising and falling as before, and your ribs, sides and back will be gently opening and releasing as before; they will simply be doing so over a designated period of time.

When you feel comfortable with the two/four count, extend the in-breath to a three count and the out-breath to a six count, backing off if you feel yourself forcing the breath in or out.

When you feel comfortable with the three/six count, extend the in-breath to a four count and the out-breath to an eight count. As always, if this is uncomfortable, drop back to the lower count and then gradually try to work your way back up.

After a couple of minutes of working with the four/eight count, take a stretch and a wriggle.

Return to the four/eight count for a few breath cycles, and then leave the in-breath at four, but extend the out-breath to ten. Work with this for a couple of minutes until it feels comfortable.

Next, cut the in-breath to a three count. Your body will have to bring the air in more quickly, so you will have to let the abdominal muscles release completely and engage the ribs just as the impulse to inhale kicks in. Work with this for a minute or so.

Keep the in-breath at a three count and extend the out-breath to a twelve count, switching from speaking the numbers to chanting (i.e. intoning) them.

As you work with this long extension of the out-breath, imagine that your throat and neck are one big empty pipe and that the vibrations are flowing up in a steady column from centre. Work with this for a couple of minutes.

Finally, take the in-breath down to a two count and switch between chanting and speaking as you count to twelve: e.g. count once chanting and then once speaking; count to six chanting and then switch to speaking on seven to twelve – you can play around with moving between the two. As always, if you can't get to twelve comfortably, go as far as you can. Your ability to extend and support your voice with ease will grow as you practise this exercise.

Take a stretch and a wriggle as you finish.

Teaching tip

Counting exercises are usually most successful in the context of vocal training that extends over a year or two rather than just one term.

These three counting exercises work best as a continuous sequence, but it may be necessary to do them separately to begin with, especially for students who find it hard to stay on the floor for long periods of time.

It will help the students to work consistently if you count out loud for them: e.g. 'In two, three; out two, three, four, five, six', etc. Each count should take about a second. Do remind the students that if they can't comfortably reach a given number, there's no shame in dropping out and waiting for the next cycle. They can't expect to master this skill right off the bat.

If the students are starting to drone or sitting back on their vocal folds, creating a creaky sound, ask them to picture some nice things that they can count – candy bars or puppies – or anything that will make them smile and help them stay present in the act of counting.

Beach ball breathing (4–5 minutes each)

I. Begin standing with your feet roughly parallel, about hip-width apart, knees soft, back and neck long.

Place your hands on your chest – at the level of your heart.

Move your hands out away from your chest about two feet and imagine that you are holding a beach ball against your body. Take time to imagine what the beach ball looks like – what colour is it; what is it made of; what does it feel like?

As you breathe out, make a continuous 'ssss' sound. Imagine this is the sound of the air escaping from the beach ball. As you make the sound, move your hands gradually in towards your chest and lower your elbows towards your sides, imagining that you are putting pressure on the beach ball.

When you have come to the end of your breath (just before your chest starts to tighten), release the pressure on your beach ball with your hands, and imagine the ball springing back into shape as you breathe in again.

Repeat this cycle of breathing and moving the hands, and as you become more familiar with it, start to vary the speed and intensity with which the air escapes from the beach ball. Sometimes the 'ssss' may be very slow and soft, and at other times it may be swift and loud.

Continue on the 'ssss' for several cycles; then imagine that the beach ball is filled with vibrations. As you gently press against it, an easy flow of 'zzzz' will come from where the beach ball is resting against your body.

Once the 'zzzz' is established, progress to an open-mouth 'mmmm' and then 'maaah'.

If you need to, take a little break and shake out your arms from time to time.

As you work with this exercise, notice how your ribcage responds to the inflation and deflation of the beach ball – your ribs will probably open up as you imagine the ball inflating and gradually return to their rest position as it deflates.

II. This part of the exercise builds on Cow Belly from earlier in the chapter, so you may find it useful to revisit it before continuing.

Begin standing with your feet roughly parallel, about hip-width apart, knees soft, back and neck long.

This time place your hands on your lower belly – about three inches below your navel.

Move your hands out away from your belly about a foot and pretend that you are holding the beach ball against your lower stomach.

On the out-breath, think of sending up a column of air from centre, shaping it into a 'ffff' at your lips. As you do so, move your hands gradually in towards your stomach, imagining that you are putting pressure on the beach ball. This will help you to engage your abdominal muscles easily, as they are drawn in towards your spine as in Cow Belly.

When you have come to the end of your breath (just before your chest starts to tighten), release the pressure on your beach ball with your hands, imagining the ball springing back into shape. This will help the abdominals release quickly, allowing the in-breath to drop right in, as in Cow Belly.

Continue on the 'ffff' for several cycles; then imagine that the beach ball is filled with vibrations. As you gently press against it, an easy flow of 'vvvv' will come up from your centre, where the beach ball is resting against your body.

Once the 'vvvv' is established, progress to an open-mouth 'mmmm' and then 'maaah'.

If you need to, take a little break and shake out your arms from time to time.

All together (6–8 minutes)

Begin standing with your feet roughly parallel, about hip-width apart, knees soft, back and neck long.

Place the back of your right hand against your ribs and your left hand against your lower belly. Just let your body breathe for a moment, noticing the gentle movement in your sides and abdomen.

Start taking more energized in-breaths, breathing into centre while also focusing on the participation of the ribs.

Now add the intention to make a 'ffff' sound on the out-breath.

On the next breath cycle, notice if your ribs suddenly drop as you begin the 'ffff'. Does your breastbone pull in? Is there a feeling of collapse in your chest? If so, the next step will help you find the energy to start the 'ffff' by engaging the core rather than collapsing the ribs and upper chest.

On the next breath cycle, continue to include the ribs in your in-breath; but this time, as you begin the 'ffff' sound, think about energizing your core, as in Birthday Candles.

When you feel confident with this, switch from a 'ffff' to a 'vvvv', including the ribs in the in-breath and initiating the sound with engagement at the core rather than collapse in the chest/ribs. Sustain the 'vvvv' as long as you can without squeezing. The ribs will naturally and gradually descend while the abdominal muscles continue to engage through the end of the out-breath.

Repeat for several minutes, perhaps moving on to an open-mouth 'mmmm' or 'ahhh' sound, until finding voice energy in the engagement of the core rather than the collapse of the thorax starts to become a regular pattern.

Teaching tip

This exercise may feel challenging to some students at first – like being asked to pat their heads and rub their bellies at the same time. With a little focused attention, though, most will get the hang of it the third or fourth time through. Encourage those who don't to have patience with themselves and explore the exercise on their own.

While this exercise is in some respects quite technical, the underlying principles of receiving (breathing in) with the whole torso and responding (breathing out) with engagement rather than collapse go to the heart of dynamic, compelling acting and are worth coming back to in many contexts and at many moments in an actor's training.

More counting (6–8 minutes)

Repeat the counting exercises above whilst standing.

You may find it helpful to start chanting as early as eight and to introduce either or both of the beach ball images/hand movements at that point.

When you get to twelve, start actually counting things in the room – elbows or ceiling tiles or chairs – anything.

Try counting to thirteen, fourteen and fifteen, physically pointing to things as you count them.

Speak the speech (5–6 minutes)

We learnt this exercise from Dudley Knight.

Begin standing with your feet roughly parallel, about hip-width apart, knees soft, back and neck long.

Breathe in on each of the following thoughts and then speak them on one breath, if possible, while engaging the beach ball or birthday candle muscles (whichever image works best for you) and keeping the throat and mouth soft and open as you do:

Speak the speech, I pray you

Speak the speech, I pray you, as I pronounced it to you

Speak the speech, I pray you, as I pronounced it to you, trippingly on the tongue

Speak the speech, I pray you, as I pronounced it to you, trippingly on the tongue, but if you mouth it

Speak the speech, I pray you, as I pronounced it to you, trippingly on the tongue, but if you mouth it, as many of our players do.

[At this point you may find your body really wants to take a quick catch breath at one of the commas; this isn't the worst thing in the world as long as that breath is achieved by releasing the abdominal muscles and engaging the ribs, rather than by gulping or gasping for air, and you don't let your energy drop away from the thought as you breathe. The goal is to connect intention and breath with length of thought, not to see how long you can keep speaking on one breath or how much you can fit into one breath.]

Speak the speech, I pray you, as I pronounced it to you, trippingly on the tongue, but if you mouth it, as many of our players do, I had as lief.

Speak the speech, I pray you, as I pronounced it to you, trippingly on the tongue, but if you mouth it, as many of our players do, I had as lief the town crier spoke my lines.

Teaching tip

This comes from William Shakespeare's *Hamlet*, Act III, Scene ii. Hamlet is encouraging a group of actors to speak their lines with fluidity and agility rather than forceful over-muscularity. 'I had as lief [pronounced like "leaf"] the town crier spoke my lines' means that he would just as soon have the town crier deliver the speech if the actors can't get it right.

As the thought becomes longer and longer, it can be helpful for you to repeat the new words a few times before the group tries the whole thought. As you feed it to the group, model engagement with what is being said so that it doesn't become a meaningless drone. Also, monitor that the group doesn't speed up but stays at a conversational pace.

Supporting the voice

A voice that is supported – that draws on the strength of the breath musculature to fulfil a clear intention – is a powerful thing. It can be hard to believe in the power of your voice, though, and it can be easy to get in your own way as you work to develop it. Some of us get in our own way because of fear that what we have to offer is not enough – that a simple engagement of a few layers of abdominal muscles will not create a voice powerful and passionate enough to be truly interesting, arresting, affecting. So we try to help it along by pushing or straining – by 'doing' more. Some of us, on the other hand, get in our own way because of fear that what we have to offer will be more than anyone can handle – that if we truly engage, or don't clamp down and restrain ourselves, something ugly, frightening or undesirable will be released. So we fail to commit or we push our energy down. Many of us do both, in different circumstances and for different reasons. Learning to get out of your own way is about tapping into your body's ability to support and release a strong voice. It's also about finding and using your personal power. Don't expect it to happen overnight, but don't sell yourself short and settle for less.

As we move into more energetic voice use, it is particularly important to keep the effort focused in the respiratory muscles and out of the throat. As you do these exercises, you may start to get pulled back into old habits – tightening the jaw, thrusting the back of the neck, tensing the shoulders, etc. – so it's a good idea to do some release and relaxation exercises beforehand. In addition, monitor those areas where you know you have trouble. If you find yourself pushing or straining your voice at any point, stop, shake out, take a breath, focus your energy into the respiratory muscles where it can really help you and start again. You've been developing the ability to recognize tension and release it; this is where it will really become useful. Also useful will be the image of an empty passageway between your centre and your lips. The more power you are generating, the more important it is to keep the channel open, i.e. to get out of your own way and let your body support your vocal intention.

Baby talk (3–5 minutes)

Begin in semi-supine.

Take a moment to release any unnecessary physical tension.

Imagine your legs and your upper body becoming lighter and lighter until they begin to lift up off the floor, resting your weight on your sitting bones.

Imagine that you are a baby, old enough to hold up your head, floating on a cloud. Allow your arms, legs, chest and head to move freely as you float along.

Although this will necessitate a strong engagement of the abdominal muscles, keep everything else as soft and free as possible.

As you are floating on your cloud, release a couple of baby sighs, imagining them bubbling up from your centre.

Follow the sighs with some very easy baby sounds 'ma ma ma ma', 'buh buh buh buh', etc. – still floating on a cloud, moving the torso, arms, legs and head freely.

Once you have established an easy flow of sound from centre, your baby talk can become more energetic and use more of your range. You can even enter into a baby dialogue with someone across the room.

Rest in semi-supine whenever your abdominal muscles start to ache.

The chair

I. (1–2 minutes)

Find a lightweight chair – a plastic or folding chair.

Now stand behind the chair with your feet roughly parallel, about hip-width apart, knees soft, back and neck long. Take the chair by the back legs and lift it up over your head; once it's there, let your shoulder blades slide down your back as far as they will go. Check to make sure that you are not tilting your head up towards the chair and your neck is still long. Hold the chair up for three or four breath cycles, engaging your ribs on each in-breath.

Let the chair down and shake your arms out.

Now, lift the chair again, again keeping your shoulders low, and blow out ten imaginary birthday candles on a 'fff' sound. In this position, you should be able to feel the engagement of the abdominal muscles all the way around.

Let the chair down and shake out your arms.

Teaching tip
This exercise can also be performed with a partner, as in the video.

II. (about 1 minute)

Everyone get a chair and stand behind it.

Take the chair by the legs and lift it up over your head; drop your shoulders (see Chair I video clip for a demonstration).

Encourage a strong in-breath by opening the ribs and letting the belly drop.

Engage your birthday candle muscles to send a strong column of 'vvvv's' up from your pelvis. Imagine pressure from a partner's hands on your lower belly, around your sides and across your lower back supporting the flow of sound until you start to feel pressure in your upper chest and throat.

Release and allow the breath in.

Blow out ten birthday candles with ten bursts of 'vvvv's'.

Release and allow the breath in.

Blow out ten birthday candles with ten 'vah's'. Note if any tension creeps into your throat as you open onto the 'ah' sound. If it does, stop, take a little yawn; continue to think of opening the back of your mouth and resume the 'vah's'.

Let the chair down and shake out your arms.

III. (about 1 minute per partner)

Find a partner. Partners, discuss together if you feel comfortable touching and being touched on the back of the neck. If you are, give consent to your partner. If not, check in with your instructor about modifying the exercise or doing an alternate exercise on your own.

Partner A, stand behind the chair with your feet roughly parallel, about hip-width apart, knees soft, back and neck long.

B, stand behind A.

A, take the chair by the legs and lift it up over your head (see Chair I video clip for a demonstration).

Once it's there, let your shoulder blades slide down your back as far as they will go. Check to make sure that you are not tilting your head up toward the chair and your neck is still long.

B, place one hand on the back of A's neck. Gently squeeze and release through the exercise to help A keep their neck long and soft. If at any point you feel the neck go very rigid or A start to pull their neck away from your hand, give it a little massage to remind them to keep the effort out of the neck and in the abdominal muscles.

A, engage a strong in-breath by opening the ribs and letting the belly drop.

Blow out three birthday candles with three bursts of 'vvvv's', and then blow out a fourth, opening the 'vvvv' to a long 'vvvvow'.

Release and allow the breath in.

Energetically engage the birthday candle muscles to send out an energized, 'Vvvow do I love thee? Let me count the ways!'

Release and allow the breath in.

Energetically engage the birthday candle muscles to send out an energized,

'I love thee to the depth and breadth and height my soul can reach!'

Let the chair down and shake out your arms.

Repeat with partner B holding the chair.

Teaching tip

If possible, assign the memorization of these lines from Elizabeth Barrett Browning's Sonnet 43 from *Sonnets from the Portuguese* the session before you do this exercise. Review the lines several times before the students pick up the chairs so they're not exhausting their arms while they try to sort out what they're going to say.

'Hey you, faceache!'

Begin standing with your feet roughly parallel, about hip-width apart, knees soft, back and neck long.

As in All Together, place the back of your right hand against your ribs and your left hand against your lower belly. Just let your body breathe for a moment, noticing the gentle movement in your sides and abdomen.

Start taking more energized in-breaths, breathing into centre while also focusing on the participation of the ribs.

When you're ready, add the intention to create a sustained 'mmm' sound on your next out-breath, finding your vocal energy in the engagement of your core. Continue sounding a sustained 'mmm' on each breath with full engagement, but now think that behind the 'mmm' sound is an AH vowel waiting to spring out. This is another way of finding an open-mouth hum. Notice how full the sound feels when you add the thought of the AH vowel.

When you're ready, begin the 'mmm' with the AH vowel waiting to spring out, and then let your jaw drop so that a strong, engaged AH sound is released on a sustained note. Continue working in this way, but now introduce the idea of gradually expanding your throat around the AH sound as you sustain it to the end of your breath. Resist any impulse of the throat to close as you near the end of your breath – if it helps, say to yourself 'Stay open, stay open' when you feel this happening. You will very probably feel your core muscles working very strongly to support the sound, which is the point of the exercise.

Now, with this sense of strong core engagement and open throat on the out-breath, let out an open and energized 'Hey!', as if you're calling to a friend across the street. When you feel confident with this, let the call become 'Hey, you!', as if the friend is ignoring you and you really need to attract their attention. Let this develop for a few breaths, gradually getting more annoyed with your friend for ignoring you until finally the call has to become 'Hey you, faceache!'. Continue to focus on keeping your throat open as your intention becomes more urgent, so that the strong sound can travel easily up from your centre. As your intention develops from greeting your friend to insulting them, think of really landing that final word on them, fully using the consonants to express your annoyance.

Teaching tip

It's important to monitor students' vocal usage through this sequence to ensure they keep an open throat and strong abdominal support. If working in a group setting, students are likely to start to push vocally in order to hear themselves. To avoid this, have them work individually or in small groups of three or four.

Supporting text

As important as all the technical exercises in the chapter are, nothing will help you find true engagement with dynamic breath supply and support as much as the genuine need to say something. That desire to reach someone and have an effect on them with your words gives purpose to your technique and makes it much easier to commit to it authentically.

As you start working on supporting text, we recommend using non-dramatic literature so that you can focus on incorporating your new skills into your speaking without the pressures of 'acting'. In this chapter, we encourage you to find language that is a bit more challenging than what you used in the last chapter, though: longer thoughts, more complex images and more urgent messages. You will need to bring to this strong language a strong vocal energy (which is NOT the same thing as volume) and strong muscular supply and support. Don't feel, however, that you need to work yourself up into some kind of state to demonstrate the power of the text. This approach will most likely cause you to breathe rapidly into your upper chest and cut you off from true supply and support. Continue to focus on engaging the muscles of respiration effectively and maintaining a sense of freedom and openness in the throat. Let the energy of the voice and the energy of the language complement each other; trust that that will be enough to communicate effectively. Again, these are not performances, just exercises.

At the same time, you will need to commit to what you are saying if you want to truly support your voice. It's well-nigh impossible to trick your body into providing muscular support for an act of communication that your mind and spirit are not engaged in, so pick a text that excites you, spend a bit of time making sure that you understand it and cultivate an attitude of eager readiness to share it.

Teaching tip

Some of the poems we suggest in this chapter are quite long. With these, we recommend that each student could be assigned one or two stanzas or a shorter selection from the poem. You may also wish to introduce other texts. Look for poems and/or prose passages that are energetic in tone but not overwrought. Look also for relatively long arcs of thought that will need a good supply of breath to express. As before, the texts should be memorized, although students may be able to work more effectively if they are allowed to carry the text at first. If you have any dyslexic students, they may find it helpful to receive the text well in advance of the day when they will need to use it in class.

Ideally, sessions on *Supporting Text* would start with a thorough warm-up using exercises from earlier in the chapter and then move on to individual work. Have the students simply speak their texts once, and then choose from the following exercises according to what they seem to need to help them find the energy of the voice in steady muscular engagement of the ribs, the abdomen and the pelvic floor. You may also feel inspired to refer back to work from previous chapters, introduce a new image or incorporate an aspect of an exercise for engaging the in-breath, engaging the out-breath or supporting the voice. If at any point the students start to drone the text, losing vocal energy and creating a flat, creaky sound, have them stop, shake out, jump up and down a couple of times, and start again with a smile and the intention to engage not only their muscles but also the attention of the people they are talking to.

Each of these exercises will take between 2 and 6 minutes, approximately. In all cases, stay engaged with the act of communicating your text to your listeners while consciously applying the principles of supply and support that you are working with. **Take the time to establish consent before any of the following exercises that involve touching.**

I.   Find a couple of partners and stand in a comfortable, aligned position. Have one partner place their hands on your ribs. Have another partner place their hands on your shoulders. Focus on breathing into the hands on your ribs without moving the hands on your shoulders. Breathe out. Repeat the in-breath while silently recalling the first line of your text, and then breathe out.

     Repeat while thinking of speaking the line to someone across the room, and then speak the line on the out-breath.

     Repeat the process, taking the next two lines of the poem together. Work up to a complete thought or image of at least three lines in length.

II. Stand in a comfortable, aligned position. Do a couple of cycles of Beach Ball Breathing I or II as a warm-up.

     Continuing with the beach ball hand movement as you do the following:

     hum as you go through the first two lines of your poem in your head

     chant (i.e. intone) the first two lines

     pick someone across the room and speak the two lines to them.

     Finally, speak the two lines to that person without the hand movement but maintaining an awareness of the easy engagement of the respiratory muscles.

III. Stand in a comfortable, aligned position. Do a couple of cycles of Beach Ball Breathing II as a warm-up.

     Pick someone across the room to speak to. Recite your poem (or stanzas) echoing your breathing impulses with your hands – when you feel the impulse to breathe in, release the pressure on the imaginary beach ball; when you want to sustain a long thought, maintain an even, steady pressure on the beach ball.

IV. Find two reasonably heavy bags or backpacks and a partner. Stand in a comfortable, aligned position, and lift the bags over your head, one in each hand.

     Your partner will first place their hands on your shoulders to remind you to keep them loose and low and then massage your neck. If your shoulders start to creep up, your partner should place their hands on them again and then go back to massaging your neck.

     With the bags held high, blow out five birthday candles.

     Blow out five candles with a 'Hey'.

     Blow out five candles with the first sound in the first line of your poem, and on the fifth candle, continue straight into speaking the line.

Repeat the process on the following lines, stopping to rest when your arms become tired. You may work your way up to speaking several lines on one breath.

V. Start as in the previous exercise, with two bags and a partner to check your shoulders and massage your neck.

Blow out three candles with the first sound of the first line of your poem, and on the third candle, continue straight into chanting the first line at a constant volume.

Blow out three candles with the first sound of the second line, and on the third candle, continue straight into chanting the second line at a slightly higher volume.

Blow out three candles with the first sound of the third line of your poem, and on the third one, continue straight into chanting the third line at a lower volume.

Blow out three candles with the first sound of the next line of your poem, and on the third one, continue straight into chanting a couple of lines, starting at a low volume and steadily increasing to a volume that is high, but not shouted.

Blow out three candles with the first sound of the next line of your poem, and on the third one, continue straight into chanting another couple of lines, starting at a high volume and steadily decreasing to a volume that is low, but not whispered.

Rest your arms, and then repeat speaking instead of chanting.

VI. Work through the 'Hey You, Faceache' exercise and then move straight into speaking your text with that sense of an open throat, strong abdominal support from your core muscles, and the intention to grab and hold your listener's attention.

Follow-up

Reflective practice questions:

- In which exercises did you feel the least amount of pressure and effort in your throat? In which did you feel the most? When you felt pressure and effort in your throat, were you able to move the muscular engagement to your lower torso? What images or exercises helped you to do that?

- When you feel angry or aggressive, where in your body do you feel that energy focus? What exercises, techniques and images could you use to focus that strong energy in your lower abdomen and pelvis?

- How do you know when you need to breathe in? What sensations do you feel and where are they located in your body?

- What is the relationship between your breath and your thought when you are speaking in a relaxed way? Does this change when you perform? If so, why do you think this happens?

- Draw two pictures of the inside of your torso, a front and a back view, including the ribs, the diaphragm and the abdominal muscles. Don't worry about being strictly anatomically correct; draw what you feel from the inside. With a coloured pencil, draw arrows showing where and in what direction you feel everything moving when you breathe in. With another pencil, draw arrows showing where and in what direction you feel everything moving when you breathe out.

- Add a neck and head to your front and back torsos and, using whatever colours take your fancy, draw your voice inside the drawings of your body. This will, of course, be a non-literal representation of what your voice feels like in your body. It could be anything – a red ball in your belly or a blue cloud in your chest, or both. There are no right answers; this is simply a way of heightening your awareness.

- When working on your text, when did you feel your muscles of respiration engage strongly to support the thought? What images or exercises helped you to find that engagement? When did you feel disengaged? Where did the sense of effort go when disengagement happened?

Exercises:

- On a phone call when you don't have to think too hard about what you're saying, sit in a comfortably aligned position with both feet flat on the floor, and use your hand to mirror what your breath is doing – moving it away from the body on the in-breath and continuously towards the body on the out-breath. After a while, move your hand to the abdominal 'beach ball' zone and use the movement to encourage your abdominal muscles to engage and gently support the flow of thought.

- Sometime when you are alone and doing a mundane chore like washing the dishes or taking a shower, start to count objects out loud. Start with five or six and then increase one by one. Stop and go back a number as soon as you feel any strain.

- Any time when you feel tense, try breathing in on a three count and out on a six count, thinking of the air filling your torso to the front, back and the sides on the in-breath and pouring from centre on the out-breath.

Suggested texts

Maya Angelou	'Phenomenal Woman'
Elizabeth Barrett Browning	'A Musical Instrument'
Ruth Fainlight	'Introspection of a Sibyl'
Linda Hogan	'When the Body'
Ted Hughes	'Wodwo'
Jackie Kay	'Castletown, Isle of Man'
D. H. Lawrence	'The Mess of Love'
Michael Longley	'The Butchers'
Claude McKay	'I Know My Soul'
Edna St. Vincent Millay	'Love is not all'
Edwin Muir	'The Horses'
Henry Reed	'Judging Distances'
William Shakespeare	'My mistress' eyes … ' (Sonnet 130)
Anne Stevenson	'The Spirit Is Too Blunt an Instrument'

Further reading

Berry, Cicely, *Voice and the Actor*, Virgin, London, 2000. Chapter 2: 'Relaxation and Breathing', pp. 18–42.

Houseman, Barbara, *Finding Your Voice*, Nick Hern Books, London, 2002. Chapter 3: 'Breath and Support', pp. 73–96.

McCallion, Michael, *The Voice Book* (Revised edition), Faber and Faber Ltd, London, 1998. Part Two: 'Breathing', pp. 62–3.

Nelson, Jeannette, *The Voice Exercise Book*, National Theatre Publishing, London, 2015. Chapter 2: 'Voice Exercises – Stage 1', pp. 36–7; and Chapter 3: 'Voice Exercises – Stage 2', pp. 60–4 and pp. 75–88.

Rodenburg, Patsy, *The Actor Speaks*, Methuen, London, 1997. 'Stage One: The Actor First Speaks', pp. 38–66.

4
RESONANCE AND RANGE

Framework

The human voice is a powerful thing. Its sound can rouse, soothe, chill, warm, irritate, comfort and on and on. Vocal qualities such as bright, sombre, flat, nasal, plummy, tight, raspy or clear influence how we feel about a speaker and, by extension, about what the speaker is saying. All these attributes of the voice are created by our resonance and pitch, and we use them almost unconsciously to have such effects on our listeners. Even as infants, we understand intentions communicated through pitch and resonance long before we understand words. They are a huge part of any vocal interaction. For actors, it is vitally important to be able to use a wide range of pitches and resonant qualities. In order to develop that ability, it helps to have a basic understanding of what pitch and resonance are and how they are created in the human voice.

Vocal anatomy – pitch

The pitch that we hear when someone speaks or sings (sounds that we describe as 'higher' or 'lower') is produced by the vocal folds. As we discussed in the last chapter, when the vocal folds are brought together with the right amount of pressure, the air pressure beneath them builds up until it blows them apart. They then fall back together until sufficient air pressure builds up to blow them apart again, and so forth. If the folds are thin and stretched tight, this process happens very quickly. If the folds are thick and slack, it happens more slowly. In the first instance, the sound produced has a high frequency – the folds open and close many times per second, so the sound waves come very quickly. In the second instance, the sound has a low frequency – the folds open and close fewer times per second, so the sound waves come more slowly (i.e. they come less *frequently*). When sound waves come very fast, we hear them as high pitches. When they come more slowly, we hear them as lower pitches. For example, to sing the note middle C, the vocal folds will vibrate at approximately 261 times a second; and to sing the note A above middle C, they will vibrate at 440 times a second. Folds that are physiologically thinner and lighter open and close more quickly and produce sound that is usually higher in pitch. The same principles apply in music – the thinnest, lightest strings on a violin vibrate more quickly and produce the highest sounds, while the thickest, heaviest strings on a cello produce the lowest sounds.

You can, however, get more than one note out of a violin string, and you can get more than one pitch out of your voice as well. The cartilage that your folds are attached to at the front (the thyroid cartilage – see Figure 9) can tilt. When it tilts forward, it stretches the folds; when the folds are stretched, they become thinner and tighter and open and close more quickly, making your voice 'higher'. When the thyroid cartilage tilts back, the folds become thicker and slacker. This makes them open and close more

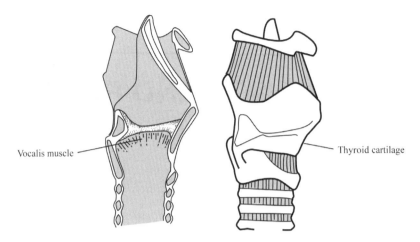

Figure 9 The larynx

slowly, producing a 'lower' voice. There are also muscles in the folds themselves – known as the *vocalis* muscles – that are particularly useful for fine-tuning the pitch of the voice. However, we don't have any direct conscious control over all this muscular activity. Although the violinist will consciously tighten the strings of the violin or move their finger up and down the string in order to change pitch, the singer or speaker cannot directly alter the thickness and tension of the vocal folds. We change pitch with our intention rather than with our fingers. It is our thoughts and feelings, or our mental image of the note we want to make, that cause our brain to unconsciously tune the muscles of the vocal folds to produce the right sound. The action of these muscles in the larynx can be affected by a number of factors: from the relatively stable – such as an individual's vocal anatomy, through those that change and develop with time and experience – for example, a speaker's accent or physical and psychological maturity, to more temporary ones – a person's general energy level and state of health, to the most immediate – one's psychological or emotional state, attitude and intention in the moment of speaking.

Vocal anatomy – resonance

The vibration of the vocal folds determines the pitch we hear. But without the resonance provided by the vocal tract, that vibration would just sound like the irritating buzzing of a fly. Resonance adds colour and size to those vibrations, giving them greater dimension and carrying power. Your vocal tract – the resonating chamber for your voice – is essentially a hollow but flexible tube which extends from the larynx through the vertical space of your throat (or pharynx) into the horizontal spaces of your nose and mouth (see Figure 10). By changing the length and shape of this tube, we alter the vocal resonance. It might be helpful to think of the vocal tract as a kind of musical instrument, perhaps a strange relative of a clarinet and a trombone. Like the clarinet, vibration is created by blowing air through a reed (in this case, the vocal folds); and like the trombone, it is flexible and can change its length. Unlike either instrument, though, it has two apertures (the nose and mouth) and can change its shape as well as its length.

Different shapes and sizes resonate different pitches in different ways. Some shapes, for example, will resonate high frequencies very well (like a violin body or a flute does), giving your voice richness, brightness, clarity and carrying power at high pitches. Other shapes resonate low frequencies very well

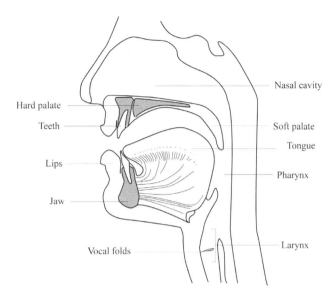

Figure 10 The vocal tract

(like a cello body or an oboe does), giving your voice warmth, body, fullness and strength at lower pitches. Try *Exploration II* to explore how a fixed shape will resonate one pitch more effectively than others.

The shape of the vocal tract also affects the quality of your voice. Some shapes will resonate in such a way that the voice sounds full and open. Some shapes will resonate in such a way that the voice sounds pinched and narrow. Essentially a longer tube produces a darker sound, and a shorter tube produces a brighter sound; a narrower tube produces a more constricted and restricted sound, and a wider tube produces a more open and generous sound.

The length and shape of your vocal tract are determined by a number of variables. While the structure of the bones and the overall amount of space available don't normally change except with age, you can alter all of the following: the height of the larynx, the width of the pharynx, the position of the soft palate (the back of the roof of your mouth), the shape and position of the tongue, the shape and position of the lips and the position of the jaw. These shapes are created by the action of a number of muscles, which we generally use for eating, swallowing and facial expression, as well as for creating speech sounds. Try *Exploration III* to get a sense of what these muscles can do. They are affected by factors similar to those that influence the pitch changing muscles – accent, age, health, energy-levels, emotion, etc.

Range and resonance and the actor

The ability of the muscles of pitch and resonance to work effectively can be limited by the habitual patterns and psychological inhibitions of our daily lives. Pitch and resonance ideally express our emotions and inner states and are responsive to the content and context of communication. But the attitudes and repressions of our parents, our peers and ourselves will often cause us to limit that expressiveness – we restrict our pitch range so as not to sound childish or silly, or because we want to sound sweet and unthreatening; we shut down our resonance when we tighten our jaw in sullen rebellion or constrict our pharynx from social anxiety. If you can move beyond such personal habits, the ability to use a full range of pitches and resonances will enable you to express the experiences and intentions of your characters with greater specificity and power.

If the parts of your vocal tract that can move are to be as free, agile and responsive as possible, the voice must be grounded in strongly supported breath. As we've discussed before, if your voice isn't getting the support it needs from your respiratory muscles, other muscles will step in and try to compensate. In particular, the muscles of the throat can constrict, the root of the tongue can tighten, and the jaw can clench all in an effort to get the sound out. This will change the shape of the vocal tract, and not in a way that gives your voice access to its full resonant possibilities. The relationship of your head and neck to the rest of your body will also change the shape of the vocal tract. If your neck is collapsed in the back or your head is jutting forward, the space between the larynx and the back of your mouth – the pharynx – will be constricted, and your resonance will be compromised. It is, therefore, important to continue to build efficient alignment and breathing habits and consciously employ them when working on resonance. Try *Exploration IV* to feel the effect of posture on resonance.

Working on range and resonance

In this chapter, we will do some specific work on the four major mobile parts of the vocal tract: the pharynx, the tongue, the soft palate and the jaw. Much of this work will focus on releasing tension so that they can move more freely and responsively. Release is, of course, only the first step. Once the muscles are free through their range of motion, you can really explore your voice's pitch range and resonant potential. As with other aspects of voice work, images and play can help you to discover possibilities that you might not find through purely technical work. The physical sensation of different pitches vibrating in your body can also inform your work on resonance, so we will work on 'feeling' resonance as well as hearing it. We'll also work on using resonance and range to help you to be heard without shouting and to speak for long periods of time without tiring the voice.

Although finding efficient resonance and power through your pitch range will give you carrying power, you should not feel that you are limited to making only 'good' sounds. All sounds have their place – having the skill to make them healthily and the freedom to use them creatively opens up a world of acting possibilities to you. When it comes to creating nuanced, vivid performances that reach audiences and affect them both intellectually and emotionally, resonance and range are, in so many ways, an actor's best friends.

Exploration

I. Listen to your friends and family speaking at different times of the day or in different circumstances, e.g. over a coffee, watching television, on the phone, out shopping. Do they change the pitch or resonance of their voices? Or do their voices stay fixed in a particular quality or part of their range? Try listening to your own voice too and see if you can tell whether you change your pitch and resonance.

II. Get a can of Pringles and empty it (what you do with the crisps is up to you). Now place the open end of the empty can lightly over your mouth and hold it there with both hands making a seal with your face so that it looks as though you have grown a long beak. (Be careful not to block your nose – you still need to breathe!) You are now going to experiment with sending different sounds and pitches into the can. Start with a gentle humming, and then open into an intoned and supported AH sound: as you open into the vowel you should start to feel the can vibrate slightly. Now try moving the pitch of the AH sound around slowly – can you feel the can vibrating more or less strongly at different pitches? At what pitches does it vibrate most strongly on the AH sound? Does it make a difference if you open your jaw and relax your tongue? Now try the same exercise with different vowel sounds – EE, AY, AW, OO. Try rounding your lips actively on the AW and OO sounds. Do you notice any differences? Ask a friend to listen while you experiment with the Pringles can – can they hear any changes? Can you find a pitch and a sound which will make the metal end of the can vibrate like a steel drum? (Note: there isn't just one.) These exercises illustrate very clearly how pitch and resonance interact in the human voice. The Pringles can is like one shape of the vocal tract. You can hear or feel how it amplifies sounds. However, you can also hear or feel how, because of its shape, it amplifies certain sounds and pitches more than others. Thankfully, the vocal tract is flexible and can create many different shapes. This makes it potentially very responsive to the sounds we make, as long as we don't get stuck in one shape or pitch.

III. If you have a mirror over your bathroom sink, take a good look at your tongue when you brush your teeth. Notice all the movements it makes as it darts out of the way of the brush – up, down, to the sides, forward, backward; it can even get thinner or fatter. When you've finished brushing, run your tongue over the roof of your mouth. There's a slight ridge behind your teeth, and then a hard, smooth plate that runs about two thirds of the way back. As your tongue gets near the back molars, that hard, smooth plate will end and a softer, spongier bit will begin; that is your soft palate. Looking in the mirror, open your mouth, stick your tongue out and see if you can make the soft palate move up and down. Most people have a little polyp of flesh, the uvula, hanging from the soft palate; as the palate raises and lowers, it too will go up and down, sometimes even seeming to disappear if the palate lifts high enough. The movements of the tongue and soft palate are two major determiners of resonant quality. Make an intoned and supported AH sound, and look at the shape your mouth makes. Now try changing that shape by altering the position of your tongue or soft palate while still intoning, or you could move the position of your jaw or lips. Notice any changes in the quality of the sound.

IV. Stand in a comfortable, aligned position. Let your jaw drop open and release a sustained, energetic AH on one note. Continuing the AH, drop your head forward and then slowly rotate it around over one shoulder, to the back, over the other shoulder, and back down. As you do this, notice how the quality of the sound changes. Try it on an EE, an OO and an OH. Rotating your head changes the shape of the vocal tract, which will change the resonant qualities of the vowels.

V. Try your hand at impressions. Start with a really distinctive sound like a New York Brooklyn, Liverpudlian or Australian Outback accent. Stop mid word and notice the shape of your mouth: where is your soft palate? What is your tongue doing? How much tension is in your lips? How much space is there at the back of your mouth and in your throat? Try a very snooty, upper-class dowager and note the same things. Try a little kid voice. A clown voice, etc. In each instance, you are changing the shape of the vocal tract in order to change the resonant properties of your voice (as well as working a specific part of your pitch range and perhaps changing accent) to change your vocal quality.

Exercises

Teaching tip

The exercises in this chapter are organized under five headings: *Working the Channel*, *Finding the Buzz*, *Expanding the Range*, *Balancing the Sound* and *Resonating Text*. In general, it's a good idea to begin any work on resonance and range with some work on freeing the vocal tract and a review of engaging breath support. It's important to transfer to the major respiratory muscles the sense of exertion that can get lodged in the throat and the back of the mouth. Tongue and jaw tension, in particular, can be very stubborn, so those exercises bear frequent repetition. Many of the exercises in *Expanding the Range* and *Resonating Text* have large pay-offs of fun and discovery. We find it useful to combine a series of more technical exercises with one or two of the more imaginative exercises per session to bring together the systematic acquisition of skill with the joy of expression.

Working the channel

The channel is your vocal tract – the space in which your voice will resonate. Much of the channel is shaped by bone, which tends to change only with age. There are, however, several components of the channel that can move; you will have already discovered some of the possibilities in the *Exploration* exercises. The first of these moving components of the vocal tract is the larynx itself. If you place your fingers lightly on your Adam's apple and then swallow, you can feel your larynx moving upwards. Similarly, if you yawn, you can feel it drop downwards. Speaking with a habitually raised or lowered larynx will reduce the amount of resonance available to you and restrict your range. For optimum range and resonance, therefore, the larynx should rest easily and be able to move freely in your neck. We will work on maintaining this relaxed position

Travelling further up the vocal tract, the next movable component we come to is the pharynx – the area between the larynx and the back of your mouth. As mentioned in the framework section, the shape of the pharynx is affected by your alignment, but it also has muscles of its own that can cause it to constrict or open. If they are over-engaged, your resonant possibilities will be narrowed. If, however, they are under-engaged and sluggish, they can also compromise your resonance. This is because sound waves generally resonate better against surfaces that are hard and firm than against surfaces that are soft and slack. Think about how much clearer, louder and fuller your voice sounds in a tiled bathroom than in a heavily curtained drawing room. We will work on finding openness and tone in this area.

We tend to think of the tongue as being part of the mouth, but in fact it descends all the way into the pharynx and attaches to the bone at the top of the larynx. Tension at the root of the tongue is very common and is one of the factors that can most affect resonance. If your tongue is bunched up at the back of your mouth, it can force some of the vibrations rising up from the larynx into your nose, which creates a very different resonance than if they are allowed to travel through the mouth. Dropping the soft palate (the back of the roof of your mouth) also prevents the vibrations from entering your mouth, sending them out the nose instead. The balance between how much sound is resonating in the oral cavity and how much is resonating in the nasal cavity has an enormous impact on vocal quality. The front of the tongue can also be an area of tension that inhibits resonance. If your tongue tends to bunch up at the front of your mouth, it can affect the size of your oral cavity. We will work to release unnecessary tension from the tongue and to engage the soft palate so that there is a greater balance of resonance between the oral and nasal cavities.

Finally, the position of the jaw determines how much resonating space there is in the mouth. The muscles that have the primary responsibility for closing the jaw are, inch for inch, among the most powerful in the body and are a favourite place for many people to carry tension. Engaging those muscles is a common way to force back emotions that we don't want to show or act on, and it can be very hard to disengage them. Think of the clenched jaw of James Bond, Dirty Harry or Sarah Connor in the *Terminator* franchise. Some people grind their teeth at night or have jaws that pop or click when they open. If you find this is the case with you or you experience any discomfort doing the jaw exercises, you may wish to consult a specialist. In any case, even after we have found a good degree of freedom in the jaw through exercises, most of us will have to consciously bring ourselves back to that release over and over again before it becomes second nature, if it ever does.

The lips also help to shape the vocal tract, and will naturally come into play in many of the exercises in this chapter. We will work with them in more detail in the next chapter on articulation.

Teaching tip

You do not need to work through every exercise for each part of the tract in sequence. Many of them get to the same muscles through slightly different angles and can be mixed and matched from session to session to prevent boredom and to reach as many students as possible, each one of whom will respond to each exercise differently. In particular, there are a number of exercises that involve yawning. Be careful not to overwork these exercises, as students can start to feel sleepy very easily.

Many of the exercises are designed to develop an inner kinaesthetic awareness of the different parts of the vocal tract, but it will also be useful for students to have access to a small hand mirror, particularly for work on the soft palate. You will also find it useful to combine the exercises in this section with exercises on articulation in the next chapter, where again a small hand mirror will be useful.

Larynx (1–2 minutes each)

For all these exercises stand or sit in a comfortable, aligned position.

I. As we described above, place your fingers lightly on your Adam's apple and then swallow slowly; you should feel your larynx moving upwards in the first phase of the swallow, and then relaxing downwards again.

   Repeat this action, but this time try to hold your larynx in a raised position at the 'top' of the swallow, i.e. don't relax your swallow.

   Now try counting out loud from 1 to 10 keeping your larynx raised. Notice the effect on your voice – you will probably sound like a cartoon character. This is because you have drastically changed your vocal resonance.

   Now relax and enjoy the sensation of your larynx descending easily.

II. Place your fingers lightly on your Adam's apple and then yawn slowly; you should feel your larynx moving downwards at the start of the yawn, and then relaxing upwards again.

Repeat this action, but this time try and hold your larynx in a lowered position at the 'bottom' of the yawn, i.e. don't relax your yawn.

Now try counting from 1 to 10 keeping your larynx lowered. Notice the effect on your voice – again, you will probably sound like a cartoon character or a comic caricature. This is because once again you have drastically changed your vocal resonance.

Now relax and enjoy the sensation of your larynx rising gently.

III. Many of the muscles which raise and lower your larynx are situated on either side of your neck. Gently massage your neck on either side of your larynx, starting underneath your jaw and working down to your collarbone.

Now, place your fingers lightly on either side of your Adam's apple and very gently move it from side to side, encouraging the muscles to relax. It's all right – this won't damage you or your larynx. You may feel some 'clicking' movements inside your larynx – these are created by the cartilages moving around and are quite normal. But if you feel nauseous at all, stop. Moving the larynx can stimulate the 'gag' reflex, particularly if there is some degree of tension in the area. The more you work on releasing tension in other ways, the easier it will become to move your larynx from side to side.

IV. A nice way to help your larynx to relax is to imagine it smiling. Think of something which genuinely makes you smile, and then think of transferring the smile down your vocal tract to your larynx. Gillyanne Kayes taught us this image, and we have found it very useful for finding a relaxed and easy larynx.

Try counting from 1 to 10 with a smiling larynx.

Now imagine your larynx frowning and count from 1 to 10. Hear the difference? Go back to the smiling larynx and try speaking to a partner for a minute or two.

Teaching tip

Some students feel uncomfortable working on the larynx. It can produce vulnerable or nauseous sensations. They can be asked to concentrate on massaging the neck muscles while imagining the larynx smiling. If it is appropriate, you might invite them to observe other students as well.

Pharynx (1–2 minutes each)

For all these exercises stand or sit in a comfortable, aligned position.

I. Take a nice, big yawn. Yawning is our bodies' reflex way of opening up the vocal tract and getting a lot of oxygen into the system quickly. It produces a long and wide-open pharynx.

Notice the sensation it creates in the throat. Try to recreate that sensation in the throat without actually yawning.

Now, try to constrict that area as tightly as you can. You can do this if you imagine that you have something caught in your throat, or that you have a sore throat, or are feeling very anxious about an interview or audition.

Go back and forth between opening it wide and constricting it, and then let it come to rest in a comfortably open position – not as wide open as for a yawn, but with an easy feeling of space.

II. Yawn, sighing out loud through the yawn.

Yawn again, and hold the pharynx in the yawning position. With the pharynx wide open, release a few easy, extended 'haaahs'. These may initially come out in the middle part of your lower range; try a couple of 'haaahs' a few notes higher and a couple a few notes lower.

With the pharynx still wide open (yawn again if you feel yourself losing it), release some 'who who' calls like a dove.

Call to someone close to you and then to someone across the room.

Release the yawning posture in the pharynx and let it come to rest in a comfortably open position.

Alternate between easily calling 'hah' and 'who' to people around the room, enjoying the sense of freedom and space in the throat.

III. Think of something which genuinely makes you smile, and then think of transferring the smile down your vocal tract to your pharynx.

Try counting from 1 to 10 with a smiling pharynx. Now imagine your pharynx frowning and count from 1 to 10. Hear the difference?

Go back to the smiling pharynx and try speaking with a partner for a minute or so.

Tongue (about 1 minute each)

Note: Not everyone's tongue will stretch to the same extent, so don't push yourself to the point of pain or discomfort when doing these exercises.

For all these exercises stand or sit in a comfortable, aligned position.

I. Place one hand at the back of your neck and the other hand on the side of your jaw. This is to help ensure that you don't push with your neck and jaw but work the tongue itself in isolation.

Imagine a big ice cream cone just in front of your mouth that you desperately want to lick. Reach for it with the tip of your tongue, but imagine that just as you are about to touch it, it is slowly pulled away from you, millimetre by millimetre. Continue reaching for it with the tip of your tongue as far as you can.

Hold the tongue there, reaching with the tip and monitoring your neck and jaw to make sure they don't try to help, until your tongue starts to ache and then another 15–20 seconds longer.

Allow your tongue to slowly retract back into your mouth.

II. Place one hand at the back of your neck and the other hand on the side of your jaw.

Let your jaw drop open and slowly curl the tip of your tongue backwards along the roof of your mouth until you can feel your palate soften.

Hold the tongue in this position, monitoring your neck and jaw to make sure they don't try to help, until your tongue starts to ache and then another 15–20 seconds longer.

Allow your tongue to slowly return to its normal position.

III. Place one hand at the back of your neck and the other hand on the side of your jaw.

Imagine the very back of your tongue slowly pushing forward, trying to get out of your mouth. This will push your whole tongue forward.

When your tongue is about as far forward as it can go, continue to push from the back until your tongue starts to ache and then another 15–20 seconds longer. Keep the neck and jaw soft and loose throughout.

Allow your tongue to slowly retract back into your mouth.

IV. Place your thumb underneath your chin and find the soft area in the angle made by your jaw. This soft area is the root of your tongue. Give it a bit of a massage while imagining that the part of your tongue that is in your mouth is softening and spreading.

Leaving your thumb under your chin, release a long, easy 'ahhh'.

Move from the 'ahh' directly into an 'ooo'. You will feel a little movement under your thumb, but if you felt the base of your tongue press against or tighten under your thumb, massage the area a bit more and think of the change from one sound to the other as happening on the roof of the mouth.

Repeat moving up and down in pitch. You may find it harder to keep your tongue root soft in some parts of your range; work in those areas particularly.

Repeat this exercise regularly until you can keep the tongue root soft as you move between vowels.

V. Let your head hang forward with the jaw dropped slightly open.

Allow your tongue to hang freely; it will probably come to rest on your bottom lip. Thinking of it as a floppy piece of meat or as giving into gravity can help you find release.

Continuing to let your tongue hang freely, slowly roll your head over to one shoulder and then over to the other shoulder before releasing it back down. Let your tongue roll in your mouth as you do so.

VI. Let your jaw hang open and place your fingertips on either side of your chin to make sure that it stays relaxed and open.

Place the tip of your tongue behind your bottom teeth.

Roll the middle of your tongue out of your mouth, leaving the tip inside, behind the bottom teeth (see Figure 11).

Hold this position until your tongue starts to ache and then another 15–20 seconds longer.

Let your middle tongue fall back into your mouth.

Next, roll the middle tongue back and forth in and out of your mouth fairly rapidly.

Make sure your jaw is not moving at all; it's important to be able to separate the movement of the tongue from the movement of the jaw.

Add some sound – an extended 'huh', which will probably come out as a 'huh-yuh-yuh-yuh' because of the movement of the tongue.

Figure 11 Tongue VI

Try the same on a pitch glide through your range.

VII. Finish your tongue release work by flicking your tongue in and out of your mouth. Start slowly and then gradually build up speed.

Try the same on a pitch glide through your range.

> ### Teaching tip
> The human tongue comes in all shapes and sizes, and so some of us are capable of achieving more flexibility than others. Students should be encouraged to work with goals appropriate to the shape and size of their own tongues, and not to compete with each other.

Soft palate (about 1 minute each)

For all these exercises stand or sit in a comfortable, aligned position.

I. Take a nice, big yawn, this time noticing what your tongue does.

    Yawn again, consciously leaving your tongue resting behind your bottom teeth, and feel the lift at the back of your mouth.

    If a mirror is available, take a look at what's happening. You should be able to see your soft palate lifting high up into your mouth.

    Let your jaw drop open and bring your mouth into position to make a 'k' sound. Before you make the sound, notice what you feel at the back of your mouth. Explode the 'k' and notice what you feel move.

    Keep your jaw relaxed and try making a 'k' sound on an in-breath and notice what you feel move.

    With your jaw relaxed, go back and forth between an out-breath 'k' and an in-breath 'k' four or five times, making each one a little more energetic.

II. Make a 'ng' sound (the sound at the end of the word 'sing') and notice what you feel at the back of your mouth. Have a look in a mirror and see what is happening to make this sound.

    Open the 'ng' into an 'ah' and notice the action at the back of the mouth. You should be able to see the tongue and soft palate separate if you have a mirror.

    Place your fingers on either side of your chin to make sure that the jaw is still and only the soft palate and the back of the tongue move as you repeat 'ng-ah-ng-ah-ng-ah' seven or eight times. Imagine the soft palate bouncing off the back of the tongue like a trampoline as you do.

    Switch to a long 'ng-ay' and then a bouncing 'ng-ay-ng-ay-ng-ay'.

    Switch to a long 'ng-ee' and then a bouncing 'ng-ee-ng-ee-ng-ee'.

Jaw (I–IV: about 1 minute each; V–VI: about 2 minutes each)

If you have a jaw that 'clicks,' don't force it to open to that point when doing these exercises. If you experience a sharp pain when massaging or moving your jaw, you should see a doctor.

    For all these exercises stand or sit in a comfortable, aligned position.

I. Clench your teeth and, with your fingers, find the muscles that pop out on either side of your jaw. These are the masseter muscles. Unclench your teeth and give these muscles a thorough massage, allowing your jaw to drop open as you do so.

    As you massage, make sure that you are keeping your shoulders loose and low.

II. Close your mouth.

    Put a finger on your chin and use it to draw your chin down, slowly opening your mouth as wide as it will comfortably go.

Close your mouth again and, this time, place your hands on either side of your face, cradling your jawbone in your palms, with the thumbs tucked behind the ears.

Keep your shoulders loose and low.

Let the weight of your hands slowly pull your jaw down.

Keep your lips together as long as possible.

Picture the space between your back molars growing as your hands draw the jaw down.

Switch back and forth a couple of times between opening your mouth by pulling down the chin and opening it by allowing the jaw to drop open at the back. Note which one gives you the feeling of having more space in your mouth.

III. Clench your teeth and place your thumbs over your masseter muscles – the ones that are popping out as you do this.

Unclench your teeth and press against your masseter muscles with enough pressure to be uncomfortable, but not enough pressure to be painful (see Figure 12).

Hold for 20–30 seconds, keeping the shoulders loose and low and breathing deeply.

Release and allow the jaw to fall open.

IV. Find the joint where your jaw hinges with your skull – it's just in front of the opening to your ear. Place your fingers here lightly, and feel how the joint moves as you open and close your jaw.

Now imagine that this joint is controlled by a wing nut (aka a butterfly nut) attached to the outside of your face. (We're indebted to Frankie Armstrong for this enjoyable image.) Tightening the nut will make you gradually clench your jaw – try it! And loosening the nut will make you gradually open your jaw – try that too!

Play with tightening and loosening the nut until you find a comfortable relaxed position for the jaw, where the lips are gently together but you can feel space between your back molars.

V. Once you have found some release in the jaw through any of the above exercises, place your thumbs under your chin and use them to gently close your jaw.

Release the thumbs and let the jaw fall open.

Imagine the masseter muscles softening, like butter melting, and see if the jaw sinks down a bit farther; do not, however, pull it down.

Figure 12 Jaw III

Repeat three or four times, keeping the shoulders loose and low and the breath free.

Take a hold of either side of your chin with the thumb and forefinger of each hand.

Use your hands to gently and slowly open and close your jaw. This requires that the jaw muscles release completely – think of them going wobbly like jelly.

When you have mastered this, add a touch of sound: a continuous 'ahhhh' from centre.

Revisiting the column of air (7–10 minutes)

You are now going to revisit the Column of Air exercise from the previous chapter with your new awareness of the vocal tract.

Start in supine or semi-supine.

Take a minute or so to release unnecessary tension from your body by imagining your head, your shoulders, your chest, your abdomen and your hips all becoming very heavy on the floor.

Visualize your throat as an empty pipe and your torso as an empty chamber with a source of energy at the base: that is, centre.

For a minute or so, just observe how centre moves your empty torso as it calls air down to itself and releases air back up: the gentle rise and fall of the stomach, the slight feeling of expansion and release in the hips, around the back and in the ribs.

Now become aware of the various elements of your vocal tract. Think of your larynx at rest in your throat. Think of the open, smiling pharynx. Let your jaw relax until you can feel there is space between your back molars. Let your tongue rest in the floor of your mouth, with the tip in contact with the back of your lower front teeth. Think of your soft palate lifting away from the back of your tongue, creating space in the back of your mouth.

Slip your lower lip under your top teeth as if you were going to make the sound 'ffff'. Simply continue to breathe, and focus on the feeling of the air sliding between your teeth and your lip.

Start to extend your out-breath so that it becomes a little bit stronger and a little bit longer. As you do, picture the air running between your centre and your lips. Think of it as being like a column of water springing up from a drinking fountain. When you feel the impulse to breathe in, breathe in – air is free, and there's little to be gained from fighting your impulses.

Notice how your body supports the flow of this fluid column of air up from centre to your lips on the exhalation and then responds to the impulse to let more air in on the inhalation.

Now, imagine that this column of air continues beyond your lips, running from centre up to the ceiling. Avoid lifting your chin as you do this.

After a couple of minutes of observing your body support the column of air on a 'ffff', imagine the air starting to vibrate, which will change it to a 'vvvv'.

Remember that the origin of this vibration is at centre.

After a couple of minutes of working with the 'vvvv', take a stretch and a wriggle.

Return to the 'vvvv' for two or three breath cycles, then close your lips around the vibrations, creating a 'mmmm'. Continue to work with the image of the sound flowing from centre and the sense of your breathing muscles easily engaging to support it.

Even as your lips are closed, remind yourself to keep the various elements of your vocal tract open: the larynx at rest in your throat; the open, smiling pharynx; the jaw relaxed and space between your back molars; your tongue resting in the floor of your mouth, with the tip in contact with the back of your lower front teeth; and your soft palate lifting away from the back of your tongue, creating space in the back of your mouth. Imagine that behind the 'mmmm' sound there is an 'aaah' sound waiting to come out. Let your mouth form the 'aaah' sound behind your lips as you make the 'mmmm'.

After a minute or so of working with the 'mmmm', open your lips and allow the 'aaah' sound to come out freely. Work with the 'aaah' for a minute or two. Imagine the sound is just pouring out of you and flowing up towards the ceiling. If at any point you find yourself disconnecting from the sense that there is a steady column of vibration flowing up from centre, go back to the 'vvvv' or the 'mmmm' to re-establish it.

Stretch and wriggle as you finish the exercise.

Finding the buzz

The work we've done so far on the vocal tract has been highly technical – working on muscles directly in order to free them and prepare them to engage in a wider range of movement with greater ease. Having laid this foundation, we'll now move on to exercises that are more imaginative and experiential as we start to work on finding full, strong resonance.

Strictly speaking, vocal resonance can only occur in the vocal tract. However, when you've found a shape for that channel that is particularly well suited to the frequencies being generated, the primary resonance can cause sympathetic vibration in other bones in your body. Well resonated lower notes can cause the breastbone to vibrate, which is one of the reasons the lower voice is often called the 'chest voice'. Well-resonated higher notes can cause a sensation of vibration in the skull, which is where we get the phrase 'head voice'. We do have a certain amount of conscious control over the vocal tract, but it's not always easy to sense the exact position of every little muscle in it or evaluate by ear how well one's own voice is resonating. Using images to find sympathetic resonance can, therefore, be very useful to help you discover new and fuller resonance in your voice.

However, resonance can't be forced – you can prepare the ground, and then you just have to experiment until it comes. Be sensitive to what you feel in your body as it will tell you a great deal about what is happening in your voice – more sometimes than what you can hear. Be aware of sensation all over your body; it's important to think of voice as a 360-degree phenomenon, not just something that is focused in the front of the body. Finally, be open to making shapes with your mouth that are unfamiliar and to working with sounds that are outside your usual repertoire – don't be afraid to be creative and bold!

Teaching tip

When a roomful of students has 'found the buzz', it's easy to spot; the sound will suddenly be very full and alive. These exercises should get students well on their way, but they may need some coaching to find full resonance. If you sense that their voices are still a bit thin or are pushed, you may want to briefly revisit some of the channel work – even just yawning to open the soft palate and pharynx. Encourage them as well to shake out from time to time. Feed them images of openness, gentleness (pushing is the number one enemy of resonance), warmth and energy throughout.

Humming (12–15 minutes)

1. Lie on the floor on your stomach with your head turned to one side.

    Take a moment to give the weight of your body to the floor and feel your body opening to the breath, particularly through the back.

    Imagine a bit of vibration coming up from centre on a 'huh'.

    On your next breath, extend the 'huh' and close your lips around it so it becomes an open-mouth 'hummmm'.

    As you hum, imagine an unbroken column of vibration between your centre and your lips.

    On your next breath, imagine all those vibrations pooling in the cheek that is next to the ground. Play with the shape of your vocal tract (by changing the position of the tongue, soft palate, lips, etc.) and with various pitches until you feel that your whole head is buzzing against the floor.

2. Next, imagine the vibrations pooling behind your collar bone. Play with the image, the vocal tract and the pitch until you feel that your upper chest is buzzing against the floor.

3. Move the pool of vibrations down to the middle of your breastbone. Spend a couple of breath cycles exploring the feeling of resonance in this area.

4. Finally, imagine the vibrations at their source, in the pelvic bowl, and experiment with pitch and vocal tract shape until you find the maximum buzzing sensation in that area.

5. Roll over onto your back.

    Connect again to the image of vibration flowing from centre as you recommence humming.

    Focus the vibrations into your head until you feel that it is buzzing against the floor.

6. Next, think of the vibrations as flowing to your shoulders and explore the feeling of resonance in this area.

7. Imagine the pool of vibrations moving to your mid-back – just above the lumbar curve, and adjust the quality of the hum correspondingly.

8. Finally, imagine the vibrations staying in the pelvis and buzzing against the floor there.

Mouths I (20–30 minutes)

This is a lengthy sequence, but it really pays dividends in your connection to resonance if you work through it slowly.

1. Lying in semi-supine, take the time to allow your breath to really settle in your body. As you breathe, imagine that you have a mouth in your belly, somewhere in the region of your navel. If it helps you to imagine it, place a hand gently on your stomach.

    When you feel you have a good image of this mouth, add vibration to the breath in the form of an easy hum, but imagine that the hum is focused in your belly mouth.

    Work with this image until you feel that the hum is really connected to the belly mouth. Now imagine that behind the hum there is an 'aaahhh' sound waiting to come out, and then visualize your belly mouth opening to release the 'aaahhh' sound just as your real mouth does so.

    Work with this sequence of breath, humming and opening into 'aaahhh' from the belly mouth for about a minute until you feel fully engaged in the image and sound. Experiment with different pitches or pitch glides on your 'aaahhh' sound.

Experiment with releasing other vowel sounds, such as 'ooooo', 'ohhhhh' or 'eeee', from this new mouth.

2. Now imagine that you have a mouth in the middle of your chest, somewhere in the region of your heart. Again, if it helps you to imagine it, place a hand gently on your chest.

    When you feel you have a good image of this mouth, add vibration to the breath in the form of an easy hum, but imagine that the hum is focused in your chest mouth.

    Work with this image until you feel that the hum is really connected to the chest mouth. Now imagine that behind the hum there is an 'aaahhh' sound waiting to come out, and then visualize your chest mouth opening to release the 'aaahhh' sound just as your real mouth does so.

    Work with this sequence of breath, humming and opening into 'aaahhh' from the chest mouth for about a minute until you feel fully engaged in the image and sound.

    Experiment with different pitches or pitch glides on your 'aaahhh' sound.

    Experiment with connecting other vowel sounds to this new mouth.

3. Roll on to your stomach with your head turned to one side.

    Take a moment to give the weight of your body to the floor and feel your body opening to the breath, particularly through the back.

    As you breathe, imagine that you have a mouth in your lumbar region, in the small of your back. If it helps you to imagine it, place a hand there.

    Now repeat the process of humming, opening into the 'aaahhh' sound and experimenting with different pitches and vowels.

4. Now imagine that you have a mouth in your upper back, in between your shoulder blades. Again, if it helps you to imagine it, place a hand there for a moment.

    Repeat the process of humming, opening into the 'aaahhh' sound and experimenting with different pitches and vowels.

5. Now roll on to one side and try combining these four mouths in the belly, chest, lower back and upper back.

    First, establish a deep connection with your breathing.

    Then, as you breathe, imagine your four new mouths. If it helps, place a hand gently on each area in turn.

    When you feel you have a good image of the four mouths, add vibration to the breath in the form of an easy hum, but imagine that the hum is centred in all four mouths.

    Work with this image until you feel that the hum is really connected to each mouth. Now imagine that behind the hum there is an 'aaahhh' sound waiting to come out, and then visualize each mouth opening to release the 'aaahhh' sound just as your real mouth does so.

    Work with this sequence of breath, humming and opening into 'aaahhh' from the four mouths for about a minute until you feel fully engaged in the image and sound.

    Roll over to your other side and experiment with connecting other vowel sounds and pitches to these new mouths.

    Continue to explore your connection to these mouths as you stretch and come up to standing.

6. Standing or sitting in a comfortable, aligned position, work through the same sequence of discovery and connection, imagining a mouth first in your forehead, next in the back of your head, and finally in the top of your head.

Try combining these three mouths in the same way that you combined the mouths in your body.

Then combine all seven mouths! What does it feel like to resonate so fully?

Working with the same principle, you can explore visualizing mouths in other areas. It is particularly useful to explore your side ribs, the palms of your hands and the soles of your feet, and then to combine them with the other mouths.

Mouths II (15–20 minutes)

1. Get a partner somewhere in the neighbourhood of your height. Partners, discuss together if you feel comfortable touching and being touched on the following places: neck, upper back, breastbone, forehead, top of head. If you are, give consent to your partner. If not, check in with your instructor about modifying the exercise or doing an alternate exercise on your own.

    Partner A, stand in front of partner B in a comfortable, aligned position. Let your head hang forward without collapsing your chest.

    Partner B, with two or three fingers of one hand, gently rub the back of A's neck.

    Partner A, let your breath settle and your jaw, tongue and face relax. Focus on your breathing. When your breath is settled, imagine a column of vibrations originating at centre and flowing up to the back of your neck to where your partner's fingers are. Play around a little with changing pitch and the shape of your vocal tract until you find a 'hmmmm' that vibrates strongly under your partner's fingers.

    When both partners agree that a strong buzz has been established, partner B, stop massaging and simply place two fingers horizontally side by side on partner A's neck. After a moment, slide the fingers about an inch away from each other. Partner A, imagine that your partner's fingers are forming a mouth at the back of your neck; continue humming and when the fingers slide away from each other, imagine that mouth opening and an 'ahhhh' sound pouring straight from your centre, out the back of your neck and up to the ceiling (your actual mouth will open as you do this).

2. Next, partner A, raise your head, and partner B use a few fingers of one hand to gently rub a spot between partner A's shoulder blades.

    Repeat the process of imagining sending a column of vibration up to that spot, finding a strong vibration beneath your partner's fingers by playing with pitch and resonant space, and finally imagining a mouth opening up and letting the sound out on a vowel as your partner glides their fingers open. The vowel may be an 'ahhh' or might be something else.

3. Repeat at the top of the breastbone, the forehead and the top of the head. You will most likely find that different pitches and vowels will resonate most strongly in each of these different areas.

4. Switch so that partner B is standing in front, and repeat the entire sequence.

Teaching tip

Some students might find the image of a mouth in different parts of the body unsettling. If students with very vivid imaginations find this too disturbing, you can suggest that they simply focus their vibrations in the particular area without visualizing the mouth very strongly.

Expanding the range

The first part of this section will concentrate on expanding and strengthening your pitch range – the number of notes you use in your voice. The second part of this section is about extending the figurative range of your voice – the arsenal of sounds that you can possibly use. Moving through your pitch range, manipulating the vocal tract and actively engaging your imagination can help you to find sounds you'd never imagine yourself making. The ability to be creative not just with your body and your mind but also with your voice is a particularly precious skill if you are an actor.

The issue of pitch is sometimes a loaded one. For one thing, it's often tied up with people's feelings about their singing voices. A belief that 'I can't sing high' can influence how one approaches using the upper register of one's speaking voice, just as a developed ability to sing bass parts can lead one to favour the lower register. There are also cultural influences. Most obviously, lower voices are often associated with masculinity and higher voices with femininity. However, both the outright acceptance and the outright rejection of gender stereotypes can lead one, unconsciously or deliberately, to limit one's use of the pitch range. We may also associate certain characteristics with pitch; lower tones may seem more sincere or assertive or domineering, or higher tones may feel more friendly or unthreatening or weak. A lot of choices made almost unconsciously as we grow up about how we want to be perceived influence how we pitch our voices. A transgendered or non-binary person's relationship with their vocal range may be a particularly complex one. The work in this chapter can be of benefit to you if you are transgendered or non-binary; please also see the *Further reading* section for a resource that will support your specific journey.

In this section, we'll start with a couple of very simple exercises to help identify what is sometimes called 'optimum pitch'. As you found with the Pringles tube, any given fixed, hollow shape will resonate one or two particular pitches more effectively than other frequencies. To the extent that the shape of your vocal tract is fixed by your bone structure, it too will resonate a couple of pitches better than others. Identifying an 'optimum pitch' doesn't mean that you should speak in that pitch all the time, but it can help you to recognize if you have a habit of either pressing your voice down lower or lifting it up higher than where it might naturally settle. If you know where your ideal pitch is, you can also use that part of your voice when you want maximum carrying power with minimum effort.

The true ideal, however, is for the voice to be free to move through a wide range of pitches. This gives you the ability to express a broad spectrum of thoughts and feelings with precision. If you are an actor, it also gives you a variety of options when creating a character. Furthermore, even if you rarely use your very highest or lowest note, working all the way through your range will strengthen your voice and add resonant depth to the notes you do use.

Optimum pitch

> **Teaching tip**
>
> Optimum pitch exercises are usually most successful in the context of vocal training that extends over a year or two rather than just one term.
>
> Identifying optimum pitch (also known as centre note) is an imprecise science, partly because this pitch will change slightly as students' voices develop. At this stage of training, it's not vital to identify precisely the exact note at which a student's voice is strongest and most resonant. Move through whichever of these exercises

you choose (doing them all is not necessary) with a minimum of fuss to help the students get a general idea of whether or not they are habitually pitching their voices above or below a range in which they might work more effectively.

I. (about 1 minute per partner)

    Get a partner. Partner A stand in front of partner B.

    Partner A, wait 15–45 seconds, and then ask B a simple question that you know they will answer with a neutral 'mm-hmm' sound; for example, 'Do you have brown [or another colour] eyes?' or 'Do you have a mobile phone?' or 'Do you like chocolate?'

    Help B to isolate the pitch that is the 'hmm' part of the 'mm-hmm'. That will usually come out at about their optimum pitch.

    B, try counting from 1 to 10 on this pitch – how does it feel? Familiar? Higher than usual? Lower than usual?

    Now, repeat with partner B asking the question. (Note that if the question is too provocative, then the pitch of the answering 'mm-hmm' will be quite extreme and will not be close to the optimum.)

II. (about 1 minute per partner)

    Get a partner. Partners, discuss together if you feel comfortable being gently pushed on your back. If you are, give consent to your partner. If not, check in with your instructor about modifying the exercise or doing an alternate exercise on your own.

    Partner A stand behind partner B.

    Partner A, wait 15–45 seconds – enough time for B to be unable to anticipate your movements, and then, without warning, give B just a little push between the shoulder blades – enough to make them lurch forward a small step, but nowhere near enough to make them lose their balance.

    B, when you are pushed, release an 'Oh!' That 'Oh' will usually come out at about your optimum pitch.

    Try counting from 1 to 10 on this pitch – how does it feel? Familiar? Higher than usual? Lower than usual?

    Now, repeat with partner B behind A.

III. (about 1 minute)

    Find the lowest comfortable note that you can make without effort (that is, don't growl!). Use that note as the bottom of a scale, and then sing up the scale for a total of eight notes (that is, an octave). The top three or four notes of the scale are likely to be in the area of your optimum pitch.

    Explore which note sounds fullest or strongest. Try humming these notes with your fingers in your ears – which one creates the loudest or richest sound in your head? Try speaking on this pitch – how does it feel? Familiar? Higher than usual? Lower than usual?

The cat sequence (6–7 minutes)

In general, high pitches resonate better in a small space – think of making sound by blowing across the top of a bottle filled with water; the less space, or air in the bottle, the higher the note that is produced.

Joan Melton has pointed out that this principle can be applied to the shape of the body when doing pitch work: small, scrunched up poses seem to encourage high notes, while stretched, expansive poses seem to make it easy to find low notes. This exercise builds on her work. As with all the pitch exercises, it's important to do some warm-up work first. You will need to engage with abdominal support in the exercise and avoid straining or pushing to reach the high or low pitches.

1. Start in extended child pose, and then bring your arms in so that your forehead is resting on your fists.

    Think of a new born kitten and, engaging the abdominal muscles of support, make a few, little mewling 'hmmm's' as high in your pitch range as you easily can.

    Next, open the little 'hmmm's' into very small, very light 'meows'.

    Move from the 'meow' into 'reow', opening your mouth wide as you do and imagining the sound travelling straight out the top of your head into the floor.

    Play with this light, newborn kitten, whimpering sound for a minute or so.

2. Come up onto your hands and knees. Allow your back to settle into its natural curves, neither slumped nor arched. Keep your head in line with your spine – neither lifted nor hanging.

    Imagine now that the helpless newborn has grown into a playful kitten.

    Engaging the abdominal muscles of support, make a few more energetic 'hmmms', still high in your pitch range, but focused less on the top of the head and more in the forehead and behind the nose.

    Open the 'hmmms' into 'meows' and 'reows'. Play with all the possibilities of this young kitten persona.

3. Still on your hands and knees, widen your stance a bit and imagine the kitten turning into a mischievous young cat.

    Lift your head up just enough to make eye contact with the other cats. Explore the possibilities of communication through young cat sounds – flirtations, idle conversation, threats. Try out some 'meows' and 'reows' in the middle of your range.

4. Next, sit back on your haunches, your arms in front of you. You are now the mature, King or Queen of the House cat. Try out some 'meows' and 'reows' lower in your range. See how little energy you can expend and still command the most respect with your meowing.

    Rise up off your haunches so you are kneeling. Open your arms to your side, with the palms facing forward. Tilt your nose up about thirty degrees, thinking length through the back of the neck as you do so. Let your jaw drop open. Imagine a wide, open pipe running from your lips to your pelvis. Yawn to re-enforce that sense of space.

    Picture an old lion. You're the most powerful animal in the room, but can't be bothered to make a lot of noise about it. Engaging the abdominal support muscles, release an easy 'raaahhhr'. Try another one a bit lower in your pitch range. Play with this deep, grumbling sound for a minute or so.

    Get into a roll-down position.

    On a 'meow' start at the top of your pitch range, and as you roll up, glide down to the bottom of your pitch range.

    Roll down, moving from the bottom of your range to the top on a 'oweem'.

Sirening (3–4 minutes)

Stand in a comfortable, aligned position.

Allow your jaw to release and your lips to hang slightly open.

Lift the back of your tongue up against your soft palate, and let the front of your tongue relax on the floor of your mouth.

Starting somewhere in the middle of your pitch range, make a gentle gliding siren sound on a long 'Ng' for 10–15 seconds.

Now, make a gliding siren starting a couple of notes (or so) higher for 10–15 seconds, then a couple of notes higher than that and so on until you are sirening at the highest notes you can easily make.

Put your hand on your lower abdomen and notice how those muscles give a little pulse of support with each pulse of the siren.

Next, come down, two (or so) notes at a time until you are sirening on the lowest notes you comfortably can.

Make one, continuous siren on 'Ng' from the top of your range through to the bottom.

Make one, continuous siren on 'Ng' from the bottom of your range through to the top.

Keep a hand on your abdomen and keep engaging support from there.

Starting back down at the bottom of your range, siren up about three notes, and then open your mouth to create a 'Ngahhh'. Sustaining the note this way will feel a bit like singing.

Siren up another three or so notes from there, and then open onto a 'Ngahhh' again. Repeat to the top of your range.

⊙ *Open angel II (3–4 minutes per partner)*

If you have ever had trouble with dislocating your shoulders, you should skip this exercise.

Find a partner who is somewhere in the neighbourhood of your height. Partners, discuss together if you feel comfortable being held at the wrists and having your partner support some of your weight. If you are, give consent to your partner. If not, check in with your instructor about modifying the exercise or doing an alternate exercise on your own.

Partner A, stand in front of partner B. Partner A should have a fairly narrow stance and B a fairly wide one.

Partner B, take A's wrists in your hands, and gently pull A's hands behind their back.

A, slowly lean forward, giving a third to a half of your weight to B. Let your chest open up, allowing your shoulder blades to be drawn together.

B, you may want to bend your knees or put one foot forward and lean slightly back to help balance A's weight.

A, you should feel a stretch across your upper chest. Tilt your nose up about thirty degrees, thinking length through the back of the neck as you do so. Let your jaw drop open. Imagine a wide, open pipe running from your lips to your pelvis. Yawn to re-enforce that sense of space.

A, release a 'Hiyiyiyi' from centre. Follow it with some Santa Claus-like 'Ho ho hos'.

'Ho ho ho' your way as far down your pitch range as you can.

On a medium low note, release from centre the phrase 'Get out of my way' a few times – don't allow the aggressiveness of the thought to drive your sense of vocal energy back up into your throat and face; let the energy from centre do your work for you.

Staying in the lower part of your range, and thinking great openness from the pelvis to the lips, release the phrase: 'How do I love thee? Let me count the ways'.

When A is finished, B gently help them come back to standing.

A, on your own two feet, take a moment to reconnect to a sense of openness from the pelvis to the lips and particularly across the upper chest.

Release some 'Ho ho hos' quite low in your pitch range and then bring them up to the lower part of your middle range.

In those lower middle notes, speak 'How do I love thee … ' again.

Speak the text one more time, letting it settle wherever it wants in your pitch range and noting where you feel the focus of the vibrations in your body.

B, stand in front of A and repeat the exercise.

More baby talk (3–4 minutes)

Teaching tip
This exercise is particularly useful for opening up the upper part of the range.

Stand in a comfortable, aligned position.

Briskly massage your neck, your face and your whole head, including the top.

As you are massaging, gently hum fairly high in your pitch range.

After a minute or so of humming, open the hum onto some easy, 'humamamamahs'.

Finish the massaging, and allow the 'humamamamahs' to develop into proper, nonsensical baby talk.

Turn to someone near you and have a nonsense baby conversation.

Turn the nonsense into an actual conversation about what you had for breakfast this morning and the route you take into school or work, still using baby tones and intonations.

Let go of the sing-song baby intonations, but stay in that open place of your upper register and talk about what your favourite foods were as a child.

Still in the high, open voice, release the following: 'How do I love thee? Let me count the ways'.

Repeat two or three times, allowing your voice to come down closer to its centre note each time.

Speak it one final time, letting it settle wherever it wants to in your pitch range and noting where you feel the focus of the vibrations in your body.

Sound pool (10–15 minutes)

1. Get into a group of 10–12 people and stand in a circle, almost touching shoulders.

   If you are comfortable, close your eyes. It isn't essential to keep your eyes shut for this exercise, however. If it makes you feel uncomfortable, you can have them slightly open and unfocused. But the exercise is about listening and giving/receiving sound with awareness, so having your eyes shut (or open and unfocused) will help you find that awareness without being distracted by the others in the group.

Imagine that in the middle of the circle there is a pool – not of water, but of sound vibrations. You can receive vibration from the pool with your in-breath and give back to it with your voice. Your responsibility as a group is to fill the pool with vibrations.

Allow your breath to deepen, and then start with some easy and sustained humming so that you establish a group sound that is centred, supported and resonant. Then begin to improvise with different vowel sounds, pitches and pitch glides.

You don't have to be making the same sound as everyone else, but don't try to be deliberately awkward or discordant. The exercise is about an experience of group resonance rather than individual sound. If you can stay aware of and connected to the group sound, you can improvise quite freely within it. Listen and receive from the pool as you breathe in, give voice to the pool as you breathe out.

On the instructor's cue, the sound will eventually fade away.

Discuss the experience with the rest of the group. What did you feel, hear or experience?

2. You are now going to repeat the exercise, but this time each member of the group will have the opportunity to take a turn 'bathing' in the pool.

Repeat the exercise up to the point where the group is improvising with vowels and pitches. Then, on the instructor's cue, take it in turns to step into the pool and listen to and feel the vibrations. There's no need to carry on vocalizing when you are in the pool; just be silent and receptive. After a short while, step out of the pool, and start sounding again. Continue until everyone in your group has had a turn. Then let the sound fade away.

Discuss the exercise with the rest of the group. What did you feel, hear or experience? Did it make a difference being in the pool? What does the exercise teach you about range and resonance?

Teaching tip

This exercise works best with a group of ten to twelve students. It can work perfectly well with eight or fourteen, however. If you have a larger group in a big enough space, you can break it into a number of smaller groups spread around the room.

In leading the exercise with just a single group, we have found it useful to be part of the group so that students don't become self-conscious about being listened to. This is not an issue when there is more than one group working at the same time. In this case, you need to stay outside the groups in order to monitor overall engagement.

One of the keys to this exercise is to let the first phase of the sound pool continue long enough to fully develop without going on so long that everyone becomes bored and disengages. There will probably be a first lull, when it seems that the sound is becoming same-y. It's worth pushing past this point to find what lies beyond the students' first impulses. This may lead to a bit of a crescendo, before the sound starts to die down again. This is a good time to murmur, 'Let's bring it down now,' and let it come to a natural fade. You can then introduce the second phase of the exercise, which has its own in-built timing.

Sound paintings I (6–10 minutes)

Stand in a comfortable, aligned position with enough space around you to stretch in all directions without invading other people's space.

Think of the space around you as the inside of your personal sphere. Begin to stretch into this space with your arms, exploring all the physical dimensions of this sphere around you: above and below you, in front of and behind you and out to either side.

As you stretch and move in your sphere, breathe out on a 'shhh' sound and fill the sphere with your breath. Think of your breath having an effect on the space around you.

Now stretch into your sphere with other parts of your body – your legs, your back, your head. Keep connected to your breath as you do so, but now breathe out on a 'ffff', filling the sphere with your sound.

Add vibration to your breath so that the sound becomes a 'vvvv'. Imagine that, as well as the vibration, the sound has a colour – brown perhaps, or green. Imagine painting that sound on the sphere around you with your breath, arms and hands and body. Use different pitches and dynamics of sound. Use different physical gestures – sweeping movements, dabbing movements, delicate movements. Think of the sound having an effect on the space around you.

Change to an 'oooo' sound and paint its colour on your sphere. Is it a blue colour, or maybe a red? What shade of that colour is it? Be specific in your intention and in your gesture.

Once you've really engaged your imagination, experiment with other vowels and consonants. What colours do you associate with them? How do they make you want to move? What visual images come to mind?

Paint your sphere as if it were a canvas – perhaps it's a landscape or an interior, or it's an abstract. Don't be general; have a specific effect on the space around you. Use different pitches and dynamics of sound. Use different physical gestures. Take some time to enjoy being an artist.

On the instructor's cue, bring your painting to a completion.

Imagine hanging it up on the wall in front of you, so that you can stand back and look at it in your mind's eye. Perhaps you'd like to sign it. Perhaps you'd like to give it a title.

Leave it hanging there while you discuss the experience with the rest of the group.

What did you feel, hear or experience in your voice? How did introducing the ides of colours change your voice use? What does the exercise teach you about range and resonance?

Teaching tip

This is another exercise which you may need to engage in at the same time as the students. If you model the work with them, they will feel less self-conscious.

You may also need to be patient and allow time for the imaginative connection to establish itself. Some groups 'get' the idea immediately; others need a bit of encouragement. When you feel that they have had sufficient time to 'create' their picture, tell them that they have another minute to finish their painting, and then bring it to a close.

Sound paintings II (10–15 minutes)

Teaching tip

We learned this exercise from Jules Craig who remembers learning it at Rose Bruford College from Lyn Darnley. For it, you will need to get decent quality reproductions of two paintings. In general, abstract paintings work best – such as Jean-Michel Basquiat's works or some of Georgia O'Keefe's more impressionistic flower paintings. Choose paintings that have several dominant colours and some distinctive shapes. The reproductions should be at least six by eight inches. If you can't find any big enough in an art book, enlarge a postcard using a colour copier. Very large posters, on the other hand, may be unwieldy. As part of the exercise, we have indicated a point where you may find it helpful to act as a conductor of the group sound by using gestures to enliven one part of the vocal orchestra or to quieten another. This can be particularly helpful for groups who are hesitant or, on the contrary, too animated.

Divide the class into two groups.

Group A, sit in a circle, facing each other, with just enough room for someone to sit in the middle of the circle. Be patient for a few minutes.

To one side, group B gather around one of the paintings.

Take a good look at the painting and think about one part of it – a line, a shape, a patch of colour – that appeals to you.

On the instructor's three count, everyone place your finger on the part of the painting you've chosen. If there is more than one person on any part, redistribute so that each person has a different detail. You are going to represent that part of the painting with your voice but without language.

Group A, close your eyes. Your job is to listen with an open mind and be aware of what pictures pop into your mind's eye or what feelings are evoked during the exercise.

Group B, stand surrounding group A, with the instructor sitting in the middle of A's circle, holding the picture so you all can see it.

B's, when your instructor points to you individually, come in with some kind of non-verbal sound inspired by your part of the painting. If the first thing that comes out of your mouth doesn't feel quite right, experiment until you find something that seems to capture the essence of your colour and shape. Keep looking at it throughout to make sure that you are continually responding to it in the moment rather than just settling into a mechanical drone of sound.

As more and more B's join in, be mindful of listening to each other and working together to capture, not only each individual part, but the overall feeling of the painting.

Once all of the B's have joined in, your instructor may conduct you – making hand signs to bring out some sounds for a little while or move others into the background.

After a minute or so, your instructor will signal you one by one to drop out until you are all silent.

Group A, open your eyes. Discuss what images and feelings were evoked over the course of the exercise. There are no wrong answers – the point of the exercise is not to guess what the picture is, but to explore the relationship between sound and images.

Finally, the instructor will show the picture to group A.

Swap groups so that B sits in a circle and A creates a new sound picture with the other painting.

Sound stories (20–30 minutes for the entire sequence)

Teaching tip

The following sequence is good for exploring the creative possibilities of vocal sound. Any number of the steps could also be used together or on their own as a warm-up to an improvisation session. However, it's easy for students to get excited by their imagination and so lose touch with a centred and supported breath. The first two steps are, therefore, designed to help integrate breath and imagination. An occasional reminder thereafter to stay connected to breath and open the throat should keep them on track. Again, the exercise works best with groups of ten to twelve students.

1. Get into a group, and sit or stand in a loose circle. Your task is simply to pass your breath around the circle. To do this, person A begins by breathing in and then, looking at person B on the left, breathes out easily. Person B 'receives' the breath by looking at A in a relaxed and open way. B then breathes in and passes the breath to C on their left, and so on round the circle.

2. Repeat the exercise in the opposite direction, but as you do so, instead of simply breathing out, use your breath to make an expressive sound: it might be a sigh, or a 'shhh' sound, a whistle, or a moan. Person B 'receives' the sound by repeating it after A as exactly as possible. B then breathes in and passes a different sound to C, and so on round the circle. Pass the sound a couple of times around the circle.

3. Now you are going to try your hand at a bit of sound storytelling. Decide on the kind of story you are going to tell – a ghost story or a fairy story is a good idea to begin with. Instead of telling the story with words, you are going to create the soundtrack of this story with your voices. Whoever begins (A), start with the opening of the story – perhaps it is the sound of wind blowing in the trees – and pass this to the person on your left (B). As in the previous step, B repeats this sound as exactly as possible before adding their sound to the story – maybe a bird whistling in the trees – and passes it on. C copies B's sound and creates their own – say, a creaking door – and passes it on. And so on round the circle until you reach a conclusion to your story.

   If you have time in the session, you could repeat this step with another type of story.

4. We'll come back to storytelling in a moment, but this time person A start by creating some kind of repeatable motion pattern with your hands. Avoid things that make sounds, such as clapping or snapping fingers. Once you've established a pattern, find a vocal sound to go along with it.

   When you have the movement and the sound, pass them to the person on your right – let them copy you until you feel that they really have things down exactly, and then stop and let them take over.

   The person who has 'received' the movement and the sound will then transform them by extending them, shrinking them, letting them grow into something new. When that person is satisfied with their new movement and sound, they pass them to the person on their right.

   Let the movement/sound go around the circle at least twice.

5. We are now ready to combine steps three and four to tell a story in both sound and movement.

   Let it be the story of a day in the life of a strange shape-changing creature. Whoever begins (A), start with the opening of the story – perhaps the sound and movement of the creature asleep – and pass it to the person on your left (B).

   B repeats both the sound and the movement as exactly as possible before transforming them into the next event in the story – maybe it's the creature waking up – and passes it on.

   C copies B's sound and movement and creates their own – the creature brushing its teeth – and passes it on. And so on round the circle until you reach a conclusion to your story.

   Discuss the experience with the rest of the group. What does the exercise teach you about range and resonance?

Balancing the sound

This work is about finding a blend of resonances that will give your voice the energy and brightness to fill large spaces without your having to think about 'talking louder'. The process of achieving this mix is different for everyone, but people commonly experience a sense of their voices coming forward into the face (i.e. the energy is not focused in the throat), feeling strong and being naturally connected to support from centre. This is sometimes called forward placement. It gives you power without push – a cornerstone not only of good voice work but of great acting as well.

Round and round (3–5 minutes)

1. Stand in a comfortable, aligned position.
    Take a moment to allow your breath to settle.
    Imagine a bit of vibration coming up from centre on a 'huh'.
    On the next breath, extend the 'huh' and close your lips around it so it becomes a 'hummmmm'. As you hum, imagine an unbroken column of vibration between your centre and your lips.
    On your next breath, think of focusing the energy of the vibration onto your lips. Over the course of the next few breath cycles, play with the position of your pharynx, soft palate, tongue, jaw and lips to see how you can find the most buzz on your lips. Play with different pitches as well.
2. Next, think of focusing the energy of the hum in your nose. Again, play with the shape of the vocal tract as well as with various pitches to find the maximum buzz in the nose.
3. After the nose, focus the vibrations as far back in your mouth as you can.
4. Finally, try to find as much buzz as you can in the middle of your mouth.
5. On one breath, see if you can move the focus of the vibrations from your lips, up to your nose, back to the very back of your mouth and then to the middle of your mouth.
    Finally, return the vibrations to the middle of your mouth, finding as much buzz as you can. Then open your lips so the sound flows out on a full and easy 'maaahhh'.

☙ *Nasal into oral (5–10 minutes)*

Some elements of this exercise have their origins in the work of Kristin Linklater.
1. Stand in a comfortable, aligned position.
    Allow your jaw to release and your lips to hang slightly open.
    Place the front of your tongue against the back of your bottom teeth and let it rest gently there.
    On a note somewhere in the middle of your pitch range, make a gliding siren sound on a 'NnnnNnnnNnnn' for 10–15 seconds.
    Massaging the sides of your nose and the sinuses alongside them, turn the 'NnnnNnnn' siren into a straight 'nnnnn' drone.
2. Finish the massage, and open the 'nnnnn' onto the nastiest 'nyah' that you can, wrinkling your nose as you do.
    As well as wrinkling your nose, wag your bottom a bit too, to keep everything loose, and try a really mean, taunting, little-kid 'nyah nyah nyah nyah nyah'. The sound should be strong, shrill and, frankly, not very pretty.

Moving from 'nyah', try a 'neee' and then a 'meee'. Use the same, taunting tune on a 'meee meee meee meee meee'.

3. Now think of screwing your face up into a witch's mask – use the same wrinkled nose that you did with the 'nyah' sound.

Thinking support from centre and openness in the throat and back of the neck, try a witch's cackle on 'me hee hee hee hee'. If it's not quite clicking, you can try one of the suggestions in the *Teaching tip*.

If at any point you feel strain in your throat, stop, shake out, yawn a couple of times and then return to the exercise thinking of keeping the throat open and soft, placing the effort in your abdominal muscles and focusing the vibrations squarely in your nose.

In your strong and brassy (and probably not very pleasant) witch's voice, try on a few witch's phrases, such as 'Toil, toil, boil and bubble' or 'I'll get you my pretty!'

4. Having fully explored the witch voice, return to a simple 'meeee', massaging your nose and sinuses and focusing the sound there.

Sustaining the 'meeee', move your fingers from the sides of your nose out across the top of your cheekbones. When you get to the area just under the middle of your eyes, switch to a quick 'may', flicking your fingers away from your face as you do. Imagine that the sound is shooting like lasers from under your eyes – very focused and very powerful.

Move between the 'meeee' and the 'may' a few times.

Finally, move from a 'meee' to a 'may', and hold it. Then, slowly open your arms until they are held fully out to the sides and change to a 'maaaah'. Imagine your entire body opening around the sound.

Repeat two or three times.

Pick a spot across the room, and use your wide, open 'maaah' voice to send the following to that spot: 'How do I love thee? Let me count the ways. I love thee to the depth and breadth and height my soul can reach!'

5. To check that you have moved sufficiently from nasal placement to oral placement as you've opened from the 'may' to the 'maaah', say the following sentence in your 'maaah' voice: 'All the happy dogs eat cheese every other day'.

Pinch your nose shut and say it again; the quality of your voice should be essentially unchanged. If your voice sounds muffled with your nose closed, think a big smile across the back of your mouth to lift the soft palate.

Teaching tip

This exercise is very useful for giving students an experience of both nasal and oral resonance and of moving between them. In the exercise, it's well worth taking the time to listen to each student individually, particularly when doing the witch's laugh. This can be quite difficult for some students to find, and they may need some help. If the sound is somewhat weak, moving back and forth between the 'nya nya' and the 'mee hee hee' can help. Putting one foot in front of the other and leaning forward with a finger outstretched, as if to bore a hole with the voice, can also work. If the student is producing a muffled sound, wrinkling the nose and thinking of lifting the soft palate off the tongue a bit will be useful.

Another point at which it's good to listen to the students individually is when they are plugging and unplugging their noses. The quality of sound should not change substantially at all except on 'm', 'n' and 'ng' sounds. If it does, ask the student to try to smile at the back of the mouth to lift the soft palate.

Wall work (10–12 minutes)

This exercise grew out of work Rebecca did with Nigel Rideout.

1. Find a bit of open wall that you can stand in front of.

   Stand facing the wall in a comfortable, aligned position. Your toes should be just a few inches away from it.

   Keeping your shoulders loose and low, bring your hands up to form a megaphone around your mouth. The outer edge of your hands should be touching or almost touching the wall.

   Find a supported 'meeee' that is strongly focused in your nose; then, move into a 'maaay' that is strongly focused under your eyes; finally, open the sound into a 'maaah' and imagine that the vibrations are forming a ball between your hands.

   Repeat a couple of times.

2. On your next time through the 'meeee, maaay, maaah' cycle, when you get to the 'maaah', slowly back away from the wall a foot or two, your hands still at your mouth. Imagine, however, that you are leaving the buzzy ball of 'maaah' vibrations at the wall.

   Check to make sure that you are not thrusting your head forward – focus on the image that you are backing away from the sound rather than pushing the sound forward.

   It will take a fair amount of abdominal support to do this – if you feel that you lack power or are straining in your throat at all, take a moment to get in touch with your beach ball breathing muscles and consciously focus your sense of engagement there.

   If you feel that you are losing the connection with the wall, simply go back and start again.

   Repeat until you are able to back away three or four feet and still feel that the energy of your voice is staying at the wall and that you are not having to push or strain to keep it there.

3. Return to the wall, and establish the ball of vibration between your hands with the 'meeee, maaay, maaah' and then, as you back away from the wall, move into chanting (i.e. intoning) the nursery rhyme 'Humpty Dumpty Sat on a Wall' or another simple, short text.

   Repeat the entire process on a higher note.

   Repeat on a note higher still.

   Return to your centre note.

   Repeat on a lower note.

   Repeat on a note lower still.

   Return to your centre note.

   Begin to chant and back away from the wall again, but this time switch into your speaking voice half way through.

   Repeat the process entirely in your speaking voice.

   Try the exercise with some other nursery rhymes – chanting first, then moving from chanting to speaking and finally using just your speaking voice.

4. Now, turn so that your back is to the wall.

   Bend your knees a bit so that you can press your back against the wall. Your head should not quite touch the wall behind it.

   Take a moment to make sure your thighs and the wall are doing the work of holding you up so that your lower belly can release.

   Open your arms against the wall at the level of your mid chest.

   Pick a point across the room from you. Go through the 'meeee, maaay, maaah' sequence once, thinking of placing the ball of vibration at that point. You will not have your hands at your face to help you focus the sound, so you will have to engage your imagination particularly strongly.

5. Move on to chanting your text, still placing the energy of the sound at that particular point across the room.

   Let a breath drop in and switch to speaking your text, concentrating on directing the energy of the sound to that point across the room.

6. Stop and shake out.

   Check that your jaw and tongue are loose.

   Consciously allow your ribs, abdomen and pelvis to open to a full in-breath, and then hum a bit while engaging your muscles of support.

   Return to your position with your back against the wall.

   Repeat the above step with the full version of 'Humpty Dumpty' or another nursery rhyme. Pick a person to be the focus of your sound rather than a point in the room.

Teaching tip

Wall work is wonderful for finding and developing forward resonance. Make sure that students stand up straight when they initially position themselves against the wall, i.e. make sure their bottoms are not sticking out and they are not dropping their heads or thrusting them forward. Make sure, as well, that they keep their shoulders loose and low as they raise their hands up to their mouths. As the students are working, if you see any shoulders starting to creep up, you can give a gentle reminder to keep them soft. It can also be helpful to remind them to keep the area between the shoulder blades open to vibration. We've divided the exercise into steps; if students are becoming physically rigid, have them step away from the wall and shake out between steps.

Straw phonation II (4–5 minutes)

Get a normal drinking straw (eco-friendly, where possible), and start humming through it, as in Straw Phonation I. Add in some 'car-revving' changes in pitch and loudness, making sure that the abdominal muscles are doing the work, not your throat muscles.

Now, try humming a familiar tune into the straw – one with lots of pitch and loudness changes is good. When you're done, put the straw down and speak the text of the song out loud, engaging the same energy and focus that you brought to the straw phonation. How does your voice sound? Where is it placed? Does it feel less effortful?

☁ *Slug tongue (3–4 minutes)*

Stand in a comfortable, aligned position.

Give your jaw muscles a bit of a massage, and then let the jaw hang comfortably open.

Allow your tongue to slowly creep forward – like a slug or oozing goo – until it is resting on your bottom lip. It should be soft and fat.

Leaving your jaw and the front of your tongue where they are, try to speak the nursery rhyme 'Jack and Jill' or another short text.

Because only the back of your tongue and soft palate can move, you will not be able to form many of the sounds in the text, particularly the consonants – don't worry about this; just give voice to the tune of the rhyme and as many of the vowel sounds as you can.

If you feel that your jaw wants to 'help' by moving up and down, gently place the thumb and forefinger of one hand to either side of your chin to encourage it to stay still and open.

If you feel that your tongue wants to pull back into your mouth, gently hold the tip with the thumb and forefinger of one hand to remind it to stay put.

Note where the energy of your voice seems to be focused. It will probably be at the front of your mouth, just behind your upper teeth.

Go through the rhyme again, noticing how the muscles of breath support engage to help power the sound.

Repeat the rhyme as you let your tongue slowly creep back into your mouth. As the tongue moves back and starts to become involved in articulating the sounds of the words, imagine the focus of the sound staying forward, just behind the top teeth. The jaw may start to move a bit, but should stay mostly released.

Speak the rhyme again with energy and intention, thinking not only of the focus of the sound staying forward, but also of the muscles of support engaging.

> **Teaching tip**
>
> This is a great 'quick fix' exercise. It encourages a release of tension in the tongue and jaw and brings the sound forward in the mouth. It can also help to enliven articulation, and so is useful to apply to any piece of text a student is working on.

Soundball (5–10 minutes)

As a group, form as large a circle as the room will allow.

The first person, A, begin with a simple hum. Hold your hands cupped in front of your mouth, and imagine the hum forming a ball of vibration between them.

Keeping your hands in front of your mouth, begin to move them – in and out, up and down, wiggling the fingers, anything – and allow the movement of the hands to shape the ball of sound. Maybe it will stay a hum but get very nasal or very low in pitch. Maybe it will open up into a light, high 'ahyahyah' or become a bright, brassy 'wahwahwah'. Anything goes, just think of keeping the vibrations focused in your hands.

Once you have found a shape for your vibrations, use your arm to 'throw' the sound to someone across the circle, i.e. make the physical gesture of throwing, and allow your voice to follow across the space.

That person will 'catch' the sound by repeating it and copying the movement of the hands. They will then find a new hand movement, which will change the shape of the sound, and so forth.

Repeat until everyone in the circle has had a chance to throw at least two or three sounds.

> **Teaching tip**
>
> This is another exercise which is good for exploring the creative possibilities of vocal sound. However, as with the Sound Stories exercise, it's easy for students to get carried away by their imaginations and so lose touch with a centred and supported breath. An occasional reminder to stay connected to their breath and open the throat will help keep them on track.

Resonating text

A word on resonating text: we've found that it's not at all uncommon to do a long session on resonance in which you employ a glorious range of full, interesting sounds, and then come on to text and return to a narrow repertoire of pinched, muffled resonances. This is quite natural – it can take some time and attention to find resonance in language. The group exercise in this section is designed to help you discover how sense and sound can work together and how resonance can contribute to expression. While you may find readings of the text that might be exciting transferred into a performance context, there is a danger in becoming too concerned about whether or not one would really 'do it this way'. An exploration of exaggerated pitch and resonance possibilities is a good way to open up the voice, which is a worthy end in itself. Increased flexibility and sensitivity to nuances of thought and sound will eventually bring life and colour to even the most naturalistic of performances.

Puck (15–20 minutes)

> **Teaching tip**
>
> You will need to prepare the text, preferably double-spaced, in a large, easy-to-read font, to hand out to the class. If you are aware of having any dyslexic students in your class, it may help them if you copy the text on to paper that is not white (green is often a good colour) and hand it out the session before you do the exercise. See *Suggested texts* for the passage.

1. The group should stand in a circle.

    Read through the text, with each student taking one line.

    If there are more than twelve students, simply read through it again until each student has had the chance to speak a line. If there are fewer, continue to read through to get the sense of the full passage; in the exercise, however, each student should work with only the first line they read.

Have a seat and discuss the meaning of the text. In line 2, 'behowls' means 'to howl at'. In line 4, the ploughman (someone who pushes a plough) is worn out ('foredone') by their work. In line 5, the last embers ('wasted brands') of the evening fire are burning out. In lines 6–8, the owl makes the poor, wretched person ('the wretch that lies in woe') think of the cloth that dead people are wrapped in ('a shroud') and, by extension, death itself. In lines 10–11, the graves are opening ('gaping') wide to let out the spirits ('sprites') to haunt the graveyard.

Take the line that you read, and read it out loud to yourself, drawing out the vowel sounds a bit. Note that we're working with the sounds here, not the letters. For example, the letter 'o' in 'now' makes an 'ow' sound, not an 'oh' sound. Pick three vowel sounds in the line that you think are particularly juicy or expressive. For example, in line 1, you might pick the 'ow' in 'now' over the short, non-descript 'uh' in 'the'.

Memorize those three sounds.

2. As a group, close your eyes and use the vowel sounds that you have picked to create the sounds of a haunted graveyard at midnight on Halloween.

You can work with one vowel for a while or move back and forth between vowels frequently.

Challenge yourself to find as many possible variations in pitch, resonant placement, volume and duration in each vowel. For example, the 'ow' could be made quite quietly with a very tight, high-pitched nasal resonance in short little bursts, or it could be made quite loudly with a wide, back-of-the-mouth resonant focus low in the pitch range and sustained for a long time.

Listen to what is going on around you and try to contribute to a complete, varied soundscape. For example, if there are lots of low, moaning sounds, try a high squeak.

On the instructor's cue, the sounds will eventually fade away.

3. In this step, you will create the soundscape again, but using all the consonant and vowel sounds in your line in sequence. In effect, you will be speaking the line, but some of the sounds may be so distorted that the words are unrecognizable. You can stop on any sound for a while and play with it before moving on to the next.

If you get to the end of your line before the instructor has cued the fade, start again at the beginning.

Keep your eyes open so you can read the line if necessary.

4. Next, stand up and find a comfortable, aligned stance.

In this step, you will go around the circle one at a time and each read your line keeping in as many varied graveyard sounds as you can, but stringing them together so that the words are recognizable. The focus, however, is very much on the sounds, rather than the words.

Next, shift the focus from the sounds to the words, but let some of the graveyard sounds bubble to the surface from time to time, for example, a bit of a howl on an 'ow' sound or a screech on an 'ee'. Don't worry about whether or not you would actually 'do it this way'; look for how the sound can help communicate the meaning or the mood of the words.

5. Everybody shake out and run around the room.

Return to the circle, and without thinking too hard about anything but communicating with energy and specificity, go around the circle and speak your lines one at a time.

Have a seat and discuss the process and any discoveries you've made.

Teaching tip

As with the Sound Pool exercise, one of the keys to this exercise is to let the sound-scape continue long enough to fully develop without going on so long that everyone becomes bored and disengages. There will probably be a first lull, when it seems that all the sounds are becoming very same-y. It's worth pushing past this to find what lies beyond the students' first impulses. This may lead to a bit of a crescendo. As with other imaginative work, students can easily lose touch with centre and support – a specific reminder to stay connected to their breathing may be necessary from time to time. It may also be useful for you to contribute some unexpected sounds along the way to prompt the students to dig a bit deeper. After the second or third natural build, whisper, 'Let's bring it down now,' and let it come to a natural fade.

When the group begins to integrate the graveyard vowels into the text, there can be a tendency for students to get stuck in one kind of sound – e.g. everyone starts using 'spooky ghost' voices or 'creaky' voices. Encourage the students to try something different with each of the vowels.

Individual work

Teaching tip

The discoveries made in group work can next be brought to bear in individual work. We have given some suggestions for texts at the end of the chapter and advise that each student should memorize one; or in the case of longer poems, a stanza or two. If you would like to use other texts, look for poems or passages that are rich in imagistic detail and have a lushness of sound and expression. Each session of text work should begin with a good general warm-up, emphasizing freeing the channel and finding the buzz. Let each student simply speak their piece, and then choose from the Individual Work exercises or adapt other resonance exercises to suit the student's needs.

Each of these exercises will take between 5 and 10 minutes. **Take the time to establish consent before any of the following exercises that involve touching.**

I. Stand in a comfortable, aligned position in the corner of the room, facing the wall. Have a partner stand behind you and massage your back. Begin an open-mouth hum and focus on filling the corner with the vibrations of your voice.

Open the hum onto a 'mmaaaa'. Your partner should now place their hands in the middle of your back and you should focus on filling their hands with your vibrations. After a couple of breath cycles, move onto chanting the first line of your text. On the second line, move from chanting to speaking.

As you continue speaking the text, you partner should move their hands to a different place on your back or neck with each new line, and you should think of allowing your sense of vibration to move into that area.

When you have finished the piece, turn from the wall. Your partner should move behind you and place their hands on your back again.

Speak the text again, still focusing on sending the vibration back into your partner's hands. This should encourage a fullness of resonance through your pitch range as you speak.

II. Lie on the floor in semi-supine and chant your text. With each line, switch to a different note and move your hand to the area of your body where you feel the strongest sense of secondary resonance.

Roll over into extended child pose. Chant the first half of your text and then move into your speaking voice for the second half, imagining the vibrations pouring out of your body and pooling onto the floor beneath you.

Bring yourself to standing and give your temples and the muscles that run along the side of your jaw a good massage. Leave the jaw hanging open.

Allow your tongue to slowly creep forward – think of it as a slug or oozing goo – until it is resting on your bottom lip. It should be soft and fat.

Leaving your jaw and the front of your tongue where they are, try to speak the first half of your text. It won't make much sense, which is just fine.

For the second half of the text, allow your tongue to slide back into your mouth, but leave the focus of your voice forward – imagine your voice forming a small ball of energy floating just in front of your lips.

III. Pick a particularly vivid image or sequence of images from your text.

Stand in a comfortable, aligned position five or six feet in front of a big, blank section of wall.

Warm up with a few easy hums and hah's, and then use your voice to 'paint' the image on the wall, using only sounds, no words. Feel free to move around as you look for ways to vocally express the precise colours, shapes, textures and moods of the images in detail.

Next, 'paint' the images on the wall using the sounds from the words of the text. The words themselves will probably be very distorted as you draw out, abbreviate or repeat different sounds as you see fit. Do be mindful of staying connected to a supported breath and keeping the sense of effort out of your throat as you work.

Next, use your hand to 'paint' the images as you speak through the section of the text you are working with again. Let the words take intelligible form this time, but try too to let your voice move with your hand.

Finally, turn around and simply speak the text, letting the movement and colours you've discovered inform your voice.

IV. Go through your text with a pencil and circle all the vowel sounds, with the exception of short sounds in short words (e.g. the 'uh' in 'the' or 'of').

Find a partner and stand in a comfortable, aligned position about four feet in front of them.

Try to communicate the thoughts and images of your text to this partner by speaking only the vowels. You may draw them out, repeat them, separate them from each other, run them together and move through your pitch range as you see fit.

Finally, speak the entire text to your partner, focusing on communicating with the words but allowing the vowel sounds to be part of the expression of the thoughts and images.

V. Find a partner.

As you speak your text, your partner will move their hand up and down (not too suddenly or violently). You must follow the movements of your partner's hand with your body and your voice – moving up when the hand goes up and down when the hand goes down or maintaining a constant pitch and physical posture when the hand is still.

Next, work on your own. Move your own hand and follow it with your voice and body as you speak the text.

Finally, simply stand and speak the text, allowing your voice to move freely up and down with the images and rhythms of the text.

VI. Stand in a comfortable, aligned position.

Have a partner stand behind you and hold your neck to remind you that you don't need to push or press from there.

Hold your hands cupped in front of your mouth and chant just the first word of your text a couple of times, feeling a ball of vibration forming between your hands.

When you feel that the energy of your voice is strong in your hands, make the motion of easily throwing the vibrations to someone across the room as you speak the word.

Repeat with each word in the first line of your text.

If you feel any tightening or jerking in your jaw or any strain in your throat, chant the word using beach ball breathing or think of blowing out a couple of birthday candles with it to get back in touch with your breath support, and then return to the throwing.

When you have worked your way through the line, chant the first word into your hands again a couple of times, and then throw the first phrase (three to five words). Chant the first word of the next phrase and then throw that phrase. Continue through the piece.

Finally, stand across the room from the rest of the group. With each line, find someone new to talk to and move your hand in an arc towards that person as you speak (i.e. start with your hand at your shoulder and move it forward and slightly up through the length of the line.)

VII. Stand in a comfortable, aligned position.

Chant the first couple of lines of your text to get warmed up.

After those first two lines, the instructor will call out a musical instrument. With your body, mime playing the instrument, and with your voice look for the particular resonance of that instrument (e.g. something low and rumbling for a cello, bright and brash for a trumpet, etc.) as you speak the next two lines.

Your instructor will call out a different instrument every couple of lines until you finish the text.

As soon as you finish, speak the text again letting your voice move through different resonances at will.

Follow-up

Reflective practice questions:

- Which exercises and images best help you release your jaw?
- Which exercises give you the greatest sense of space in the back of your mouth?
- In what area of your body do you most easily feel secondary resonance?
- Do you find that you have a tendency to favour either higher or lower pitches?
- What words or images would you use to describe your 'normal' voice?

- Were there any exercises in which you felt you were using a voice that was not 'your own'? If so, what words or images would you use to describe this 'other' voice or voices? How did producing this 'other' voice feel physically different from producing your 'normal' voice?

- In the *Balancing the Sound* exercises, when did you feel your voice had the most energy with the least amount of effort? Where was the effort focused in your body? Where did you feel the 'buzz'?

- Did you find that introducing language expanded or narrowed the resonances you were able to find in your voice? Why do you think you had this experience?

- In doing individual text work, what discoveries did you make about your voice? Did the resonance work lead to any discoveries about the text?

Exercises:

- As part of your brief morning warm-up, spend a minute or two chanting 'mah, may, mee, moh, moo' over and over on different pitches.

- Play with finding the place in your voice where you can get the strongest feeling of buzz in a variety of spaces. For example, chant and then speak some nursery rhymes in the shower, in a closet, in the kitchen, facing curtained windows in a small room, facing a blank wall in a large room, etc. and try to find where your voice feels the most energetic with the least amount of effort. If theatre spaces are available to you, try the same in them. Look for the most effective resonant placement from the lip of the stage, the back of the stage, facing stage right, stage left, sending your voice to the front row, the back of the house, etc.

Suggested texts

Puck

Now the hungry lion roars
And the wolf behowls the moon,
Whilst the heavy ploughman snores,
All with weary task fordone.
Now the wasted brands do glow
Whilst the screech-owl, screeching loud,
Puts the wretch that lies in woe
In remembrance of a shroud.
Now it is the time of night
That the graves all gaping wide,
Every one lets forth his sprite
In the churchway paths to glide.
    From *A Midsummer Night's Dream* by William Shakespeare

Aphra Behn	'Song: Love Arm'd'
Lewis Carroll	'Jabberwocky'
e e cummings	'i thank You God for most this amazing'
Carol Ann Duffy	'Warming Her Pearls'
Laurie Ann Guerrero	'Last Meal: Breakfast Tacos, San Antonio, Tejas'
Joy Harjo	'Once the World Was Perfect'
Langston Hughes	'The Weary Blues'
Gerard Manley Hopkins	'As Kingfishers Catch Fire'
Michael Ondaatje	'The Cinnamon Peeler'
Alice Oswald	'Wedding'
Sylvia Plath	'Blackberrying'
Christina Rossetti	'Goblin Market'
Wole Soyinka	'In the Small Hours'
Dylan Thomas	'Fern Hill'

Further reading

Houseman, Barbara, *Finding Your Voice*, Nick Hern Books, London, 2002. Chapter 5: 'Releasing the Sound: Freeing the Voice', pp. 138–52; and Chapters 6 and 7, pp. 162–92.

Kayes, Gillyanne, *Singing and the Actor* (Second edition), A&C Black, London, 2004. Chapter 5: 'Developing the Three Octave Siren', pp. 45–57; and Chapter 8: 'Tuning the Oral Resonator', pp. 90–8.

Linklater, Kristin, *Freeing the Natural Voice* (Revised edition), Drama Book Publishers, New York, 2006. Chapter 4: 'Workday Four' to Chapter 10: 'Workday Ten', pp. 87–197.

McCallion, Michael, *The Voice Book* (Revised edition), Faber and Faber Ltd, London, 1998. Part Three: 'Tuning', pp. 81–6 and 93–117.

Mills, Matthew and Stoneham, Gillie, *The Voice Book for Trans and Non-Binary People: A Practical Guide to Creating and Sustaining Authentic Voice and Communication*, Jessica Kingsley Publishers, London, 2017.

Nelson, Jeannette, *The Voice Exercise Book*, National Theatre Publishing, London, 2015. Chapter 2: 'Voice Exercises – Stage 1', pp. 42–8; and 'Voice Exercises – Stage 2', pp. 65–73.

Rodenburg, Patsy, *The Actor Speaks*, Methuen, London, 1997. 'Stage Two: Extending the Voice into Resonance, Range and Speech', pp. 91–103.

Turner, J. Clifford, *Voice and Speech in the Theatre* (Sixth edition, edited by Jane Boston), A&C Black, London, 2007. Chapter 3: 'The Tone', pp. 26–36 and pp. 47–52; and Chapter 4: 'The Note', pp. 53–65.

5
ARTICULATION AND MUSCULARITY

Framework

Speech is one of the most important tools we have to convey thoughts and feelings to others. Muscular articulation gives clarity and precision to speech, enabling a performer to make verbal expression more affecting and effective. If a dancer's steps are vague or mistimed, or if a guitarist's fingering is fumbled or misplaced, their artistic interpretation of the choreography or music is severely limited. For actors, the lips, tongue and other articulators are the equivalent of the dancer's feet and the guitarist's fingers: if they do not move with precision and energy, they cannot be responsive to the artistic intention.

Articulation work is not the same thing as elocution, however. Making sounds with purpose and exactness is not necessarily the same thing as making sounds 'beautifully'. Nor is it the exclusive domain of 'classical' performance: for example, the use of uncompromisingly muscular articulation at lightning speed in the service of complex language is a hallmark of Lin-Manuel Miranda's *Hamilton* throughout the world. The aim of articulation work is simply to form all the sounds needed to make each word easily understood with an economy of effort, and to use those sounds to advance the speaker's intention.

Meeting these aims as an actor does not require that you change your accent. You may have some specific habits that are common to the region where you grew up – for example, dropping 't' sounds at the ends of words, as many UK and US speakers do – which you may want to modify in certain plays and certain theatrical spaces so that you can fulfil the cadences of the text and be better understood on stage, but, in most instances, you do not have to fundamentally change the way you speak to attain effective articulation.

In some cases, there may be sounds that are difficult for a person to pronounce clearly. In general, the practising of individual sounds is done in speech rather than voice classes, so this book does not address the specific formation of each English sound, nor does it give extensive drills for each one. There are many excellent resources listed in the *Further reading* section at the end of the chapter that describe in detail the most efficient way to form individual speech sounds. If a particular sound proves particularly difficult for you to make in a standard way ('s' and 'r' are commonly problematic), and you are seriously planning to make acting your career, it may be worth your while to find a personal speech tutor to help you with them. What we do want to accomplish in this voice course is the releasing and toning of the muscles of articulation so that they can move with freedom and precision.

Vocal anatomy

Those muscles involved in forming speech sounds are numerous. There are, for example, four different sets of muscles that make up the body of your tongue and then another four sets of muscles that attach

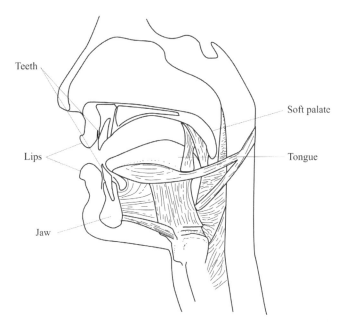

Figure 13 The articulators

to your tongue and help to move it around. These muscles are also attached to the jaw, the soft palate, the wall of the pharynx and the bone at the top of your larynx (see Figure 13). Unnecessary tension or movement in the tongue when you are speaking, therefore, can affect the overall quality of your voice by pulling the soft palate down or raising the larynx up.

The soft palate itself functions as an articulator when we lower it to send the air out of the nasal passage in making the 'n', 'm' and 'ng' sounds. This is one of the simpler articulation movements – only four muscles are involved in lowering and raising the soft palate. There are, however, ten different sets of muscles that can be used to move your lips. Some are within the lips themselves, but some run up to your cheekbones and others go out to your cheeks and down to your chin (see Figure 14). It takes great co-ordination for all these muscles of the tongue, the soft palate and the lips to come together and make sounds – the years that it takes young children to learn how to talk understandably is a witness to this. Even after we have left our toddler-hood well behind, we can still learn to use these muscles more efficiently, much as an athlete learns to perform common acts like running and jumping more effectively.

We've mentioned the tongue, the soft palate and the lips – there is one other active articulator of importance, and that is the jaw. The jaw, however, is tricky. While we often want the tongue and the lips to become livelier and more engaged, we usually want the jaw to become less so. The tongue and the lower lip are attached to the jaw, so when it moves, they move

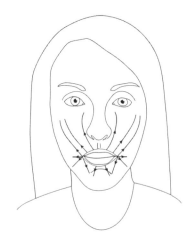

Figure 14 Lip muscles

too. Sometimes, instead of moving the lip or the tongue on its own to make speech sounds, we just move the jaw up and let the lip and tongue go along for the ride. As an illustration, first allow your jaw to drop open about a finger's width. Leaving the jaw where it is, make a 'duh' sound by moving just the tip of your tongue. Now bring your tongue down so that the tip is behind the lower teeth. Leave the tongue where it is and make a 'duh' sound by moving your jaw up. It's rare to consistently make speech sounds exclusively with the jaw, but it is quite common to 'help' with the jaw. This 'help', however, actually serves to make the sounds less sharp and defined. It also narrows the space in your mouth, decreasing resonance – a lose/lose situation. It will be helpful, therefore, if the lips and the tongue learn to work independently of the jaw.

Articulation and breath

While freeing the actions of the lips and the tongue from the jaw, it is important to also connect them to a strongly supported breath. As with just about anything to do with speaking, articulation will flow most easily if the body is aligned and the channel from the lips to the pelvic bowl is released and open. Focusing the effort of speaking in the muscles of support at one end of the channel and in the articulators at the other can help to keep that passage clear. Furthermore, the muscles of support and the articulators have a kind of symbiotic relationship with each other: commitment in one area can encourage commitment in the other. If you are having trouble at any point finding a good, strong engagement of your articulators, try working on your breath support for a little while. Conversely, if you feel that you are losing touch with a solid, supported breath, try working with some articulation exercises. Waking up one area can send a message to the brain that you are serious about the act of communication, which wakes up the other area. In its essence, good articulation is about this very commitment to communication. It's about focusing and specifying the strong need to make yourself understood.

Exploration

   I. Bring your jaw up so that your back teeth are almost touching but there is still a bit of space between your lips. Keep your jaw held in this position and speak the alphabet moving your lips and tongue as little as possible. Note how this affects your sense of your voice and your overall energy.

  II. Speak the alphabet again, this time moving your jaw as much as you can, almost as if you were chewing each sound. Note how this affects your sense of your voice and your overall energy.

III. Purse your lips tightly and then blow through the most powerful 'puh' sound you can.

      Repeat, adding your voice to make a 'buh'.

      Place your lips together as lightly as possible and blow through as little air as you can to make a tiny 'puh'.

      Repeat, adding your voice to make a 'buh'.

      Press the tip of your tongue as hard as you can up against the ridge behind your top teeth (the alveolar ridge), then blow through a strong 'tuh'.

      Repeat, adding your voice to make a 'duh'.

      Place the tip of the tongue so that it is just barely touching the alveolar ridge and blow through just enough air to make a small 'tuh'.

      Repeat, adding your voice to make a 'duh'.

Push the back of the tongue up hard onto your soft palate and blow through a 'kuh'.

Repeat, adding your voice to make a 'guh'.

Let the back of your tongue sit lightly on your soft palate and blow through just barely enough air to make a 'kuh'.

Repeat, adding your voice to make a 'guh'.

Note how both the very tense and the very lax articulations affect your sense of your voice and your overall energy.

Return to each of the sounds and play with the amount of effort you use to produce them. Look for an engagement that is energetic but not tense.

Exercises

Teaching tip

The exercises in this chapter are organized under three headings: *Toning the Articulators*, *Specifying the Sounds* and *Articulating Text*. Work on *Toning the Articulators* can be introduced fairly early in a course of voice work. Frequent repetition of a repertoire of exercises over a long period of time is probably the most effective approach. It is also useful to work on these muscles in conjunction with breath work; as noted, effective breath support and effective articulation often go hand in hand. However, it is also worth noting that a focus on articulation work can distract students from breath support, release and alignment. It is vital, therefore, to remind students to pay attention to their alignment, to keep released and to stay connected to a centred breath. Work on *Articulating Text* can be introduced at any time, but is often most useful after students have become adept at connecting breath to the act of speaking, supporting long, energetic thoughts and employing a full range of resonant sounds within language. Articulation work is a good way to segue between technical voice work and the specific communication of an idea that is the concern of text and acting work.

Toning the articulators

The same principles apply here as in all the physical work we have done; the goal is to release tension so that the muscles can learn effective patterns of engagement. Many of the muscles involved in articulation are found in the vocal tract, and we've already done some release work on them in the resonance chapter. In this chapter, we will continue that work as well as develop the ability of all the muscles involved in articulation to work independently and with precision. This will allow you to use the appropriate tool for the job. For example, if you can separate the action of the tip of your tongue from the action of the middle of your tongue, you will be able to make a 't' sound with less effort and more clarity – why use a shovel when a teaspoon will do?

Teaching tip

As with any muscles, it takes time and repetition of exercises for the articulators to learn a new pattern of usage. In any given voice session, you may want to do just a couple of exercises for each of them. Rotating through all the exercises will help to prevent boredom and give each muscle group a slightly different work out from day to day.

Jaw (about 1 minute each)

For all these exercises stand or sit in a comfortable, aligned position. Any of the jaw exercises from Chapter 4 are also good for finding release in this area.

I. Give the masseter muscles a gentle massage, allowing the space between your back molars to gradually increase as you do.

Hold your hands in front of you and extend your thumbs. Place your hands on the sides of your face with your thumbs hooking under your ears. Your jawbone should be nestled in the centre of your palms.

Slowly draw your hands down the length of your jaw. When you get to the chin, let your hands slide forward off your face, and make a small gesture of throwing away all the tension through your fingertips.

Repeat three or four times, adding a small sigh the last couple of times.

II. Place the tips of your fingers along the side of your jaw at the level of your lower gums, under the back molars and wisdom teeth.

Let the weight of your arms hang from your fingers and allow that weight to gradually draw your jaw open. Imagine that the jaw muscles are clay, slowly yielding beneath your fingers. Keep the shoulders soft and low.

When the jaw is open as far as it will comfortably go, take a hold of either side of your chin with the thumb and forefinger of each hand and use your hands to gently and slowly open and close your jaw.

Soft palate

Tone up the soft palate with the exercises from Chapter 4.

Tongue (about 1 minute each)

Note: Not everyone's tongue will stretch to the same extent, so don't push yourself to the point of pain or discomfort when doing these exercises.

For all these exercises stand or sit in a comfortable, aligned position and place one hand at the back of your neck and the other hand on the side of your jaw; this is to help ensure that you don't push with your neck and jaw but work the tongue in isolation.

I. Push the whole of your tongue straight out of your mouth and hold for a few seconds.

Reach for your nose with the tip of your tongue and hold for a few seconds.

Reach for your left ear and hold for a few seconds.

Reach for your chin and hold for a few seconds.

Reach for your right ear and hold for a few seconds.

Repeat this sequence several times, gradually building up speed.

Now, make a huge circle from the nose to the left ear to the chin to the right ear and then another in the opposite direction. Repeat several times.

Allow your tongue to slowly retract back into your mouth.

II. Imagine that each of your teeth is covered with a different flavour of ice cream. Use your tongue to taste each tooth one at a time, front, bottom and back.

Be particularly mindful of keeping the jaw as still as possible without locking it while the tongue moves.

III. Get a mirror to look at your tongue.

Stick your tongue out of your mouth about an inch.

Try to make it as thin and wide as possible.

Without retracting your tongue or sticking it out more than a further half an inch, try to make it as thick and narrow as possible.

Go back and forth between thin and thick several times.

IV. Imagine that you are a cat lapping milk with your tongue. Be particularly careful that the jaw and the back of the neck don't tighten or push forward as you do this.

V. Imagine that you've been eating ice cream in a fancy restaurant, and now there's some of it on your upper lip.

Try to lick the ice cream away as discretely as possible. See if you can move just the tip of your tongue along your upper lip while keeping the rest of it in your mouth.

Next, imagine ice cream on your bottom lip and try to lick it away with just the tip of your tongue.

Finally, move the tip all the way around your lips, keeping the body of the tongue in your mouth.

Lips (about 1 minute each)

For all these exercises stand or sit in a comfortable, aligned position.

I. Massage your face. Start around your lips and then move up the sides of the nose, out across the cheeks and cheekbones, around the eyes, onto the temples and then up across the forehead.

Pull your face in as if you were making a fist with it – eyes scrunched closed, lips tightly pursed. Then, open your face out as wide as it will go – eyebrows up, mouth stretched open. Go back and forth a couple of times.

II. Make sure your hands are clean for this one. Hook your pinkies into the corners of your mouth and pull them out as far as they'll go. Move the pinkies around your lips, pulling them in all directions.

Take your fingers out of your mouth and blow through your lips, making a noise like a horse.

Add some voiced vibrations, making a shivering sound.

Continuing to blow through your lips, move from the bottom of your pitch range to the top and back.

III. Place one hand at the back of your neck and the thumb and forefinger of the other hand on the sides of your chin; this is to help ensure that you don't push with your neck and jaw but work the lips in isolation.

Lift just your top lip – thinking of sneering can help. Move it up and down six or seven times.

Try to lift just the left half of your upper lip and then just the right. Move back and forth between the two. This is something that you can getter better at with practice.

Now lower just your bottom lip – thinking of a ventriloquist's dummy or of a little kid who is about to cry can help. Move it down and up six or seven times.

Try to pull down just the left half of your lower lip and then just the right. Move back and forth between the two.

IV. Keep one hand at the back of the neck and the other monitoring your jaw at the chin.

Push both lips straight out as far as possible, as if you were going to give someone a cartoon kiss. Open and close your lips as much as you can while keeping them stretched forward. Don't let the jaw become involved.

Next, pull your lips in over your teeth.

Keeping your jaw more or less still, move your lips back and forth from pushed out to pulled in six or seven times, ending with your lips out.

Leaving the top lip pushed out, pull just the bottom lip in.

Pull the top lip in as well.

Push out just the bottom lip, leaving the top in.

Push out the top lip as well.

Continue pulling in and pushing out each lip in isolation until you have gone through the cycle four or five times.

End by blowing out through your lips.

V. Keep one hand at the back of the neck and the other monitoring your jaw at the chin. Push your lips out and make an OO sound (as in 'food').

Now spread your lips and make an EE sound.

Move between these two sounds as accurately and agilely as you can.

Now, build up the following sequence of vowels, starting slowly and increasing the speed as you repeat the sequence six or seven times: OO-EE-OO-AY-OO-AH-OO-OH-OO-AW.

Note the following:

OO = the vowel sound in 'food'

EE = the vowel in 'speak'

AY = the vowel in 'say'

AH = the first vowel sound in 'father'

OH = the vowel sound in 'hope'

AW = the vowel sound in 'awe'

Specifying the sounds

The focus in this section is not on mastering the ideal formation of every English speech sound. As mentioned, that is more commonly the domain of the speech class. Rather, the work here is designed to develop the articulators' capacity to move economically and precisely. Nimbleness – of the mouth and of the mind – is a wonderful characteristic in an actor; it brings liveliness and dynamism to performance.

Before beginning these exercises, it can be useful to revisit the pre-class exploration of using too little and too much effort to form sounds. In the exercises that follow, you will be looking for a happy medium – an engagement of the articulators that is energized but not forced. One indicator that they are working well is that they can move between sounds quickly. Speed, itself, however, is not the point; it's a neat trick to be able to rattle off text in record time, but it will rarely be the most effective way to pursue an intention onstage. The goal is easy clarity; speed is just a tool to help you gauge your progress.

In this section, we recommend that you frequently monitor that your jaw is not trying to do the work of the other articulators by placing the forefinger and thumb of one hand on either side of your chin. Ideally, your jaw should rest in a comfortably open position that will allow you to work your other articulators freely. It may feel that you have to stretch your tongue and lips more than you are used to in order to make certain sounds without closing the jaw. Give yourself some time to get used to the new sensations and to become comfortable with the new movement patterns. With time and practice they will become more second nature. Do note, though, that to cleanly make the sounds 's', 'sh', 'z', 'zh' (the sound in the middle of the word 'pleasure'), 'ch' (in 'church') and 'dg' (in 'judge') the jaw will probably have to close a bit. The trick then is to learn to let it release again when it is not needed.

You may have found in exercises from the previous chapter that an easily released jaw also allows you to find fuller resonances. The movements of other articulators can affect resonance as well. For example, if your tongue root tenses and your soft palate drops every time you make an 'l' sound, the vowel that follows will have only a small space to resonate in. If you can isolate the action in the tip of the tongue, the resonance will stay open and full. You may find it useful to move back and forth between the *Working the Channel* and *Finding the Buzz* exercises from Chapter 4 and the exercises here to develop a good relationship between articulation and resonance.

Teaching tip

It is helpful to do a bit of warming up with exercises from *Toning the Articulators* before moving into *Specifying the Sounds*. This section lists a number of sound and word combinations that are useful as drills and then some tongue-twisters to practise crisp, engaged articulation. There are many resources for other tongue-twisters, and introducing new ones frequently can help to prevent boredom while also running the articulators through a wide range of sound combinations. You may want to occasionally have elimination rounds with a tongue-twister in which each person in a circle has to speak it more quickly than the previous person and drops out if they make a mistake. Or do tag team tongue-twisters, with partners in pairs alternating lines in a race with other pairs. A little bit of fun encourages the lightness of touch that is a hallmark of good articulation.

The basics

I.   (2–3 minutes)

Stand or sit in a comfortable, aligned position.

Allow the jaw to drop open about a knuckle width. Place the forefinger and thumb of one hand on either side of your chin to encourage your jaw to stay easily open. You may feel a little tug on the skin beneath your fingers, but the jawbone underneath should stay more or less still.

Breathe in, and then bring your lips together energetically (but not too forcefully), and release them energetically to make a voiceless 'puh'. Repeat four or five times in rapid succession.

With the same motion of the lips, add voicing to make a 'buh'. Repeat four or five times in rapid succession.

Leaving the jaw where it is, breathe in and lift the tip of your tongue up to make firm contact with your alveolar ridge (right behind the top teeth), and then release it vigorously to make a voiceless 'tuh'. Repeat four or five times in rapid succession.

With the same motion of the tongue, add voicing to make a 'duh'. Repeat four or five times in rapid succession.

Still leaving the jaw comfortably open, breathe in and bring the soft palate and the back of the tongue together with a firm contact, and then let them spring quickly apart to make a voiceless 'kuh'. Repeat four or five times in rapid succession.

With the same motion of the soft palate and tongue, add voicing to make a 'guh'. Repeat four or five times in rapid succession.

Now put these three motions together into a sequence. Start first with a slow, distinct 'puh tuh kuh'.

Keeping the jaw released and the motions distinct, gradually increase your speed in repeating 'puh tuh kuh' until you are going quite quickly indeed. Remember to keep your breath flowing and to stay released in the back of your neck. Place a hand there, if it helps.

Next, put the motions together in a slow, distinct 'kuh tuh puh'. Repeat seven or eight times, increasing speed.

Now, put the two patterns together: 'puh tuh kuh kuh tuh puh'. Slowly build up speed, keeping your jaw released.

Next, put the motions together in a slow, distinct 'buh duh guh'.

Keeping the jaw released and the motions distinct, gradually increase your speed in repeating 'buh duh guh' until you are going quite quickly indeed. Remember to keep your breath flowing and to stay released in the back of your neck.

Next, put the motions together in a slow, distinct 'guh duh buh'. Repeat seven or eight times, increasing speed.

Finally, put the two patterns together: 'buh duh guh guh duh buh'. Slowly build up speed, moving through your pitch range as you do so and keeping your jaw released.

II. (5–6 minutes)

Stand or sit in a comfortable, aligned position.

Allow the jaw to drop open about a knuckle width. Place the forefinger and thumb of one hand on either side of your chin to encourage your jaw to stay easily open, although note that it will probably need to close a little when making 'ss' and 'zz'.

Go through the following sound combinations at a conversational speed, breathing as necessary and thinking of moving your articulators in a purposeful but not overly deliberate manner.

Make sure that you fully form each sound in the combinations. For example, on 'BAYLD' you may find that you have a tendency to stop just short of making a full 'L' sound, replacing it with a 'W' sound, or to make an incomplete 'D' sound. If you find that you have dropped or not quite completed a sound, go back and repeat the entire line two or three times focusing on finishing that sound without overstressing it.

Note the following:

OO = the vowel sound in 'food'
OH = the vowel sound in 'hope'
AW = the vowel sound in 'awe'
AH = the first vowel sound in 'father'
AY = the vowel in 'say'
EE = the vowel in 'speak'

LOOPT	LOHPT	LAWPT	LAHPT	LAYPT	LEEPT
LOOBD	LOHBD	LAWBD	LAHBD	LAYBD	LEEBD
GOOKT	GOHKT	GAWKT	GAHKT	GAYKT	GEEKT
GOOGD	GOHGD	GAWGD	GAHGD	GAYGD	GEEGD

BOOLT	BOHLT	BAWLT	BAHLT	BAYLT	BEELT
BOOLD	BOHLD	BAWLD	BAHLD	BAYLD	BEELD
MOOMD	MOHMD	MAWMD	MAHMD	MAYMD	MEEMD
ROOFT	ROHFT	RAWFT	RAHFT	RAYFT	REEFT
ROOVD	ROHVD	RAWVD	RAHVD	RAYVD	REEVD
TOOST	TOHST	TAWST	TAHST	TAYST	TEEST
TOOZD	TOHZD	TAWZD	TAHZD	TAYZD	TEEZD

Take a little break to give your jaw a massage, blow through your lips, massage under your chin and flap your tongue in and out. Continue with the following, making sure you pronounce those L sounds:

PROOLN	PROHLN	PRAWLN	PRAHLN	PRAYLN	PREELN
PROOLM	PROHLM	PRAWLM	PRAHLM	PRAYLM	PREELM
PROOLZ	PROHLZ	PRAWLZ	PRAHLZ	PRAYLZ	PREELZ
TROOPL	TROHPL	TRAWPL	TRAHPL	TRAYPL	TREEPL
TROOBL	TROHBL	TRAWBL	TRAHBL	TRAYBL	TREEBL
BROOTL	BROHTL	BRAWTL	BRAHTL	BRAYTL	BREETL
BROODL	BROHDL	BRAWDL	BRAHDL	BRAYDL	BREEDL
DROOKL	DROHKL	DRAWKL	DRAHKL	DRAYKL	DREEKL
DROOGL	DROHGL	DRAWGL	DRAHGL	DRAYGL	DREEGL
KROOFL	KROHFL	KRAWFL	KRAHFL	KRAYFL	KREEFL
KROOVL	KROHVL	KRAWVL	KRAHVL	KRAYVL	KREEVL
GROOSL	GROHSL	GRAWSL	GRAHSL	GRAYSL	GREESL
GROONL	GROHNL	GRAWNL	GRAHNL	GRAYNL	GREENL

Take a little break to give your jaw a massage, blow through your lips, massage under your chin and flap your tongue in and out. Continue with the following:

SPOOSTS	SPOHSTS	SPAWSTS	SPAHSTS	SPAYSTS	SPEESTS
SPOOFTS	SPOHFTS	SPAWFTS	SPAHFTS	SPAYFTS	SPEEFTS
SPOOVST	SPOHVST	SPAWVST	SPAHVST	SPAYVST	SPEEVST
SNOOKST	SNOHKST	SNAWKST	SNAHKST	SNAYKST	SNEEKST

(for the following, use the voiceless 'TH' sound in 'thin')

SNOOTTH	SNOHTTH	SNAWTTH	SNAHTTH	SNAYTTH	SNEETTH
SLOOTTHS	SLOHTTHS	SLAWTTHS	SLAHTTHS	SLAYTTHS	SLEETTHS
SLOOTHT	SLOHTHT	SLAWTHT	SLAHTHT	SLAYTHT	SLEETHT

(for the following, use the voiced 'TH' sound in 'this')

SLOOTHD	SLOHTHD	SLAWTHD	SLAHTHD	SLAYTHD	SLEETHD
SKOOTHZ	SKOHTHZ	SKAWTHZ	SKAHTHZ	SKAYTHZ	SKEETHZ
SKOOLVZ	SKOHLVZ	SKAWLVZ	SKAHLVZ	SKAYLVZ	SKEELVZ

STROONDL   STROHNDL   STRAWNDL   STRAHNDL   STRAYNDL   STREENDL
STROOMBL   STROHMBL   STRAWMBL   STRAHMBL STRAYMBL   STREEMBL

III. (2–3 minutes)

Monitoring the jaw with your fingers, repeat each of the following phrases four times at a conversational pace, slightly exaggerating the specific movements that each combination of sounds requires:

Paper poppy

Lily lolly

Mommala poppala

Unique New York

Red leather yellow leather

Will you won't you (be sure on this one that you are really saying 'won't you', not 'won chew')

Go through the sequence again at a conversational pace. This time don't exaggerate the movements, but do notice them.

Repeat three or four times, increasing your speed each time.

Consonant combinations (10–30 seconds per tongue-twister)

Repeat the following tongue-twisters seven or eight times each, gradually increasing your speed. You may want to slightly exaggerate the movement of the lips and tongue initially and then relax into them:

Peggy Babcock.

Toy boat.

Three tree twigs.

Find five fine friends.

The Leith police dismisseth us.

Rubber baby buggy bumper.

Let little Nelly run.

A cheep chick sleeps in cheap sheets.

Strange strategic statistics.

The sixth sheik's sixth sheep's sick.

Do daily deeds diligently. Don't dilly dally.

Two toads totally tired of trying to trot to Tewksbury.

A regal rural ruler.

Around the rough and rugged rock, the ragged rascal ran.

One smart fellow, he felt smart; two smart fellows, they felt smart; three smart fellows, they all felt smart.

A thin little fellow picked six thick thistle sticks.

Can you imagine an imaginary menagerie manager managing an imaginary menagerie?

Articulating text

Articulation work is, of course, important to help actors make text clear, but it also can help actors make text fun. Spoken language doesn't just convey information, it also stimulates our brains through sound – sharp sounds, smooth sounds, long sounds, short sounds, repeated sounds, rhythmic sounds. When approaching text, look for how the texture of the sounds can help support your intention as a speaker. Engaged, energetic articulation will then start to feel necessary and organic, rather than obligatory and technical. The text work that we've included in this chapter is not only intended to drill the mechanics of articulation, but also to encourage mental focus and creative exploration.

Henry V (15–20 minutes)

> **Teaching tip**
>
> You will need to prepare the text, preferably double-spaced, in a large, easy-to-read font, to hand out to the class. If you are aware of having any dyslexic students in your class, it may help them if you copy the text onto paper that is not white and hand it out the session before you do the exercise. See *Suggested texts* for the passage.
>
> If you have already done the Puck exercise from the previous chapter, the group should catch on to this pretty quickly. As in that exercise, there may be a moment when everyone seems stuck making very similar sounds, at which point it is worth staying with the exercise a bit longer to see what direction it might take. After the second or third natural build, whisper, 'Let's bring it down now,' and let it come to a natural fade.

1. The group should stand in a circle.

    Read through the text with each student taking one line.

    If there are more than fourteen students, simply read through it again until each student has had the chance to speak a line. If there are fewer, continue to read through to get the sense of the full passage, but in the exercise each student should work with only the first line they read.

    Have a seat and discuss the meaning of the text. It is the Chorus's introduction to the fourth act of Shakespeare's *Henry V.* At this point in the play, it is late the night before a major battle, and the English and French armies are camped out making their final preparations. In lines 1–3, the listener is invited to imagine ('entertain conjecture') a specific scene. In line 5, the sounds made by both armies are said to move between the camps 'stilly', or 'quietly' so that, in lines 6–7, the guards on either side ('fixed sentinels') can almost hear each other's whispers. In lines 8–9, the campfires on either side seem to be communicating, and through the pale ('paly') flames, each army ('battle') can see the darkened ('umbered') faces of the other. In lines 12–14, the armourers are doing their job, which is to use hammers and rivets to secure the armour on the knights – 'accomplishing', or finishing their preparation. This sound could fill the listener with dread of what's to come.

Take the line that you read, and read it out loud to yourself, leaning into the consonant sounds a bit. Note that we're working with the sounds here, not the letters. For example, the letter 'c' in 'conjecture' makes a 'k' sound, not a 'see' sound.

Pick three consonant sounds or combinations of consonant sounds (such as the 'kt' in 'conje<u>ct</u>ure') in the line that you think might be particularly evocative of the scene that is being described.

Memorize those three sounds.

2. As a group, you will now close your eyes and use the consonant sounds that you have picked to create the soundscape of armies preparing for battle and of the battle itself. Think about the whispers and clangs that Shakespeare is describing. Think too about the sounds that will come – the clink of sword on sword, the swish of arrows, the moans of the dying, the laboured breathing.

You can work with one consonant for a while or move back and forth between consonants frequently. Challenge yourself to find as many possible variations in each consonant. For example, the 'k' could be made lightly and frequently, like crickets chirping in the night, or it could be strongly exploded, like a sword hitting another sword. The quality of the sound will change too depending on whether the lips are spread or pursed. Play around and try to find as many qualities of sound with each consonant as you can.

Listen to what is going on around you and try to contribute to a complete, varied soundscape.

On the instructor's cue, the soundscape will eventually fade away.

3. Now, in the next step, you will create the soundscape with all the sounds in your line in sequence. In effect, you will be speaking the line, but some of the sounds may be so distorted that it is unrecognizable. Feel free to stop on any sound for a while and play with it before moving on to the next. If you get to the end of your line before the instructor has cued the fade, start again at the beginning. Keep your eyes open so you can read the line.

4. After the complete line soundscape, stand up and find a comfortable, aligned stance.

In this step, you will go around the circle one at a time and each read your line keeping in as many varied sounds as you can, but stringing them together so that the words are recognizable. The focus, however, is very much on the sounds, rather than the words.

Next, shift the focus from the sounds to the words, but let some of the military sounds bubble to the surface from time to time, for example, a bit of an explosion on a 't' or a murmur on an 'm'. Don't worry about whether or not you would actually 'do it this way'; look for how the sound can help communicate the meaning or the mood of the words.

5. Everybody shake out and run around the room.

Return to the circle, and without thinking too hard about anything but communicating with energy and specificity, go around the circle and speak your lines one at a time.

Have a seat and discuss the process and any discoveries you've made.

The Windhover (12–15 minutes)

> **Teaching tip**
> You will need to prepare the text, preferably double-spaced, in a large, easy to read font, to hand out to the class. If you are aware of having any dyslexic students in your class, it may help them if you copy the text onto

paper that is not white and hand it out the session before you do the exercise. See *Suggested texts* for the passage. If there are not enough groups to take all the lines, don't worry about completing the poem.

Divide into groups of two or three students.

Each group should take two lines of the text.

In your group, identify the three or four consonant sounds that seem to dominate your lines of text.

Identify what exactly you do with your articulators to make each of those sounds.

For each sound, create a large, total body movement that echoes the movement of the articulators. For example, you may pull your body into a tight circle on a 'w' sound or bring your elbows to your knees and then pull them up and away on a 'k'.

Integrate the movements into the speaking of the lines.

Practise the lines a few times.

The groups should form a circle in the order that their lines appear and, one by one, share what they've done so far.

Go around the circle again, and this time, make your physical movements only half as big.

Go around the circle again, and let your body be still, but your articulators full of life and movement.

Go around the circle one last time, and don't think of anything but sharing the text with the other groups.

Have a seat and discuss the process and any discoveries you've made.

Subway Wind (5–6 minutes)

Teaching tip

You will need to prepare the text, preferably double-spaced, in a large, easy-to-read font, to hand out to the class. If you are aware of having any dyslexic students in your class, it may help them if you copy the text onto paper that is not white and hand it out the session before you do the exercise. See *Suggested texts* for the passage.

Stand in a circle in a comfortable, aligned position.

As a group, read the entire piece aloud at a conversational pace, focusing only on making sense of what you're reading.

Go back to the beginning and read the first four lines at a slower pace, focusing on keeping your jaw released as much as possible.

Speak the second four lines at more of a conversational pace again, focusing now on fully forming each sound with the articulators. This doesn't mean you have to exaggerate them – just use the muscles you need to make them clear and distinct.

Speak the next four lines at the same pace, shifting your focus to your breathing – engaging the muscles of support as you speak and allowing them to spring open on the in-breath, like a beach ball springing back into shape. Place a hand on your lower abdomen and a hand alongside the ribs if it helps you.

Speak the last four lines at the same conversational pace, focusing on engaging both the breathing muscles and the articulators in harmony with each other.

Now, speak the whole poem with a focus on communicating the author's intention, while continuing to engage both the breathing muscles and the articulators in harmony with each other.

Individual work

> ### Teaching tip
> The discoveries made in group work can next be brought to bear in individual work. We have indicated some suggested texts at the end of the chapter and advise that each student should memorize one, or in the case of longer poems, a stanza or two. If you would like to use other texts, look for poems or passages that feature strong sounds requiring a high degree of muscular commitment. Each session of text work should begin with a good general warm-up, emphasizing toning the articulators and specifying the sounds. Let each student simply speak their piece, and then choose from the Individual Work exercises or adapt other articulation exercises to suit the student's needs.

Each of these exercises will take 3–6 minutes. **Take the time to establish consent before any of the following exercises that involve touching.**

I. Stand in a comfortable, aligned position.

Have a partner hold your neck to remind you not to push from there.

Do a couple of cycles of beach ball breathing on 'ffff'.

Keeping one hand on the lower belly to encourage connection and support, whisper your text. This should be a true whisper, not a stage whisper – no voice should be involved, nor should the breath be forced or strained. With no voice energy involved, the focus of your impulse to communicate will be solely on your articulators.

When you come to the end of your text, go back and repeat it with voicing. Engage your articulators, however, as if you were still whispering. Notice the effect this has on your speech – does it feel more energized, or more present, or perhaps loud and domineering?

Finally, simply stand and speak the text.

II. Stand in a comfortable, aligned position. If you don't have your text memorized, have a partner hold it in front of you.

Hold your hands in front of you, one on top of the other.

Speak the first few lines of your text extremely slowly. As you do so, use your hands to recreate the movements inside your mouth. For example, on a 't' sound, the fingers of the bottom hand may rise up and flick against the fingers of the top hand. On a 'ng' sound, the heels of the top and bottom hands may join together.

Now let your hands drop. Close your eyes and speak those lines a bit more quickly than before, but still rather slowly. Focus your attention on the movement of the articulators.

Repeat these steps until you have worked your way through the entire text.

Finally, speak the text at a conversational speed, focusing on communicating with your audience while maintaining an awareness of your muscularity.

III. Stand in a comfortable, aligned position.

Place the thumb and forefinger of one hand on either side of your chin to encourage your jaw to stay loosely open as much as possible.

Have a partner set up two chairs in front of you, about ten feet apart.

When your partner stands at the chair to your left, you will speak as slowly as you can. When your partner stands at the chair to your right, you will speak as quickly as you can.

When your partner stands in the middle of the space between the chairs, you will speak at a conversational pace.

You must speed up as they move to the right and slow down as they move to the left. They can choose to stand still from time to time, to move more quickly or slowly, or to double back before reaching a chair. Their intent should be to keep you on your toes but not trip you up.

When you have reached the end of your text, go back and speak it again at a conversational pace.

IV. Stand in a comfortable, aligned position as far away from the rest of the group as possible.

Have a partner hold your neck to remind you not to push from there.

Begin speaking your text at a fairly loud volume, but not shouting.

Gradually take the energy out of the volume and put it into the articulation, so that you are speaking increasingly more quietly but more distinctly.

When the group can no longer make out what you are saying, they will raise their hands.

Return to the volume/energy of articulation that you were using a couple of moments before the group could no long understand you. Staying at this volume, let your articulation become progressively lighter – less effortful. Again, the group will raise their hands when they can no longer make out the distinct sounds in each word.

Return to a conversational tone and speak the text with just the articulatory energy necessary to reach the group across the room.

V. Sit in a comfortably aligned position. The rest of the class should sit on the floor around you.

Imagine that your text is a story that you are going to tell to a group of four-year olds (note: childish behaviour is not needed from the group – these are very interested, well-behaved four-year olds).

Without allowing your pitch to go up more than a couple of notes above your ordinary speaking range, speak the text, using the sounds of the consonants and vowels to draw the children into the story.

The class should return to their normal positions and adult personas. Stand and speak the text to them, using as much of the storytelling energy of articulation as is appropriate.

Follow-up

Reflective practice questions:

- Which sounds does your jaw most like to 'help' with?

- Which consonant combinations are hardest for you to say?

- When drilling sounds or tongue-twisters, which articulators get the most tired? The lips? The tip of the tongue? The back of the tongue? The jaw?

- What, if anything, did you notice about the relationship between breath and articulation?

- In line nine of the *Henry V* passage, why do you think Shakespeare chose the word 'battle' when 'army' probably would have been easier to understand? In line ten, why did he pick the less common 'steed' over 'horse'? Are there other words that may have been picked for their sound?

- In the text that you worked on individually, are there any words that you think were picked for their sound?

- In doing your own text work and watching others, how did the articulation work contribute to the overall energy and clarity of the final performance?

- When you watch theatre, TV or films, note which actors' articulation is particularly well-suited to the storytelling. Which actors are sometimes not clear in their speech? Which actors seem to overdo their enunciation of sounds? How is this related to the characters they play? How well would the film actors' articulation work on stage? How would the stage actors' articulation work on screen?

Exercises:

- Work a couple of minutes of tongue-twisters into your morning warm-up, always taking the time to release the jaw before you start.

- In situations where you might ordinarily use volume to reach someone, see to what extent you can get your message across by sharpening the clarity of the speech sounds.

- From time to time, try reading aloud, concentrating on bringing together the energy of the thought, the energy of the breath and the energy of the articulation.

Suggested texts

Chorus from *Henry V* by William Shakespeare

1. Now entertain conjecture of a time
2. When creeping murmur and the poring dark
3. Fills the wide vessel of the universe.
4. From camp to camp through the foul womb of night
5. The hum of either army stilly sounds,
6. That the fixed sentinels almost receive
7. The secret whispers of each other's watch.
8. Fire answers fire, and through their paly flames
9. Each battle sees the other's umbered face.
10. Steed threatens steed in high and boastful neighs
11. Piercing the night's dull ear, and from the tents
12. The armourers, accomplishing the knights,
13. With busy hammers closing rivets up,
14. Give dreadful note of preparation.

The Windhover by Gerard Manley Hopkins

I caught this morning morning's minion, king-
    dom of daylight's dauphin, dapple-dawn-drawn Falcon, in his riding
    Of the rolling level underneath him steady air, and striding
High there, how he rung upon the rein of a wimpling wing
In his ecstasy! then off, off forth on swing,
    As a skate's heel sweeps smooth on a bow-bend: the hurl and gliding
    Rebuffed the big wind. My heart in hiding
Stirred for a bird, – the achieve of, the mastery of the thing!

Brute beauty and valour and act, oh, air, pride, plume, here
    Buckle! AND the fire that breaks from thee then, a billion
Times told lovelier, more dangerous, O my chevalier!
No wonder of it: shéer plód makes plough down sillion
Shine, and blue-bleak embers, ah my dear,
    Fall, gall themselves, and gash gold-vermilion.

Subway Wind by Claude McKay

Far down, down through the city's great gaunt gut
    The gray train rushing bears the weary wind;
In the packed cars the fans the crowd's breath cut,
    Leaving the sick and heavy air behind.
And pale-cheeked children seek the upper door
    To give their summer jackets to the breeze;
Their laugh is swallowed in the deafening roar
    Of captive wind that moans for fields and seas;
Seas cooling warm where native schooners drift
    Through sleepy waters, while gulls wheel and sweep,
Waiting for windy waves the keels to lift
    Lightly among the islands of the deep;
Islands of lofty palm trees blooming white
    That led their perfume to the tropic sea,
Where fields lie idle in the dew-drenched night,
    And the Trades float above them fresh and free.

Julia Alvarez	'New Clothes'
Maya Angelou	'Touched by an Angel'
Hilaire Belloc	'Tarantella'
John Betjeman	'A Subaltern's Love Song'
Sharon Bryan	'Sweater Weather: A Love Song to Language'
Rita Dove	'Teach Us to Number Our Days'
T. S. Eliot	'Skimbleshanks: The Railway Cat'
W. S. Gilbert	'My Name is John Wellington Wells'
Cathy Park Hong	'All the Aphrodisiacs'

| Liz Lochhead | 'Bawd' |
| William Shakespeare | 'When I Do Count the Clock ....' (Sonnet 12) |

Liz Lochhead   'Bawd'
Dorothy Parker   'One Perfect Rose'
Harold Pinter   'The Ventriloquists'
Vikram Seth   'Round and Round'
William Shakespeare   'When I Do Count the Clock ....' (Sonnet 12)

Further reading

Berry, Cicely, *Voice and the Actor*, Virgin, London, 2000. Chapter 3: 'Muscularity and Word', pp. 43–75.

Houseman, Barbara, *Finding Your Voice*, Nick Hern Books, London, 2002. Chapter 8: 'Shaping the Sound: Firming Up Your Articulation', pp. 193–229.

Knight, Dudley, *Speaking with Skill: An Introduction to Knight-Thompson Speechwork*, Methuen Drama, London, 2012.

Lessac, Arthur, *The Use and Training of the Human Voice*, Mayfield Publishing Company, California, 1997. Chapter 5: 'The Dynamics of Consonant NRG', pp. 63–121.

Linklater, Kristin, *Freeing the Natural Voice* (Revised edition), Drama Book Publishers, New York, 2006. Chapter 19: 'Workdays Nineteen, Twenty, Twenty-one and Thereafter', pp. 295–311.

McCallion, Michael, *The Voice Book* (Revised edition), Faber and Faber Ltd, London, 1998. Part Four: 'Speech', pp. 125–90.

Nelson, Jeannette, *The Voice Exercise Book*, National Theatre Publishing, London, 2015. Chapter 1: 'Getting to Know Your Voice', pp. 24–5; Chapter 2: 'Voice Exercises – Stage 1', pp.49–51; and Chapter 3: 'Voice Exercises – Stage 2', p. 74.

Rodenburg, Patsy, *The Actor Speaks*, Methuen, London, 1997. Stage Two: 'Extending the Voice into Resonance, Range and Speech', pp. 104–22.

Skinner, Edith, *Speak with Distinction* (Revised edition, edited by Lilene Mansell), Applause Books, New York, 2000.

Turner, J. Clifford, *Voice and Speech in the Theatre* (Sixth edition, edited by Jane Boston), A&C Black, London, 2007. Chapter 5: 'The Word', pp. 66–102.

Appendix 1
VOCAL WORKOUT

In this appendix we provide you with a short vocal workout that can be easily performed at home or at work, in a classroom, office space or dressing room. It assumes a familiarity with all five chapters of *The Vocal Arts Workbook*. We would like to thank those former students who helped to refine it: Jonathan Bonnici, Sonya Cassidy, Lauren Crace, Katie Georgiou, Mike Grady-Hall, Antonia Kinlay, Siu Hun Li, Antonio Magro, Tim Pritchett, Georgina White and Jonathan Wright.

1. Begin on the floor, lying in semi-supine, and connect to your breathing, focusing particularly on the movement of your ribs, as in Counting I.

   - Now, on an out-breath, release a steady, sustained SH sound for a mental count of 10.
   - Breathe in, and then produce an easy, sustained SS sound for a mental count of 12.
   - Repeat, and then produce a clear, sustained ZZ sound for a mental count of 12.
   - Repeat, aiming to keep the sound at a steady intensity for its whole length.

2. Now bring your lips gently together to create a hum (MM) on your next out-breath. As you do so, imagine there is an AH vowel waiting behind the hum. On your next out-breath, begin humming in this way and then let the jaw drop open to release the AH vowel, aiming to maintain the vowel for a mental count of 12.

   - Repeat, and then do the same with the vowels OO and EE.

   (If you find yourself running out of breath before you reach 12, don't worry – just keep exercising regularly and the muscles will respond. If you can sustain for longer than 12, keep up the good work.)

3. Still on the floor in semi-supine, move your attention to your abdominal muscles as they respond to the movement of your diaphragm. Encourage your abdominal muscles to release as you breathe in and to engage as you breathe out – place the impulse for breathing in your centre, as in The Column of Air exercise.

   - Now, on the out-breath, produce a sustained SH sound with a steady engagement of the abdominal muscles throughout.
   - Repeat, but this time complete the sound with a CH, and feel the added contraction of the abdominal muscles supporting this sound.
   - Repeat, producing a long FF sound, feeling the engagement of the abdominal muscles sending the air to where the sound is shaped at the teeth and lip.
   - Repeat on a long VV sound, feeling the vibrating air focused on your teeth and lip.

- Now use the engagement of the abdominal muscles to touch off a short, easy HUH sound – think of it as a little dart of sound going up to the ceiling.

- Repeat, feeling the support of the abdominal muscles.

- Repeat with a HAY sound, but give yourself an imaginative impulse – for example, calling to a friend across the street.

- Repeat, and then do the same with a HI sound (greeting a friend you haven't seen for a while, for example).

4. Now bring yourself up on to all fours, as in the Cow Belly exercise. In this position, think of your back lengthening and widening as you breathe.

- As you breathe in, think of your ribs widening in your back.

- As you breathe out, release on to a hum (MM), imagining an AH vowel waiting behind it. Repeat and open the jaw to release the AH vowel, thinking of sending the sound into the floor.

- Repeat, and then do the same with the vowels OO and EE.

- Now focus your attention on your abdominal muscles. As in Cow Belly, think of engaging the muscles to lift your stomach up towards your spine as you breathe out, and then release the muscles to allow the stomach to drop towards the floor as you breathe in. Release your out-breath on a SH sound.

- Repeat, but this time complete the sound with a CH, and feel the added contraction of the abdominal muscles supporting this sound.

- Repeat the exercises from step (3) in this position.

5. Now sit well forward in a chair, and think of your back lengthening and widening as you breathe. Think of your neck being free not fixed, and your head facing forward with the top of your head parallel with the ceiling.

- As you breathe in, think of your ribs widening out to the sides from the spine as you breathe in.

- Release your out-breath on a hum (MM), imagining an AH vowel waiting behind it. Repeat and open the jaw to release the AH vowel, thinking of sending the sound across the room.

- Repeat, and then do the same with the vowels OO and EE.

- Now focus your attention on your abdominal muscles. As in Cow Belly, think of engaging the muscles to move your stomach towards your spine as you breathe out, and then relax the muscles to allow the stomach to release as you breathe in. Release your out-breath on a SH sound.

- Repeat, but this time complete the sound with a CH, and feel the added contraction of the abdominal muscles supporting this sound.

- Now combine your awareness of the ribs and the abdominal muscles. Allow the ribs to widen and the abdominal muscles to release as you breathe in. Release your out-breath on a hum (MM), imagining an AH vowel waiting behind it. Feel your abdominal muscles actively engaged to support this sound.

- Repeat and open the jaw to release the AH vowel, thinking of sending the sound across the room.

- Repeat several times, focusing on the AH vowel and think of lifting the soft palate away from the back of the tongue to create space in the back of the mouth.

- Repeat with the vowel sounds AY (as in 'hay') and OH (as in 'hoe'), feeling the space in the back of your mouth.

- Continuing to use a supported breath, begin to work your pitch range as in the Sirening exercise, using first a NG sound (as in 'si<u>ng</u>') and then an AH.

6. Stand up and continue to sound on AH while shaking out, swinging your arms and sirening through your range.

   - Now stand easy and, thinking of your back lengthening and widening as you breathe, allow the ribs to open outwards and the abdominal muscles to release as you breathe in. Release your out-breath on a hum (MM), imagining an AH vowel waiting behind it. Feel your abdominal muscles actively engaged to support this sound.

   - Repeat and open the jaw to release the AH vowel, thinking of sending the sound across the room.

   - Repeat several times, focusing on the AH vowel, and think of lifting the soft palate away from the back of the tongue to create space in the back of the mouth.

   - Repeat with the vowel sounds OO, OH, AW, AH, AY, EE.

7. Complete the workout with the following work on the articulators.

   - Enjoy a full, open-mouthed yawn, and then scrunch the face up and release.

   - Repeat several times, to waken up the muscles in the face.

   - Massage the muscles of the jaw to encourage it to open fully.

   - Massage the muscles around the lips.

   - Now blow your lips out on a BRRR sound (the 'shivering' sound we make when we are cold) – glide this sound through your pitch range.

   - Flick your tongue in and out of your mouth very quickly, making a rapid series of LA sounds – and glide this sound through your pitch range.

   - Now stick your tongue out and point it and flatten it several times.

   - Anchor the tip of your tongue behind your lower front teeth, then stretch the body of your tongue forward into a hump over the lower front teeth, and then release it back into your mouth.

   - Do this several times, making a YA-YA-YA sound as the tongue moves forward and back. The jaw should stay loosely open rather than moving up and down. Glide this sound through your pitch range.

   - Finish up by working your articulatory muscles on the following sound sequences:

BUH-BUH-BUH **BUH**-BUH-BUH **BAH**

PUH-PUH-PUH **PUH**-PUH-PUH **PAH**

MUH-MUH-MUH **MUH**-MUH-MUH **MAH**

DUH-DUH-DUH **DUH**-DUH-DUH **DAH**

TUH-TUH-TUH **TUH**-TUH-TUH **TAH**

NUH-NUH-NUH **NUH**-NUH-NUH **NAH**

GUH-GUH-GUH **GUH**-GUH-GUH **GAH**

KUH-KUH-KUH **KUH**-KUH-KUH **KAH**

NGUH-NGUH-NGUH **NGUH**-NGUH-NGUH **NGAH**

Play with your pitch range on these sequences, and instead of AH at the end of each sequence, try substituting other vowel sounds. Let your body be free and keep your neck and jaw relaxed.

Appendix 2
SAMPLE CURRICULA

These outline programmes are provided to indicate two ways in which the work of this book may be incorporated into a formal curriculum. These are not meant to be definitive models, as it is expected that teachers will adapt them to suit the learning needs of their particular students. We have assumed a minimum of 3 hours a week.

15-week model (one semester)

Block 1   *Introduction*

Week 1   Initial work from Chapter 1 on *Stretching*, *Floor Work*, *Roll-ups* and *Keeping It Loose*. Work on *Opening the Breath* from Chapter 2.

Week 2   Revisit work of week 1, and add initial work on *Coming on to Voice* from Chapter 2.

Week 3   Continue as above, and add later work from Chapters 1 and 2, including work on *Breath and Voice in Action*.

Week 4   Continue as above as appropriate, but focus on *Engaging the In-breath* from Chapter 3.

Week 5   Continue as above as appropriate, but focus on *Engaging the Out-breath* from Chapter 3. Work on *Connecting to Text* from Chapter 2.

Block 2   *Development*

Week 6   Review the work of Weeks 1–5.

Week 7   Continue with the work of Weeks 1–5, and add work on *Working the Channel* from Chapter 4. Further work on *Connecting to Text* from Chapter 2.

Week 8   Continue as above as appropriate, but focus on *Supporting the Voice* from Chapter 3.

Week 9   Revisit work of Week 8, and add initial work on *Finding the Buzz* from Chapter 4.

Week 10   Revisit work of Week 8, and add initial work on *Expanding the Range* from Chapter 4. Work on *Supporting Text* from Chapter 3.

Block 3   *Consolidation*

Week 11   Review the work of Weeks 7–10, and add later work on *Finding the Buzz* and *Expanding the Range*.

Week 12   Continue as above as appropriate, but focus on *Toning the Articulators* from Chapter 5. Work on *Resonating Text* from Chapter 4.

Week 13   Continue as above as appropriate, but focus on *Balancing the Sound* from Chapter 4.

Week 14   Continue as above as appropriate, but focus on *Specifying the Sounds* from Chapter 5.

Week 15   Warm up. Work on *Resonating Text* from Chapter 4 and *Articulating Text* from Chapter 5.

30-week model (three terms)

Term 1	*Introduction*
Week 1	Initial work from Chapter 1 on *Stretching*, *Floor Work*, *Roll-ups* and *Keeping It Loose*.
Week 2	Work on *Opening the Breath* from Chapter 2.
Week 3	Revisit work of Weeks 1 and 2, and add initial work on *Coming on to Voice* from Chapter 2.
Week 4	Continue as above.
Week 5	Continue as above, and add later work from Chapters 1 and 2.
Week 6	Continue as for Week 5 and add work on *Breath and Voice in Action* from Chapter 2.
Week 7	Continue as above as appropriate. Work on *Connecting to Text* from Chapter 2.
Week 8	Continue but add work on *Engaging the In-breath* from Chapter 3.
Week 9	Continue as above as appropriate, but focus on *Engaging the Out-breath* from Chapter 3.
Week 10	Warm up. Further work on *Connecting to Text* from Chapter 2.
Term 2	*Development*
Week 1	Review the work of Term 1.
Week 2	Continue review of Term 1, including *Connecting to Text* work as appropriate.
Week 3	Continue with the work of Term 1, and add exercises from *Working the Channel* in Chapter 4.
Week 4	Continue as for Week 3 as appropriate.
Week 5	Continue as for Week 3 as appropriate, but add work on *Supporting the Voice* from Chapter 3.
Week 6	Continue work on *Supporting the Voice*. Work on *Supporting Text* from Chapter 3.
Week 7	Revisit work of Weeks 5 and 6, and add initial work on *Finding the Buzz* from Chapter 4.
Week 8	Continue as for Week 7.
Week 9	Continue as for Weeks 5 and 6, and add initial work on *Expanding the Range* from Chapter 4.
Week 10	Continue as for Week 9. Further work on *Supporting Text* from Chapter 3.
Term 3	*Consolidation*
Week 1	Review the work of Term 2, and add later work on *Finding the Buzz* and *Expanding the Range*.
Week 2	Continue as for Week 1.
Week 3	Continue as above as appropriate, but focus on *Toning the Articulators* from Chapter 5.
Week 4	Continue as for Week 3.
Week 5	Continue as for Week 3, and add work on *Balancing the Sound* from Chapter 4.
Week 6	Continue as for Week 5. Work on *Resonating Text* from Chapter 4.
Week 7	Continue as above as appropriate, and add work on *Specifying the Sounds* from Chapter 5.
Week 8	Review the work from Chapter 4.
Week 9	Review the work from Chapter 5.
Week 10	Warm up. Work on *Resonating Text* from Chapter 4 and *Articulating Text* from Chapter 5.

Appendix 3
VOCAL HEALTH

Because we speak quite freely on a daily base throughout our lives, it can be easy to take vocal health for granted. Many performers, however, will at some point be in danger of having their voices compromised by illness or injury, and it can be a scary experience. In this appendix, we'll explore the most common causes of occasional voice loss and the treatments and preventive measures that you can take to relieve it.

As we explored in Chapter 3, your voice is produced by your breath interacting with your vocal folds – two folds of tissue and muscle situated in your larynx. When you are physically well and engaging your out-breath with good abdominal support, this interaction occurs in a healthy way and your vocal folds function normally. However, as we described in Chapter 3, sometimes when we want to sound louder, e.g. shouting at a soccer match or talking over loud music at a party, we try to force our voice from the throat rather than using more abdominal support. We do this by bringing the vocal folds together more tightly. This causes them to interact quite violently and, since your vocal folds are like any other tissue in your body, they will eventually become irritated if they're banged and slammed around too much. Imagine clapping or rubbing your hands together as hard as you can for ten minutes; the surface of your vocal folds will suffer every bit as much as the skin on the palms of your hands if they are subjected to the stress of rubbing up against each other violently for extended periods of time. They can even develop a kind of callus (called a nodule) which can seriously affect your vocal quality and, if left untreated, may permanently damage your voice. We're not suggesting that you don't shout at soccer matches or talk at loud parties, but giving some thought to your vocal usage in these situations will really help sustain your vocal health. Increasing abdominal support, using an optimum pitch, finding strong resonance in the mask of your face, and focusing on muscular articulation will all serve you well in these situations.

Similarly, if you are playing a demanding role where a character has to shout or scream a lot, or where you have to project your voice quite strongly, then a good warm-up which focuses on those same features will be essential to avoid wearing out your voice after a couple of performances. In these circumstances it's also a good idea to make use of a good cool-down procedure to help the vocal muscles relax. Some gentle release work from Chapter 1 coupled with yawning and downward pitch glides on vowels and voiced consonants for 10 minutes or so will do the trick.

Bringing the vocal folds together too tightly in order to create a louder sound is not the only thing that can have an adverse effect on them. Dehydration can also make them more vulnerable. Drinking plenty of water keeps your folds lubricated from the inside and is essential for good vocal health. Alcohol and caffeinated drinks, on the other hand, are actually dehydrating, so do try to limit your intake. Using a humidifier and/or a steam inhaler will help counteract the feeling of dryness. A good indication of how well hydrated you are is if you 'pee pale', that is, if your urine is a pale yellow colour.

One of the most destructive substances that can harm the folds is cigarette smoke, as it not only dries them out but also acts as an irritant (although cannabis is actually more irritating). Some people will be able to smoke longer than others before any damage becomes audible, but damage will happen, and there's no way of telling when. The most useful thing you can do, if at all possible, is to stop smoking.

Even with the best will in the world, however, it's impossible to completely avoid coughs, colds, viral laryngitis or hay fever and other allergic reactions, all of which affect the vocal folds and can lead to inflammation. Inhaling steam will alleviate this, perhaps with a couple of drops of Olbas oil or tea tree oil to offset any infection. Also, try to avoid excessive throat clearing and coughing as these can only cause more irritation to the vocal folds. In extreme circumstances of vocal fatigue, you may need to undertake some vocal rest – anything from limiting the amount of talking you do during the day up to a day or two of complete silence.

Eating habits can also disrupt the voice at inconvenient times, particularly if you are prone to acid reflux. This happens when acidic juices from your stomach flow back out of your oesophagus, potentially falling into your larynx and damaging your vocal folds. Certain foods have been linked to this, including spicy foods, tomatoes, carbonated drinks, chocolate, coffee, tea and citrus fruits and drinks. Eating late at night, smoking and drinking alcohol can all be contributory factors as well. You may not be aware that you suffer from reflux, as it often happens at night. So, typical signs of it are feeling your voice is 'rough' in the morning with an unpleasant taste in your mouth, frequent coughing and throat clearing particularly after eating, and/or vocal problems with no obvious cause. If you are regularly experiencing any of these symptoms, it's best to have them checked out by a doctor to prevent long-term damage to your voice.

In fact, if you're experiencing any persistent disturbance to your voice, you should get it checked out by a doctor. Don't be a hero! Your voice is your profession – look after it closely.

Further reading

Davies, D. Garfield and Jahn, Anthony F., *Care of the Professional Voice: A Guide to Voice Management for Singers, Actors and Professional Voice Users*, Methuen Drama, London, 2004.
Shewell, Christina, *Voice Work: Art and Science in Changing Voices*, Wiley-Blackwell, Chichester, 2009.

Appendix 4
BIBLIOGRAPHY AND RESOURCES

Recommended books

Practical voice and speech

Berry, Cicely, *Voice and the Actor*, Virgin, London, 2000.

Berry, Cicely, *Your Voice and How To Use It*, Virgin, London, 2000.

Bunch Dayme, Meribeth, *The Performer's Voice: Realizing Your Vocal Potential*, W. W. Norton & Company, New York, 2005.

Fletcher, Patricia, *Classically Speaking: Dialects for Actors* (Fourth edition), XanEdu, Acton, MA, 2017.

Houseman, Barbara, *Finding Your Voice*, Nick Hern Books, London, 2002.

Kayes, Gillyanne, *Singing and the Actor* (Second edition), A&C Black, London, 2004.

Knight, Dudley, *Speaking with Skill: An Introduction to Knight-Thompson Speechwork*, Methuen Drama, London, 2012.

Lessac, Arthur, *The Use and Training of the Human Voice*, Mayfield Publishing Company, California, 1997.

Linklater, Kristin, *Freeing the Natural Voice* (Revised edition), Drama Book Publishers, New York, 2006.

Martin, Stephanie and Darnley, Lyn, *The Teaching Voice* (Second edition), Whurr Publishers, London and Philadelphia, 2004.

McCallion, Michael, *The Voice Book* (Revised edition), Faber and Faber Ltd, London, 1998.

Melton, Joan (with Kenneth Tom), *One Voice*, Heinemann, Portsmouth, NH, 2003.

Mills, Matthew and Stoneham, Gillie, *The Voice Book for Trans and Non-Binary People: A Practical Guide to Creating and Sustaining Authentic Voice and Communication*, Jessica Kingsley Publishers, London, 2017.

Morrison, Malcolm, *Clear Speech* (Fourth edition), A&C Black, London, 2001.

Nelson, Jeannette, *The Voice Exercise Book: A Guide to Healthy and Effective Voice Use*, National Theatre Publishing, London, 2015.

Rodenburg, Patsy, *The Actor Speaks*, Methuen, London, 1997.

Shewell, Christina, *Voice Work: Art and Science in Changing Voices*, Wiley-Blackwell, Chichester, 2009.

Skinner, Edith, *Speak with Distinction* (Revised edition), edited by Lilene Mansell, Applause Books, New York, 2000.

Turner, J. Clifford, *Voice and Speech in the Theatre* (Sixth edition, edited by Jane Boston), A&C Black Publishers, London, 2007.

Vocal anatomy and vocal health

Borden, Gloria J. and Harris, Katherine S., *Speech Science Primer*, Williams & Wilkins, Philadelphia, 1980.

Bunch, Meribeth, *Dynamics of the Singing Voice* (Fourth edition), Springer-Verlag, Austria, 2001.

Davies, D. Garfield and Jahn, Anthony F., *Care of the Professional Voice: A Guide to Voice Management for Singers, Actors and Professional Voice Users*, Methuen Drama, London, 2004.

Mathieson, Lesley, *Greene and Mathieson's The Voice and Its Disorders* (Sixth edition), Whurr Publishers, London and Philadelphia, 2001.

Shewell, Christina, *Voice Work: Art and Science in Changing Voices*, Wiley-Blackwell, Chichester, 2009.

Bodywork

Lam Kam Chuen, Master, *The Way of Energy*, Simon & Schuster, New York, 1991.
Macdonald, Glynn, *The Complete Illustrated Guide to Alexander Technique*, Element, Dorset, 1998.
McEvenue, Kelly, *The Alexander Technique for Actors*, Methuen, London 2001.

Recommended poetry anthologies

Being Alive, edited by Neil Astley, Bloodaxe Books, Northumberland, 2004.
Looking Out, Looking In: Anthology of Latino Poetry, edited by William Luis, Arte Publico Press, Houston, Texas, 2012.
Out of Bounds: British Black & Asian Poets, edited by Jackie Kay, James Proctor, Gemma Robertson, Bloodaxe Books, Northumberland, 2012.
Poems for Life, selected by Laura Barber, Penguin Books, London, 2007.
The 100 Best African American Poems, edited by Nikki Giovanni, Sourcebooks Inc, Illinois, 2010.
The School Bag, edited by Seamus Heaney and Ted Hughes, Faber and Faber Ltd, London, 1997.
When the Light of the World Was Subdued: A Norton Anthology of Native Nations Poetry, edited by Joy Harjo, W. W. Norton & Company, New York, 2020.

Recommended poetry websites

www.famouspoetsandpoems.com
www.poemhunter.com
www.poetryarchive.org
www.poetryfoundation.org
www.poets.org

Appendix 5
PROFESSIONAL HISTORIES

David Carey

David Carey trained during the 1970s as a speech and drama teacher at the Royal Scottish Academy of Music and Drama in Glasgow, where his voice teachers were John Colson, Jacqui Crago and Jim House. John was the husband of Greta Colson, Co-Director of the New College of Speech and Drama, London. Greta Colson was a graduate of the Central School of Speech and Drama and author or co-author of a number of books on voice, speech and phonetics. The New College of Speech and Drama, which was later absorbed by Middlesex Polytechnic (later Middlesex University), was one of a number of drama schools in the 1960s which were training voice teachers in the UK. Jacqui Crago and Jim House were both graduates of New College. Jacqui's classes in phonetics and poetry were a particular influence on David's decision to become a voice teacher.

However, David's initial introduction to voice and speech work was literally at his mother's knee. Elna Carey (nee Graham) trained during the 1930s as a Speech Teacher at the Central School of Speech and Drama under Elsie Fogerty. Gwynneth Thurburn and J. Clifford Turner were also on the Central faculty at this time. She married actor Brian Carey, who came from a theatrical family in Dublin, and so David was brought up with a deep awareness of the importance of voice, speech and articulate communication.

Following his training in Glasgow, David completed a BA degree in English Language and Linguistics at Edinburgh University before taking up a position as Lecturer in Voice and Speech at Queen Margaret College, Edinburgh, where he taught on the College's undergraduate drama programme for five years. His work at this time was strongly influenced by both Cicely Berry and Kristin Linklater through their seminal books, *Voice and the Actor* (first published in 1973) and *Freeing the Natural Voice* (first published in 1976). Berry had trained under and worked with Gwynneth Thurburn at the Central School of Speech and Drama (CSSD), while Linklater had trained under and worked with Iris Warren at the London Academy of Music and Dramatic Art (LAMDA). David found that the rigorous and muscular work of Berry was complemented by the more kinaesthetic and image-based approach of Linklater, and that a combination of the two was well suited to the needs of developing students.

David left Edinburgh in 1982 to join the Royal Shakespeare Company as Assistant Voice Director, working under Cicely Berry and alongside Patsy Rodenburg. The four years that David spent at the RSC were a rich period in the company's history. Judi Dench, Fiona Shaw, Juliet Stevenson and Harriet Walter, Kenneth Branagh, Brian Cox, Derek Jacobi, Alan Rickman and Antony Sher were all members of the acting company. In addition to Joint Artistic Directors, Terry Hands and Trevor Nunn, other directors included Bill Alexander, John Barton, Ron Daniels, Howard Davies, Barry Kyle and Adrian Noble. Notable plays and productions of this period with which David was associated were *Richard III* with

Antony Sher, *Henry V* with Kenneth Branagh and the world premieres of *Les Liaisons Dangereuses* and Howard Barker's *The Castle*. David's understanding of voice, text and acting was deeply informed by the opportunity to observe these actors and directors, but most especially by the experience of watching Cicely Berry's unique collaboration with these theatre artists. Her passion for language and its ability to express the human experience, particularly through the work of Shakespeare, left an indelible impression on David and continues to influence his work to this day.

David left the RSC to take up the post of Senior Lecturer (later, Principal Lecturer) in Voice Studies at the Central School of Speech and Drama, where he was responsible for developing and sustaining the school's postgraduate programme in Voice Studies, a course of professional development for graduates who wished to follow a career in voice teaching. David was responsible for all aspects of teaching and learning, from course design and admissions to assessment, timetabling and pastoral care. He taught modules in vocal anatomy, vocal pedagogy, voice and text, and phonetics, as well as supervising dissertations and independent practical projects.

Under his leadership, the course became recognized as a national and international benchmark in the field.

David left Central in 2003, returning to the vocal training of actors as a senior voice tutor at the Royal Academy of Dramatic Art. While at RADA he established a relationship with the Oregon Shakespeare Festival, where he was a guest voice and text director in 2005, 2008 and 2010. He was also an Associate Editor for the *Voice and Speech Review,* the journal of the Voice and Speech Trainers Association, from 2002 to 2009.

David left his position at RADA at the end of 2010 to become a Resident Voice and Text Director with the Oregon Shakespeare Festival, where he is currently responsible for voice, text and dialect for four to five productions each season.

David's pedagogy is an eclectic one which draws on the work of the leading voice teachers of the past fifty years, such as Cicely Berry, Kristin Linklater and Patsy Rodenburg. His academic interest in Linguistics – he has a Masters in Contemporary English Language and Linguistics from Reading University – also informs his practice through a deep understanding of language, vocal anatomy, phonetics and dialects. He also draws actively on his experience of Alexander Technique and T'ai Chi. He places emphasis on exploring and developing the natural potential of the voice, with equal attention paid to physiological function and imaginative intention, so that fundamental work on breathing, alignment, resonance and articulation is integrated with expressive work on text and communication.

David was awarded a prestigious National Teaching Fellowship in 2007 by the UK's Higher Education Academy in recognition of his contribution to vocal pedagogy.

Rebecca Clark Carey

Rebecca Clark Carey trained as an actor in the University of California at Irvine's Master of Fine Arts programme. Her principal voice and speech teacher there was the late Dudley Knight, and she continues to draw heavily on Dudley's teaching in her own work. Dudley himself studied voice with Kristin Linklater and Catherine Fitzmaurice, both of whom did their initial training in London; Kristin at the London Academy of Music and Dramatic Art with Iris Warren and Catherine at the Central School of Speech and Drama with Cicely Berry and Gwynneth Thurburn.

Dudley Knight was a Master Teacher of Fitzmaurice Voicework, a method of training that draws on and adapts various disciplines such as hatha yoga and shiatsu to free and strengthen the voice. Dudley was also an internationally respected teacher of speech who regularly conducted workshops on Knight-Thompson Speechwork. While this book does not address speech as an independent discipline, the chapter on articulation has been greatly informed by Dudley's emphasis on agility and clarity.

Rebecca continued her training at the Central School of Speech and Drama in London. While working on her MA in Voice Studies there, she had the opportunity to receive instruction from many leading voice practitioners, including Cicely Berry, Andrew Wade, Joanna Weir-Ouston, Gillyanne Kayes and Meribeth Bunch Dayme. Her dissertation was on speaking Shakespeare's late plays (an edited version was published in *Voice and Speech Review: Film, Broadcast and Electronic Media Coaching*, 2003).

Shortly after completing the Central course with distinction, Rebecca joined the Oregon Shakespeare Festival, working in both the education department and as an assistant to voice and text directors Scott Kaiser and Ursula Meyer. Their expertise and generosity continue to inform and inspire her coaching work. She went on to become a regular guest voice and text director and, eventually, the head of voice at OSF.

Rebecca has also worked in England as a voice teacher at the Central School of Speech and Drama, The Italia Conti Academy of Theatre Arts, The Oxford School of Drama, and for five years as a senior voice tutor at the Royal Academy of Dramatic Art. She frequently coaches British actors on American accents and was the accent coach for the Royal and Derngate's productions of Tennessee William's *Spring Storm* and Eugene O'Neill's *Beyond the Horizon* and their revivals at the Royal National Theatre in 2010. She was also the accent coach for Robert Schenkkan's Tony Award-winning *All the Way* at the American Repertory Theatre and on Broadway.

Links to the videos can be found at: https://vimeo.com/channels/vocalarts/videos

INDEX